**NIGHT+**

The critics are tal

MW01178632

"Extraordinary detail, itineraries organized by theme, and a unique up-to-the-minute black book of what's hot provides readers with the ultimate guide." — **Forbes.com**

"Opening chapters set the spirited tone ... a host of food-focused entries accommodate all tastes." —*Travel + Leisure*

"Focus[es] their information to attract vacationers who don't want cookie-cutter itineraries." —*Wall Street Journal*

"Well-written, cleverly organized ... remarkably comprehensive."
—*Passport Magazine*

"The most enjoyable feature may be the various three-day itineraries ... I don't know that I'd want a manicure and a martini at the Beauty Bar around 10 p.m. on a Friday night, but I'm delighted to know it's possible." —*New York Times*

"Perfect for the business person or jet-setter who's in town for a few days and has little time to research a visit. But area residents can pluck a few gems from its pages, too."—*Sacramento Bee*

"Numerous three-day itineraries to mix and match to your heart's delight."—*Chicago Tribune*

"Your one-stop guide to shopping, nightlife, restaurants, hotels and other attractions in the city."—*DC Style Magazine*

But it's your opinion that counts.
Let us know what you think at pulseguides.com.

PULSEGUIDES

Pulse Guides' **Night+Day Toronto** is an independent guide. We do not accept payment of any kind from events or establishments for inclusion in this book. We welcome your views on our selections. Please email us: **feedback@pulseguides.com**.

The information contained in this book was checked as rigorously as possible before going to press. The publisher accepts no responsibility for any changes that may have occurred since, or for any other variance of fact from that recorded here in good faith.

Distributed worldwide by Publishers Group West (PGW).
First Edition. Printed in the United States. 30% postconsumer content.
Copyright © 2008 ASDavis Media Group, Inc. All rights reserved.
ISBN-10: 1-934724-02-5; ISBN-13: 978-1-934724-02-6

Credits

Executive Editor	Alan S. Davis
Editor	Christina Henry de Tessan
Author	Neil Carlson
Contributors	Waheeda Harris, Anya Wassenberg
Copy Editors	Gail Nelson-Bonebrake, Elizabeth Stroud
Maps	Chris Gillis
Fact Checker	Gina Quinn
Production	Samia Afra, Jo Farrell, Samantha Glorioso, Tess Herrmann

Photo Credits: (Front cover, left to right) *martini,* Les Byerley; *couple dining,* Ultra Supper Club; *The Crystal at the Royal Ontario Museum*, Mary Lou Dauray. (Back cover, left to right) *C-Lounge*, Stipco Photos; *Body Blitz Spa*, Body Blitz Spa; *The Rex Hotel Jazz & Blues Bar*, The Rex; *Colborne Lane*, Paula Wilson. (Inside cover, top to bottom) *Susur*, Susur; *The Drake Hotel,* Keith Pace Asciak Photography; *Casa Loma*, Andrew Ross. (p.4) *Alan Davis*, Mary Lou Dauray. (p.12) *Piers Handling*, Jeff Vespa/WireImage for the Toronto International Film Festival Group.

Special Sales

For information about bulk purchases of Pulse Guides (ten copies or more), email us at bookorders@pulseguides.com. Special bulk rates are available for charities, corporations, institutions, and online and mail-order catalogs, and our books can be customized to suit your company's needs.

NIGHT+DAY
the Cool Cities series from **PULSE**GUIDES

P.O. Box 590780, San Francisco, CA 94159
pulseguides.com

Pulse Guides is an imprint of ASDavis Media Group, Inc.

NIGHT+DAY
TORONTO

By Neil Carlson

PULSE GUIDES

From the Publisher

My brief retirement more than ten years ago came to an end when I set out on a journey to find the 100 most fun places to be in the world at the right time. The challenge of unearthing the world's greatest events—from the Opera Ball in Vienna to the Calgary Stampede—led me to write a guidebook. In fact, it was two guidebooks, *The Fun Also Rises North America* and *The Fun Also Rises International*, named after Ernest Hemingway's *The Sun Also Rises*, which helped popularize what has become perhaps the most thrilling party on earth (Pamplona's Fiesta de San Fermín, also known as the Running of the Bulls).

Over a five-year period I attended approximately 150 events, among them Caribana in Toronto. A Caribbean festival in Toronto? I just had to see how this northern city celebrated the steamy Caribbean spirit. While Caribana was the reason that originally drew me to Toronto, it immediately became clear that the city had infinitely more to offer.

As I pursued my research and traveled the world, I became aware of a gaping hole in the travel guide industry. Not a single guide adequately served my needs. There was budget, gourmet, upscale, historic, and more, but none provided the kinds of details I needed to hit the ground running and make the most of my limited time. I wanted a selective list of options provided by reliable local sources with valuable insider tips. I decided to fill the hole myself, and Pulse Guides was born. Night+Day, the first series from Pulse Guides, presents the best that a city has to offer, in a totally new format that allows you to find the places that are right for you quickly and easily. The goal is to provide the best content available in the travel business—and based on the first reviews, we are off to a fine start. We hope that you'll agree.

Pulse Guides abides by one guiding principle: Never settle for the ordinary. I hope that our new approach allows you to experience the very best the city has to offer.

Wishing you extraordinary times,

Alan S. Davis, Publisher and Executive Editor
Pulse Guides

P.S. To contact me, or for updated information on all of our **Night+Day** guides, please visit our website at **pulseguides.com**.

The Night+Day Difference

The Pulse of the City

Our job is to point you to all of the city's peak experiences: amazing museums, unique spas, and spectacular views. But the complete *urbanista* experience is more than just impressions—it is grown-up fun, the kind that thrives by night as well as by day. Urban fun is a hip nightclub or a trendy restaurant. It is people-watching and people-meeting. Lonely planet? We don't think so. **Night+Day** celebrates our lively planet.

The Right Place. The Right Time. It Matters.

A **Night+Day** city must have exemplary restaurants, a vibrant nightlife scene, and enough attractions to keep a visitor busy for six days without having to do the same thing twice. In selecting restaurants, food is important, but so is the scene. Our hotels, most of which are 4- and 5-star properties, are rated for the quality of the concierge staff (can they get you into a hot restaurant?) as well as the rooms. You won't find kids with fake IDs at our nightlife choices. And the attractions must be truly worthy of your time. But experienced travelers know that timing is almost everything. Going to a restaurant at 7pm can be a very different experience (and probably less fun) than at 9pm; a champagne boat cruise might be ordinary in the morning but spectacular at sunset. We believe providing the reader with this level of detail makes the difference between a good experience and a great one.

The Bottom Line

Your time is precious. Our guide must be easy to use and dead-on accurate. That is why our executive editor, editors, and writers (locals who are in touch with what is great—and what is not) spend hundreds of hours researching, writing, and debating selections for each guide. The results are presented in four unique ways: The *99 Best* with our top three choices in 33 categories that highlight what is great about the city; the *Experience* chapters, in which our selections are organized by distinct themes or personalities (Hot & Cool, Hip, and Classic); a *Perfect Plan* (3 Nights and Days) for each theme, showing how to get the most out of the city in a short period of time; and the *Toronto Black Book*, listing all the hotels, restaurants, nightlife, and attractions, with key details, contact information, and page references.

Our bottom line is this: If you find our guide easy to use and enjoyable to read, and with our help you have an extraordinary time, we have succeeded. We review and value all feedback from our readers, so please contact us at **feedback@pulseguides.com**.

TOC

INTRODUCTION 9
   Night+Day's Toronto Urbie 12

THE 99 BEST OF TORONTO 15
   Always-Trendy Tables 16
   Brunches 17
   Canadian Cuisine 18
   Celebrity Hangouts 19
   Classic Hotel Bars 20
   Contemporary Art and Design Spaces 21
   Dance Clubs 22
   Ethnic Dining 23
   Fine Dining 24
   Gay Scenes 25
   Guided Tours 26
   Historic Buildings 27
   Hot Chefs 28
   Jazz Clubs 29
   Late-Night Eats 30
   Live Music 31
   Martinis 32
   Meet Markets 33
   Nouvelle Asian Restaurants 34
   Of-the-Moment Dining 35
   Only-in-Toronto Museums 36
   Power Lunches 37
   Restaurant-Lounges 38
   Romantic Rendezvous 39
   Scene Bars 40
   Seafood Restaurants 41
   Sexy Lounges 42
   Spas 43
   Summer Patios 44
   Views 45
   Ways to Enjoy a Sunny Day 46
   Ways to Escape a Rainy Day 47
   West Queen West Art Spaces 48

EXPERIENCE TORONTO 49
Hot & Cool Toronto 50
The Perfect Plan (3 Nights and Days) 51
The Key Neighborhoods 55
The Shopping Blocks 56
The Hotels 57
The Restaurants 60
The Nightlife 67
The Attractions 74
Hip Toronto 80
The Perfect Plan (3 Nights and Days) 81
The Key Neighborhoods 85
The Shopping Blocks 86
The Hotels 87
The Restaurants 89
The Nightlife 96
The Attractions 103
Classic Toronto 108
The Perfect Plan (3 Nights and Days) 109
The Key Neighborhoods 113
The Shopping Blocks 114
The Hotels 115
The Restaurants 119
The Nightlife 133
The Attractions 138

PRIME TIME TORONTO 143
Prime Time Basics 144
Eating and Drinking 144
Weather and Tourism 144
National Holidays 145
The Best Events Calendar 146
The Best Events 147

HIT THE GROUND RUNNING 159
City Essentials 160
Getting to Toronto: By Air 160
Getting to Toronto: By Land 164
Toronto: Lay of the Land 165
Getting Around Toronto 165

Other Practical Information (Money Matters; Safety; Gay and Lesbian Travel; Traveling with Disabilities, Radio Stations, Print Media, Shopping Hours, Size Conversion, Attire, When Drinking Is Legal, Smoking, Drugs, Time Zone, Numbers to Know, Additional Resources for Visitors) 167
Party Conversation—A Few Surprising Facts 174
The Cheat Sheet (The Very Least You Ought to Know About Toronto) (Neighborhoods, Performing Arts Venues, City Parks, Streets, Retail Centers, Pro-Sport Teams, Famous People Who Attended North Toronto Collegiate Institute, Area Codes, Expressways, Singular Sensation, and Coffee) 175
Just for Business and Conventions 182

Toronto Region Map 184

LEAVING TORONTO 185
Overnight Trips
    Cottage Country 186
    Niagara Falls 188
    Niagara-on-the-Lake 190
    Stratford 192
    Thousand Islands 194
Day Trips
    Hamilton and Burlington 196
    Kleinburg 197
    St. Jacobs 198

TORONTO BLACK BOOK 199
Toronto Black Book 200
Toronto Black Book by Neighborhood 214

Toronto Neighborhoods Map 219

Toronto Unique Shopping Index 220

Toronto Action Central Map 221

About the Author and Contributors, Acknowledgments 223

Introduction

Toronto: What It Was

In 1793, John Graves Simcoe, the first Lieutenant-Governor of Upper Canada, set up house with his wife Elizabeth and three children at Garrison Creek at Toronto Bay—establishing the first permanent settlement at York, which would later be renamed Toronto. It was shortly after the American Revolution, and construction of Fort York quickly began near this strategic location in anticipation of trouble with the revolutionaries to the south, trouble that soon came knocking during the War of 1812. American forces occupied the small trading town in April of 1813, burning down the city's Parliament buildings when they withdrew again a few days later. It was one of the more vicious episodes in the conflict, and in retaliation, the British marched on Washington and torched America's government buildings—giving the White House its name, since it had to be whitewashed to hide the scorch marks.

It was a rough beginning for this bustling modern city of 2.5 million, Canada's largest, nestled on the shores of bright blue Lake Ontario and today a model of peaceful coexistence. Toronto means "fishing weir" (a type of fishing trap) in the Huron language, and for centuries before Simcoe and the British arrived, the area was home to Native American encampments, many of them on the east bank of the Humber River in what is now Etobicoke. The area was also a hub for fur traders. Known as the Toronto Portage or Toronto Carrying Place, it was first visited by Europeans in 1615 and was heavily used by both Native Americans and traders in the 17th century as a meeting place and camp. The fur trade wars grew so heated that the French set up an military outpost in the area for a few years between 1720 and 1759, calling it Fort Rouillé. Today, you'll find the outlines of Fort Rouillé marked in concrete at Exhibition Place, just west of the Rose Garden.

> **Known as the Toronto Portage or Toronto Carrying Place, it was first visited by Europeans in 1615 and was heavily used by both Native Americans and traders in the 17th century as a meeting place and camp.**

After the hostilities ceased, the city was incorporated in 1834 and began to grow. Not much in the way of monuments remain from those very early days, but the foundations of the city's many neighborhoods were laid. Yonge Street, at the city's heart, was established by Simcoe along an ancient Huron trail, and he demarcated the city's first intersection at what is now Yonge-Dundas Square. The Bank of Upper Canada building at 252 Adelaide Street East dates from 1830, and is one of the few buildings to survive the Great Fire of 1849, which burned hundreds of buildings to the ground and left many residents homeless.

The city's growth in the 19th century was prodigious, as industrialization drew in more and more people from outlying areas, birth rates boomed, and overseas events like the Irish Potato Famine sent waves of immigrants. Lake steamers and the arrival of the Canadian National Railroad (CN) further fueled Toronto's growth and turned the waterfront into an industrial center. By the 1880s, the city that had once been dubbed "Muddy Toronto" for its lack of paved roads had reached a population of 100,000. The eclectic neighborhood now known as Kensington Market originated on land originally owned by a single family—the Denisons—who sold it off piecemeal to create the city's first large development. The University of Toronto opened its doors in 1843, and a booming bacon trade with England resulted in a thriving meat-packing industry and gave the city one of its nicknames—Hogtown.

As the 19th century turned into the 20th, the city became caught up in the era's rampant industrialism. Some of Toronto's grander structures bear witness to this moneyed era, like the ultra-posh King Edward Hotel and the regal Royal Alexandra Theatre. Casa Loma, the brooding castle with medieval turrets that looks down on the city from Spadina and Davenport roads, was begun in 1911. The fairy-tale house was built by Toronto's own robber baron, Sir Henry Pellatt, who brought hydroelectric power to the city. Although Casa Loma was never completed, the family moved in in 1914 to enjoy amenities that included 52 phones, 5,000 lights, and 25 fireplaces in what was then the largest home in North America.

In the 1920s and '30s, the area saw the arrival of a host of European immigrants, many of them Jews fleeing persecution in Eastern Europe and elsewhere. Kensington Market became known as the "Jewish Market," and was home to 30 synagogues serving about 60,000 Jews. While their descendants have mostly moved out of the area (Bathurst Street is now the center of the city's Jewish population), people seeking refuge from subsequent trouble spots in the world, from Latin America to Cambodia and Somalia, have always found a home in Kensington Market.

The first few decades of the 20th century also saw the beginnings of a wave of modernism in architecture, with the building of the landmark Union Station on Front Street, as well as the original Toronto Stock Exchange on Bay, in what is now the Design Exchange museum.

The war effort turned into the post-war boom, which brought an immediate influx of some 400,000 European immigrants, creating some of the city's most vibrant ethnic neighborhoods—Little Italy in the west, and Greektown in the east end—and bringing some continental flair to Waspy Toronto. The then prim and proper city saw the opening of its first sidewalk cafes and patios, now a Toronto staple.

The city's infatuation with modernism continued into the 1960s and '70s as the economy boomed. In 1966, world-renowned sculptor Henry Moore graced the city's new City Hall with his sculpture, *The Archer*. Toronto grew into its role as Canada's financial capital and the engine of its economy, and the Financial District expanded correspondingly as its suitably impressive home. The original Toronto Dominion Plaza, the downtown's largest conglomeration of skyscrapers at the corner of Bay and Wellington Streets, was the last project designed by famed architect Mies Van Der Rohe, completed just after his death in 1969. The Royal Bank Plaza, at 200 Bay Street, opened in March 1977, its dizzying height covered with a thin film of real gold, 2,500 ounces in all.

In the latter part of the 20th century, another wave of immigration, this time from Asia, began to change the city's cultural landscape, cementing Toronto's

Key Dates

1793   The first European settlement is established, followed quickly by the building of Fort York.

1834   Toronto incorporates as a city.

1835   Sections of Yonge Street, the longest street in the world, are paved.

1904   The Great Fire of Toronto begins in a factory on Wellington Street, and by the next day has destroyed much of the downtown around Front, Yonge, and Bay Streets.

1964   Toronto's "new" City Hall opens at Nathan Phillips Square.

1967   Caribana, the world's largest street party, is initiated as a gift to the city from its Afro-Caribbean community in honor of Canada's centennial.

1976   The Festival of Festivals, precursor to the Toronto International Film Festival, holds its first event.

1989   The Skydome (now called the Rogers Centre) opens, becoming the first stadium in the world to feature a fully retractable roof.

1992-3   The Toronto Blue Jays become the first franchise to win back-to-back World Series victories.

1998   The population of the city of Toronto swells to 5 million with the creation of the Greater Toronto Area, an amalgamation of seven surrounding municipalities into one.

Night+Day's Toronto Urbie

THE URBIE AWARD: Piers Handling

Piers Handling has transformed staid and respectable Toronto into a sexy and desirable city—not just in the eyes of the numerous travelers and tourists who come to the largest city in Canada, but to the residents whose traditionally cautious nature has made it such a conservative metropolis for the past 20 years. With his effortless grace and presence as the artistic director of the Toronto International Film Festival, Handling has transformed a small regional festival into a world-renowned event. Handling attended the world's film hot spots every year—Hollywood, Cannes, New York—and cajoled the movers and shakers into putting Toronto on their annual schedule to showcase their films in the number three movie market in North America. For ten days each September, heavyweight producers, dazzling red-carpet mainstays, and obsessed movie viewers crowd the streets. And Toronto has a chance to preen before the world. Having ascended the ranks to become artistic director of the festival in 1994 and now in transition to become its CEO, Handling continues his promotion of TIFF and the city of Toronto to a global network of influencers. TIFF's glow extends far beyond the festival itself. Residents are taking renewed pride in their hometown, and the entire city is experiencing a renaissance: the downtown core is vibrant with trendy condos, upscale shopping, and lively nightlife. The arts scene is thriving. Impressive restoration projects have created the underground glories of the Gladstone and Drake Hotels. The Crystal at the Royal Ontario Museum and the Four Seasons Centre for the Performing Arts gave the city a huge cultural boost. The redevelopment of forgotten 19th-century relics like the Distillery District and the Brickworks have encouraged restoration, while on the horizon sits the reinvention of the Art Gallery of Ontario by native son Frank Gehry. Thanks to Handling's shining the spotlight on Toronto, the city has fallen in love with itself again—and is more eager than ever before to show off to the world.

Night+Day cities are chosen because they have a vibrant nightlife scene, standard-setting and innovative restaurants, cutting-edge hotels, and enough attractions to keep a visitor busy for six days without doing the same thing twice. In short, they are fun. They represent the quintessential *urbanista* experience. This phenomenon wouldn't exist but for the creativity and talents of many people and organizations. In honor of all who have played a role in making Toronto one of the world's coolest cities, Pulse Guides is pleased to give special recognition, and our Urbie Award, to one individual whose contribution is exemplary.

reputation for ethnic, racial, linguistic, and religious diversity. Official slogans such as "Toronto: Home to the World," "Toronto: The World Within a City," and "Diversity: Our Strength" were coined to celebrate the city's uniquely multicultural make-up, and an enduring and oft-reported urban myth—that UNESCO had named Toronto the world's most diverse city—was born.

> The post-war boom brought some 400,000 European immigrants, creating some of the city's most vibrant areas and bringing continental flair to Waspy Toronto.

Toronto: What It Is

Modern Toronto is North America's fifth largest city, and recent census figures show that fully half that population was born outside the country. Over 90 nationalities and ethnic groups speak over 100 languages—and if UNESCO ever does grant a city the title of "Most Diverse," the honor might very well be Toronto's to claim. What began as a meeting place has become the intersection of world cultures. In this city of festivals, you'll find many ethnic celebrations, from the Chinese New Year to the Hindu Diwali, or Festival of Lights, and over 8,000 restaurants to tempt your palate with flavors from around the globe.

The television and film industries have transformed large areas of the city, particularly in the East and West Ends, taking what were blocks of empty warehouse and industrial spaces and turning them into studios and lofts. Toronto's lakeshore still retains traces of its industrial roots, but a new mix of public spaces like the Harbourfront Centre for the Arts and glass condos have sprung up all over the downtown area, chasing away urban blight with stellar restaurants, hip clubs, and designer furniture shops.

The arts have risen in importance, and today only London and New York can boast more stages than Toronto. Some 200 professional theater and dance companies put on over 10,000 live performances every year, and the city is seen as a testing ground for major performances like *The Lord Of The Rings,* which debuted in Toronto before making the jump to Broadway.

All that show biz hasn't gone to the city's head, though, and its famously friendly and down-to-earth vibe has made the annual Toronto International Film Festival as much a hit with the stars as with the spectators. The beautiful people, including international glitterati, are now regular fixtures on the Toronto streetscape, either pausing for makeup during a shoot or partying down in the Entertainment District. Film and television shoots have become so commonplace all over town that they're rarely greeted with anything other than passing curiosity. The Toronto Film Festival has grown into a celebration of film second only to Cannes, bringing more waves of sophisticated visitors—and the nightlife scene to cater to their tastes. Canadian actors have often complained of the lack of a "star" system in Canada, but it's the very lack of hype that proves so attractive to the celeb set. For years, the Rolling Stones have begun their world tours by coming to Toronto to rehearse for a few months, drawn by the same laid-back attitude that makes the Film Festival so popular with both fans and stars.

> Toronto's lakeshore still retains traces of its industrial roots, but a new mix of public spaces like the Harbourfront Centre for the Arts and glass condos that have sprung up all over the downtown area are chasing away urban blight with stellar restaurants, hip clubs, and designer furniture shops.

Since star power has helped Toronto spread its message as one of the world's most cosmopolitan cities, it's not surprising that the city has called on the stars to reinvigorate the landscape in the form of a contemporary architectural renaissance. Internationally heralded luminaries such as Daniel Libeskind, Norman Foster, Will Alsop, and local-born superstar Frank Gehry have all recently contributed landmark buildings to the city's streetscape, and even acclaimed cellist Yo-Yo Ma has gotten in on the act, partnering to design the outdoor Toronto Music Garden, and helping to brand the city as a destination for architecture buffs.

While Vancouver will always reign as Canada's gateway to Asia, and Montreal can rightfully claim the title as Canada's—and arguably North America's—most European city, Toronto long ago shook off the dowdy cobwebs of its Victorian past to emerge as one of the world's most truly vibrant cities. You'll find every ethnicity, from Albanian to Zimbabwean, represented in the city's many pocket-sized ethnic neighborhoods, and should you ever tire of exploration, you can head to one of the buzzing rooftop patios to recharge with a cocktail alongside a beautiful, international who's-who.

Noted social historian Jane Jacobs called Toronto "the city that works," and you won't doubt that characterization once you've spent a few days here. You're in for a roaring good time.

Welcome to fabulous Toronto ...

THE 99 BEST of TORONTO

Who needs another "Best" list? You do—if it comes with details and insider tips that make the difference between a good experience and a great one. We've pinpointed the 33 categories that make Toronto exciting, magnetic, and unforgettable, and picked the absolute three best places to go for each. With a little help from Night+Day, Toronto is yours for the taking.

Always-Trendy Tables

#1–3: Toronto's style setters know what makes a restaurant hot—it's a magical mix of flash, glamour, and, of course, great food. But only a few hot spots can withstand the test of time. When one manages to find the right combination of ingredients to keep it fresh and fun, it makes the leap from hot to legendary.

Lee
603 King St. W., Entertainment District, 416-504-7867 • Hot & Cool

The Draw: The crowds come to Lee, funky spiritual sister to super-refined Susur just next door, to sample the imaginative creations of star chef Susur Lee in a more casual setting.

The Scene: Foodies and fashionistas mix and mingle at the pink Lucite tables on purple upholstered banquettes. Stylish servers guide guests through a menu of over 30 small-plate selections. *Mon-Sat 5:30-11:15pm.* $$ ≡

Hot Tip: A plate-glass wall faces the street—ask for a table near it for a prime see-and-be-seen spot.

Sassafraz*
100 Cumberland St., Bloor/Yorkville, 416-964-2222 • Hot & Cool

The Draw: One of Toronto's most popular see-and-be-seen restaurants, this longstanding hot spot is the perfect place to enjoy delicious, locally inspired cuisine surrounded by a glamorous international jet-set crowd.

The Scene: Sassafraz oozes a measured coolness, and Hollywood A-listers jockey with a coterie of beautiful and deep-pocketed locals to experience the venerable, gorgeously reborn space to dine on dishes like Clare Island organic salmon cooked sous vide with white beans, Swiss chard, and tomato horseradish broth. *Daily 11am-2am.* $$$ B ≡

Hot Tip: If you can't score a reservation for dinner, drop by for wine and a mouthwatering plate of gourmet Canadian artisan cheeses.

Swan
892 Queen St. W., West Queen West, 416-532-0452 • Hip

The Draw: Big crowds congregate here to savor nouvelle-diner cuisine served in a slightly ironic retro-diner setting.

The Scene: It's Andy of Mayberry meets Basquiat: Artists, gallery owners, and myriad other hipsters retire to the lunch counter and wooden booths, dining on updated comfort food dishes and discussing the latest must-see exhibition. *Mon-Fri noon-3:30pm and 5-10:30pm, Sat 10am-3:30pm and 5-11pm, Sun 10:30am-3:30pm and 5-10:30pm.* $$ ≡

Hot Tip: The art-infused action continues on weekends when Swan hosts one of the city's trendiest brunches.

Brunches

#4–6: After a late night out on the town, Torontonians love to come out to refuel on Sundays. With so many restaurants offering a decadent brunch, it can be hard to choose. But the best places offer a lively scene and beautiful setting in addition to a satisfying feast that is sure to ease your entry into the day.

Gallery Grill

7 Hart House Cir., 2nd Fl., University of Toronto, 416-978-2445 • Classic

The Draw: The flawless combination of old-world charm and refined, inventive cuisine makes it a consistent favorite.

The Scene: Though the guests represent a cross-section of Toronto, the Harry Potter–esque room oozes classic style—think vaulted ceilings, stained-glass windows, coat-of-arms flatware, carved furniture, and Gothic Revival masonry. The architecture raises expectations, and the chef delivers, with items like smoked trout and braised beef cheeks. *Mon-Fri noon-2:30pm, Sun noon-3pm.* $$ –

Hot Tip: After your meal, head downstairs to the JM Barnicke Gallery, a hidden gem that exhibits significant historical and contemporary Canadian art.

Jamie Kennedy Wine Bar and Restaurant

9 Church St., St. Lawrence, 416-362-1957 • Hot & Cool

The Draw: Jamie Kennedy's impeccable culinary style has made this one of Toronto's most popular dining spots.

The Scene: The brunch crowd that gathers in this simple dining room every Sunday consists of a high quotient of the food-obsessed with a sprinkling of hipsters. This isn't traditional brunch with eggs Benny and Western omelette—consider instead a tartelette with cherry tomatoes and smoked sheep's milk cheese, mushroom ragout with polenta and organic egg, or beef brisket hash with horseradish crème fraîche. *Tue-Sat 11:30am-11pm, Sun 11am-3pm.* $$$$ =

Hot Tip: Make an early reservation so you can order the best dishes off the menu before items run out.

Mitzi's Café & Gallery

100 Sorauren Ave., Parkdale, 416-588-1234 • Hip

The Draw: These updated-yet-homey interpretations of breakfast classics have given Mitzi a cultlike local following.

The Scene: Urban scenesters recovering post-clubbing, couples, young families—yes, kids—and a mix of people drawn from the neighborhood drop in to dine on Mitzi Gaynor's talk-of-the-town brunch. Homemade granola with fruit and vanilla yogurt, fluffy French toast, and syrups made from seasonal fruits are the stuff of local legend. *Mon-Fri 7:30am-4pm, Sat-Sun 9am-4pm.* $ =

Hot Tip: Don't be deterred by the weekend lineup; tables turn over quickly and you'll be glad you waited.

Best Canadian Cuisine

#7-9: Canadian cuisine is inspired by traditional European cooking styles and highlights locally sourced ingredients. For Canadian chefs the focus is on seasonal delights from the southern Niagara region, eastern Prince Edward County, or the southwestern Guelph area.

Canoe Restaurant & Bar*

66 Wellington St. W., 54th Fl., Financial District, 416-364-0054 • Classic

The Draw: A stunning view of the Toronto Islands enhances the sublime cuisine.

The Scene: The view from the 54th floor of the Toronto-Dominion Tower, along with the elegant décor, seduces patrons even before the menu arrives to win them over completely. Some of the finest examples of inventive Canadian cuisine emerge from this kitchen, such as truffle ravioli with porcini foam. *Mon-Wed noon-2:30pm and 5-10pm, Thu-Fri noon-2:30pm and 5-10:30pm. $$$* B =

Hot Tip: Everything on the tasting menus is also available à la carte, so you don't have to miss out if you don't want multiple courses.

Czehoski*

678 Queen St. W., Queen Street, 416-366-6787• Hip

The Draw: One of the city's fast-rising culinary stars, Nathan Isberg is reason enough to come.

The Scene: This is one of the trendiest tables in one of the city's trendiest neighborhoods. Expect local artists, media types, dating couples, Queen Street's usual gang of hipsters, and, increasingly, an out-of-town crowd that's gotten the inside scoop. Whenever a magazine covers Toronto's thriving arts reputation, Czehoski gets a mention. Note that while the food is highly regarded, service can be slow. *Daily 11:30am-10:30pm (bar until 2am nightly). $$* B =

Hot Tip: The flammekuche is a delectable starter of smoked ricotta, duck bacon, and shallots on a thin crust—so good you could easily order it twice.

Drake Dining Room and Raw Bar*

1150 Queen St. W., West Queen West, 416-531-5042 • Hip

The Draw: Rising star of the Toronto restaurant scene, exec chef Anthony Rose fashions imaginative creations in the city's hippest surroundings.

The Scene: The crowd is as fashionable as the décor, which includes a gleaming raw bar and plush dining room. Artists and actors, film and television professionals, savvy local politicians and designers lounge on the green cushions waiting for Rose's fiendishly unique creations as house music plays from the lounge. *Mon-Tue 11am-2pm and 6-10pm, Wed-Sat 11am-2pm and 6-11pm, Sun 11am-2pm and 6-9pm. $$* 0 =

Hot Tip: Dinner can be your ticket to get ahead of the line for après-dinner drinks in the ever-popular lounge.

Celebrity Hangouts

#10–12: With so many productions filming on Toronto's streets and a steady stream of international sports teams hitting town, celebrity sightings have become a favorite sport of locals—especially during the Toronto International Film Festival.

Hemingway's
142 Cumberland Ave., Bloor/Yorkville, 416-968-2828 • Classic

The Draw: This casual restaurant/bar's welcoming ambience has made it a perennial favorite at all hours with locals and visiting celebs alike.

The Scene: Toronto's only heated year-round rooftop patio boasts a fine view of Yorkville's main drag, and an indoor bar and summertime streetside patio. The casual menu features typical bar items, but the crowds mainly come for the friendly party vibe—and those crowds can include Hollywood royalty and pro-sports figures. *Daily 11am-2am.* =

Hot Tip: If you need to catch that one game while you're on vacation, this is the place to see it in style.

This Is London
364 Richmond St. W., Entertainment District, 416-351-1100 • Hip

The Draw: This elite Brit-pop cool club draws wealthy, 30-something club kids with an exclusive door policy and a suitably hedonistic scene for an over-the-top night out.

The Scene: London boasts stylists in the ladies' room and authentic British music memorabilia. Room 364, the celebrity-rich VIP area, takes posh partying to its highest level. The large main floor is all dancing go-go boots and minis; the second floor overlooks the gyrating action below and includes plenty of cozy nooks where you can retire for more intimate conversation. The third floor houses the extravagant ladies' room and spa. *Fri-Sat 10pm-3am.* ℂ≡

Hot Tip: This is one of the city's hardest velvet ropes. Visit thisislondonclub.com to email your request to get on the guest list and bypass any line.

Trattoria Giancarlo
41 Clinton St., Little Italy, 416-533-9619 • Classic

The Draw: With its welcoming vibe and perfect Italian fare, this neighborhood institution has long been a favorite with high-profile locals and visiting celebs.

The Scene: One of the pioneers that transformed Little Italy from ethnic neighborhood to one of Toronto's premier hot spots, Giancarlo remains to this day a place to see and be seen. Sophia Loren loved it, and her three-hour lunch there is still talked about. Watch the mother-and-son chef team prepare your meal in an open kitchen as you enjoy the European ambience. *Mon-Sat 6-10pm.* $$$ =

Hot Tip: Definitely call ahead to get a reservation for the coveted patio in summer—its corner location makes it a prime people-watching spot.

Classic Hotel Bars

#13–15: In recent years, many of Toronto's biggest hotels have undergone a wave of renovations. What resulted was a kind of competition for stunning design. Hotel bars got buffed and shined as well, and now lure not only hotel guests but in-the-know locals to enjoy their spruced-up settings.

Avenue

Four Seasons Toronto, 21 Avenue Rd., Bloor/Yorkville, 416-964-0411 • Classic

The Draw: This is quite simply one of the most fashionable restaurant/lounges in town, in part because of its plum location in the Four Seasons.

The Scene: There may be no better place to catch up with the A-listers who frequent the hotel than in these sophisticated surroundings. Chic and sleek, this highly polished spot draws an upper-crust crowd of handsome business types, stylish shoppers, and the odd celeb. The 20-foot yellow onyx bar shines like glass. *Mon-Sat 11:45am-1am, Sun 10:30am-2:30pm and 4:30-11pm.* ☰

Hot Tip: Order from the posh snack menu, which includes mini Kobe beef, foie gras burgers, and other gourmet delights.

Azure Restaurant & Bar

InterContinental Toronto Centre, 225 Front St. W., Entertainment District, 416-597-8142 • Classic

The Draw: This restaurant/lounge may be best known for its fabulous artwork, but it also benefits from a great downtown location and sleek, modern décor.

The Scene: *Liquid Veil*, the mesmerizing azure-blue glass art installation by Stuart Reid, sets a mood of contemporary elegance that's matched by the scene of well-dressed visitors and downtowners. A soaring wall of windows provides natural light even in bad weather. The extensive martini list and fairly lengthy list of wines are complemented by a continental-based menu. *Daily 5:30am-10:30pm.* ☰

Hot Tip: Join downtowners Thursdays for happy-hour cocktails.

Library Bar

Fairmont Royal York, 100 Front St. W., Downtown/Yonge, 416-368-2511 • Classic

The Draw: Located in one of the city's poshest hotels, this old-school bar reminiscent of a gentleman's club has gained a stylish following.

The Scene: Heavy wood furniture and a carved, polished bar, leather upholstery, and richly colored drapes are the backdrop to a scene of high-powered businesspeople, politicians, and visiting VIPs, as well as upscale travelers looking for a refined place to relax. The well-suited and well-coiffed sip well-mixed drinks and nibble from a casual lounge menu. *Mon-Fri noon-1am, Sat 5pm-1am.* ☰

Hot Tip: This is a good spot for a quiet meeting during the day.

Best

Contemporary Art and Design Spaces

#16–18: Sure, West Queen West has been declared the epicenter of Toronto's modern arts and design scene, but you can find thriving cultural venues in almost any neighborhood. These off–West Queen West hot spots draw some of Toronto's savviest crowds.

Design Exchange

234 Bay St., Financial District, 416-363-6121 • Hip

The Draw: This unusual museum and exhibition space is devoted to the principles of design.

The Scene: The Design Exchange aims to elevate the importance of design in contemporary life. To that end, it offers educational programs in addition to a variety of theme-based exhibits, such as plastic (materials) or home appliances (functional design). The main exhibition hall features changing shows, while the Chalmers Design Centre showcases the work of graduating design classes, competition winners, and the latest innovations. *Mon-Fri 9am-5pm, Sat-Sun noon-5pm.* $

Hot Tip: Aficionados should call ahead to make an appointment (Mon, Wed, and Fri afternoons) to browse the archive of journals, design books, and other texts.

401 Richmond

401 Richmond St. W., Entertainment District, 416-595-5900 • Hip

The Draw: This old industrial building is now a highly desirable spot for art galleries, studios, and arts organizations, making it into a great local arts scene.

The Scene: The building itself is a rabbit warren of hallways and doors, but pick up a guide and you'll do just fine finding 401's many tenants. They include Gallery 44, devoted to contemporary photography; the collective YYZ Artists' Outlet Studio, the Dub Poets' Collective; and film festival offices, among others. Add a hip cafe, and the atmosphere is all about cutting-edge creativity. *Hours vary according to tenants, and special events occur in evenings, but galleries are typically open Tue-Sat noon-5pm.*

Hot Tip: Make your way to the rooftop patio in good weather for a laid-back place to kick back and watch the bustle of the Entertainment District.

Power Plant Gallery

231 Queen's Quay W., Harbourfront, 416-973-4949 • Hip

The Draw: Three fabulous art spaces in a contemporary and newly refurbished arts complex on the Harbourfront draw an endless stream of style-setters.

The Scene: The goal of the exhibits here is to challenge and excite in flexible indoor spaces. In addition to a smaller indoor gallery space, outdoor venues are used extensively whenever possible to showcase installations or film screenings. *Tue-Sun noon-6pm.* $

Hot Tip: The Power Plant runs an ambitious program of lectures, talks, and other special events—check the website (thepowerplant.org) for schedules.

Best Dance Clubs

#19–21: Toronto's clubs are red-hot these days and guests lists are highly competitive. You'll have to pass muster with door staff, but once inside, you can expect fab décor, long drink lists, and scads of well-dressed partiers.

Afterlife Nightclub

250 Adelaide St. W., Entertainment District, 416-593-6126 • Hot & Cool

The Draw: Three floors and four levels of over-the-top style and cutting-edge sound systems have made this a perennial favorite of 20- and 30-somethings.

The Scene: On the lower-level dance floor, splashes of colored lighting illuminate gyrating and scantily clad dancers and all the reflective surfaces of the bar in a darkened room, while the music throbs from a high-tech sound system. You can take a break from dancing in a quieter lounge upstairs, which overlooks the downstairs action. Higher still, it's stark white with blue lights for intimate conversations in sexy and more upscale surroundings. The crowd is young and fun-loving, and heats up the dance floor all night long. *Fri-Sat 10pm-3am.* C≡

Hot Tip: The roof has one of the best patios in Clubland, and if hunger strikes, head up there to sample some excellent BBQ.

BaBaLuu

136 Yorkville Ave., Bloor/Yorkville, 416-515-0587 • Classic

The Draw: This hot Latin dance club promises over-the-top décor, a sexy dance scene, and a high-fashion, celeb-studded crowd ready to party the night away.

The Scene: Mirrored walls and bright Latin-flavored colors dominate the room, where everyone, male and female, is dressed to kill and grooving to hot Latin beats. Expect a VIP scene of Hollywood stars and pro-sports icons on the other side of the velvet rope, and a sweaty dance floor. The dim lighting adds to the exclusive urban ambience. *Tue-Sun 9pm-2am.* C≡

Hot Tip: Thursdays are the best night, when a regular crowd of Latin-dance aficionados get there before 9pm to heat up the dance floor ahead of the crowds.

Gallery

132 Queen's Quay E., Harbourfront, 416-869-9444 • Hot & Cool

The Draw: Some of the city's best DJs spin in this chic and intimate setting.

The Scene: With space for only 300 clubbers to groove to progressive and house sounds, it's one of the most difficult lineups in the city. In keeping with the gorgeous room's design décor, patrons spend a lot of time getting their casual-cool looks just so, and you should too if you hope to pass the doorman's muster. *Sat 10pm-3am.* C≡

Hot Tip: Arrive before midnight to be assured of a spot on the dance floor until the wee hours.

Best Ethnic Dining

#22-24: This city has over 90 ethnicities who speak more than 100 languages, so it's no surprise that the dining scene delivers a wide array of enticing dishes to choose from. But these destinations go well beyond exciting the taste buds and promise a cosmopolitan scene and stylish ambience as well.

Babur

273 Queen St. W., Entertainment District, 416-599-7720 • Classic

The Draw: Babur offers superb Northern Indian cuisine in a polished setting.

The Scene: In the simple dining room, sitar music plays as you watch the chefs energetically assemble your meal. From foodies who've read the rave reviews to hip creative professionals who live and work in the area, people come from all over town to sample the cuisine. *Mon-Sat 11:30am-3pm and 5-10:30pm, Sun 11:30am-3pm and 5-9:30pm.* $$ =

Hot Tip: Start with pakoras and a sweet lassi to ready your palate for spicy entrées.

Caju

922 Queen St. W., West Queen West, 416-532-2550 • Hip

The Draw: This sunny slice of Brazil has a chic ambience and fantastic food.

The Scene: The crowd is Queen West hipsters and foodies who've come to check out the buzz on this unusual addition to the Toronto dining scene. Caju comes from the Brazilian word for cashew nut—only a hint of the exotic names and flavors you'll enjoy like sirloin grilled with garlic butter served with crispy cassava chips. Join the crowds in the vibrant dining room for a Brazilian-flavored cocktail, and enjoy the sophisticated, loungey aura of the place. *Tue-Thu 5:30-10pm, Fri-Sat 5:30-11pm.* $$ =

Hot Tip: Try the signature drink, the caipirinha.

Ouzeri

500A Danforth Ave., Greektown, 416-778-0500 • Classic

The Draw: The upscale Greek-Mediterranean décor is all very pleasant, but the atmospheric and bustling streetside patio is the real hook here.

The Scene: A lively European cafe ambience is perfected by blue awnings and a wrought-iron railing. Ouzeri has been packing in the crowds for years, and many fun-seekers stay for drinks after dinner. The menu features an extensive list of Greek classics. The warm ambience is complemented by outstanding food and friendly service. It's a boisterous and festive place to kick back and pretend you're on the sunny Mediterranean. *Sun-Thu 11:30am-11pm, Fri-Sat 11:30am-midnight.* $$ =

Hot Tip: Assure that you'll get a seat on the popular patio by reserving ahead of time.

Best

Fine Dining

#25–27: Torontonians love formal dining experiences, albeit with a touch of contemporary comfort and flair thrown in. Local chefs are happy to oblige, with the best places mixing old-school charm with modern manners.

Auberge du Pommier

4150 Yonge St., Uptown, 416-222-2220 • Classic

The Draw: Well-groomed locals come here to savor old-school French classics served in a rustic former woodcutter's cottage.

The Scene: The Auberge has long been synonymous with high-end French dining in Toronto. The mood here is refined, the crowd dressed elegantly to the nines. Seamless French country style is done here with panache: cut stone walls, huge barn beams, wood-burning fireplaces, and in the summer, a garden terrace. *Mon-Thu 5-9pm, Fri-Sat 5-9:30pm.* $$$ ⊟

Hot Tip: Be sure to reserve a table on the garden terrace in summer.

Opus

37 Prince Arthur Ave., Bloor/Yorkville, 416-921-3105 • Classic

The Draw: Simultaneously glamorous and intimate, Opus serves up one of the city's most refined dining experiences.

The Scene: Located in a restored Victorian townhouse, this eatery caters to an upper-class clientele with restrained elegance. In the dining room, the sexy spot lighting and grand columns, white linens, and leather seating create a sober, Manhattan-style effect. The fare is high-end French-continental and the friendly owners are the hosts. *Daily 5:30-11:30pm.* $$$ ⊟

Hot Tip: Call ahead to reserve one of the five courtyard tables in summer, shaded by a maple tree.

Sen5es Restaurant & Lounge

SoHo Metropolitan, 318 Wellington St. W., Entertainment District,
416-935-0400 • Hot & Cool

The Draw: Contemporary opulence, combined with a warm and intimate ambience, makes this an excellent choice for a special night out.

The Scene: Sen5es aims to please all the senses—and it succeeds with its elegant interior, gorgeous food, and fantastic wine list. Brazilian-born executive chef Claudio Aprile brings his South American sensibilities to the top-quality meat and seafood. *Tue-Sat 6-10pm; bar and bistro daily 4pm-1am.* $$$ B ⊟

Hot Tip: Come early to enjoy a drink in the sexy lounge beforehand.

Best

Gay Scenes

#28–30: With the continent's second-largest gay population, Toronto's Gay Village has always had a host of bars and clubs. But along with the old favorites, a growing demand for more stylish venues has resulted in a newly revitalized scene.

Byzantium*

499 Church St., Gay Village, 416-922-3859 • Hip

The Draw: A sophisticated restaurant with a busy bar-lounge and lengthy, inventive cocktail list attracts the sexy young things in droves.

The Scene: The crowd is mixed gays and hip straights, with an overall sheen of fashionable downtowners, and the bar is seldom empty. The playful Gay Village mood is sophisticated, still friendly but not so raucous as some places. A richly colored dining room with florals and formal seating offers a menu of globally inspired dishes. After dinner, the action at the bar really heats up. *Daily 5:30pm-2am.* ≡

Hot Tip: Check out the long martini list—the Byzantium original Sonomatini (vodka, cabernet sauvignon, and sweet vermouth) is great.

Fly Nightclub

8 Gloucester St., Gay Village, 416-410-5426 • Hot & Cool

The Draw: This hot gay-male dance club has multiple floors of style and flash.

The Scene: About 1,000 revelers pass through the doors of Fly on any given Saturday night, when the Canada's best DJs pump out the beats till 7am. If you've seen *Queer as Folk*, this is the series' original Babylon Club, and that's the celeb-studded scene of wild partying you'll find here, with the latest in sound and light systems cranking it out to the huge dance floor. The monster facility also includes quieter lounge areas. Locals consistently rate this best dance club in town. *Fri 10pm-3am, Sat 10pm-7am.* ⓒ≡

Hot Tip: The bistro downstairs is a good place to fuel up beforehand.

Fuzion Resto-Lounge & Garden*

580 Church St., Gay Village, 416-944-9888 • Hot & Cool

The Draw: This Gay Village hot spot has it all: fab cocktails, a buzzing scene, great food, and a house DJ to set the mood.

The Scene: Fashionable hetero and gay diners gather in this elegant cream dining room to indulge in chef Patrick Wiese's menu of locally sourced products featuring unusual options such as venison. After 10pm, the lounge and street-side courtyard fill with trendsetters, who like to see and be seen, enjoy a luscious cocktail (or three), and revel in the latest soul-house mix from the Fuzion DJ. Those looking for a romantic spot should head to the back garden, with a fish pond and waterfall to set the mood. *Tue-Wed 5pm-11pm, Thu-Sun 5pm-2am.* ≡

Hot Tip: Sunday night, the lounge becomes a very hot property in the Village, so make a dinner reservation to ensure entry to the lounge.

Best

Guided Tours

#31–33: Forget about boring buses packed with gawking tourists. In Toronto, even hipsters will find guided tours that amuse, entertain, and enlighten with little-known insights.

Artinsite

Various locations, 416-979-5704, artinsite.com • Hot & Cool

The Draw: Get the real scoop on Toronto's art scene through a guided tour of art galleries, studios, and architectural sites given by a local expert.

The Scene: See Toronto with an artist's eye. Longtime arts journalist Betty Ann Jordan is also a columnist with stylish *Toronto Life* magazine, and she leads tours of art galleries and studios. Scheduled tours can include art instruction or theory and history, even access to impressive private collections. Call ahead to book the tour of your choice. Tours available afternoons and evenings. *Call in advance to make arrangements.* $$

Hot Tip: Jordan leads a free tour of Yorkville galleries the first Thursday evening of every month starting at 6:30pm—call and ask for the starting location.

CHUM/Citytv Building

299 Queen St. W., Entertainment District, 416-591-5757 • Hot & Cool

The Draw: This is the hub of the most recognized media empire in town.

The Scene: The CHUM/City empire and its historic downtown location are home to the coolest Canadian broadcasters, including music video station Much Music. Your tour of this innovative broadcaster includes the open-studio concept newsrooms, as well as a view of cable specialties like Much. You'll get an entertaining inside view of how television is made. Bumping into local celebs is a given, and you may just run into an international superstar. *Tours offered afternoons Mon-Fri. Call ahead for details.* $

Hot Tip: Check out Speakers' Corner, a self-operated video booth where visitors tape their opinions, with the results broadcast later.

Steam Whistle Brewing Company

The Roundhouse, 255 Bremner Blvd., Harbourfront, 416-362-2337 • Hip

The Draw: This boutique brewery is one of the coolest hangouts in town.

The Scene: When upstart microbrewery Steam Whistle took over the historic John Street Roundhouse in the shadow of the CN Tower in 1998, the owners set out not only to produce a fine beer, but to be the hippest brew in town. They succeeded, and are now a mainstay in virtually every nightclub and bar in Toronto. Take a walk along the catwalks, and enjoy a tasting of their signature pilsner afterward. *Mon-Sat noon-6pm, Sun noon-5pm; tours Mon-Sat 1pm-5pm.* $

Hot Tip: Steam Whistle has become a popular venue for corporate and other events, so call ahead to be sure it isn't closing for a private party.

Historic Buildings

#34–36: While it's a thoroughly modern city, Toronto wears its history with pride. Two major fires have destroyed many of the oldest buildings, but you can glimpse the city's grand past in these carefully restored locales.

Casa Loma

1 Austin Terr., Uptown, 416-923-1171 • Classic

The Draw: This imposing medieval castle overlooks modern-day Toronto from a manicured six-acre estate.

The Scene: It took prominent early 20th-century Toronto businessman and industrialist Sir Henry Pellatt nearly three years and 300 men to build his dream home. The building includes towers and turrets, richly decorated suites with original antiques, a vast Great Hall with huge oak beams, secret passages, and an 800-foot tunnel connecting the main building with the stables and carriage house. *Daily 9:30am-5pm (last entry at 4pm); Gardens (May-Oct) daily 9:30am-4pm.* $

Hot Tip: Climb to the top of a turret for a breathtaking view of the city below.

St. Lawrence Market

92 Front St. E., St. Lawrence, 416-392-7219 • Hip

The Draw: Come for the food, or just to check out the crowds at this culinary mecca that buzzes on Saturday mornings.

The Scene: The St. Lawrence Market bustles with a cross-section of Toronto. And the Market delivers something for everyone in clean, bright efficiency, with the traditional array of meats, cheeses, and produce, as well as specialties like caviar and smoked salmon, organic coffees and teas, prepared foods, and baked goods. The first floor also houses jewelry, clothing, and gift retailers. *Tue-Thu 8am-6pm, Fri 8am-7pm, Sat 5am-5pm.*

Hot Tip: Check the Market Gallery for exhibits, open most days until 4pm.

Spadina Museum

285 Spadina Rd., Uptown, 416-392-6910 • Classic

The Draw: This beautifully restored Edwardian charmer on well-tended grounds allows visitors to see how the other half lived.

The Scene: The house began its life as a country estate in Victorian times, evolving into a townhouse in the Edwardian era as the city began to grow around it. Begun in 1866, it retains its original furnishings and chronicles the lives of the Austin family (and upper-class Torontonians in general) throughout the 20th century. *Sep 4-Dec 31 Tue-Fri noon-4pm, Sat-Sun and holidays noon-5pm; May 1-Labor Day Tue-Sun noon-5pm.* $

Hot Tip: Horticulturists will want to wander the six-acre gardens, home to some 300 varieties of plants and flowers.

Hot Chefs

#37–39: Whether they're playing to the cameras, creating a seasonal menu, or opening the newest see-and-be-seen room, this city's powerhouse chefs keep the crowds—and the international press—buzzing.

Bistro & Bakery Thuet

609 King St. W., Entertainment District, 416-603-2777 • Classic

The Draw: Unwavering culinary excellence means that food here incorporates many of this country's finest ingredients.

The Scene: Deep-pocketed locals and visitors—and those looking to splurge on something very special—book long in advance and then dress up to dine on Thuet's seasonal masterpieces. From the exacting classic décor to the refined palates of the guests and thoughtful menu, sophistication is the buzzword. *Tue-Fri 11:30am-2pm and 5:30-11pm, Sat 5:30-11pm, Sun 11am-2pm. $$$* ≡

Hot Tip: Consider dropping in for brunch—it's one of the city's most noteworthy options and features the chef's legendary charcuterie as well as Toronto's most widely acclaimed steak frites.

Colborne Lane*

45 Colborne St., St. Lawrence, 416-368-9009 • Hot & Cool

The Draw: Chef Claudio Aprile's pioneering foray into the heady world of molecular gastronomy is a foodie favorite.

The Scene: The city's who's-who, serious foodies, and curious locals with deep pockets flock to Aprile's room to see what he has brought back from his stint alongside El Bulli's Ferran Adrià. Though both the décor and the patrons look beautiful, Claudio's the star. *Tue-Wed 5:30-10:30pm, Thu-Sat 5:30-11pm. $$$* ⒷⒾ≡

Hot Tip: Go hungry—you will be strongly encouraged to try three or four courses per person to fully experience the wonders of Aprile's talents.

Susur

601 King St. W., Entertainment District, 416-603-2205 • Hot & Cool

The Draw: Polished elegance combines with food artistry from one of the world's top chefs to create a destination dining experience.

The Scene: The trendy and cosmopolitan diners of Toronto can't get enough of their hometown star chef and flock here for masterpieces of Pan-Asian fusion in streamlined and modern surroundings—think muted colors and soft lighting. Known for expert service and over-the-top plating served at a leisurely pace to an elegant crowd, Susur promises to deliver a magical evening. Reserve far in advance. *Tue-Thu 6-10pm, Fri-Sat 6-10:30pm. $$$$* ≡

Hot Tip: Order the famous five- or seven-course tasting menu to experience the best of Lee's culinary wizardry. Note that the meal is served in reverse order—meaning that it goes from the heaviest to the lightest course.

Best

Jazz Clubs

#40–42: Jazz has never gone out of style in Toronto. Fueled by the hugely successful Downtown Jazz Festival, the world's greats have made this city a home away from home—and a superb place to catch some outstanding music.

Live @ Courthouse

57 Adelaide St. E., St. Lawrence, 416-214-9379 • Classic

The Draw: The city's most sophisticated jazz crowd hangs here to check out the top talent onstage. The beautiful historic space doesn't hurt, either.

The Scene: In a room punctuated by soaring ceilings, marble floors, wrought-iron fixtures, and four fireplaces, a great-looking—and deep-pocketed—Jazzophile crowd gathers to enjoy concerts in bebop, fusion, swing, groove, and even Latin music and the blues. *Tue-Sat. Show times vary (usually around 8-9pm).* C ≡

Hot Tip: Head to the upstairs balcony Musicians Lounge for the best acoustics.

Opal Jazz Lounge

472 Queen St. W., Entertainment District, 416-646-6725 • Hot & Cool

The Draw: Opal is known for its excellent live jazz and beautiful contemporary-cool dinner room.

The Scene: With the exception of the large Miles Davis photo, every décor element in this beautiful modern space is high-design. Not everyone is here for the music, but in between drinking gorgeous cocktails and dining on chef Fawzi Kotb's skillfully crafted fare, a new wave of urban, ultra-chic jazz fans is being born. *Tue-Sat 5:30pm-late.* C =

Hot Tip: While you might flow effortlessly from dining room to lounge, your tab doesn't. Make sure you don't pay the "entertainment surcharge" twice; it's included in your order.

Rex Hotel Jazz & Blues Bar

194 Queen St. W., Entertainment District, 416-598-2475 • Classic

The Draw: This downtown beer parlor has become a venerable home of jazz and blues with an honest musician-friendly feel.

The Scene: The audience will be thick with musicians and art-school types, and music lovers dressed in anything from Prada to Levis who come first and foremost for the great music—12 different acts per week—and casual, relaxed vibe. Canada's finest musicians play here against a post-modern retro tavern-chic backdrop. The Rex is an industry and a local jazz community mainstay. *Daily 11am-late. Show times vary; call for details.* C ≡

Hot Tip: During the Downtown Jazz Festival, the Rex hosts the likes of Harry Connick Jr. and Ani DiFranco, who show up from time to time for a jam.

Late-Night Eats

#43–45: As Toronto's club scene has grown, so has the city's appetite for good eats at any hour of the day or night. From high-end to cafe-style, there's something to please every palate after the rigors of clubbing.

Bistro 333

333 King St. W., Entertainment District, 416-971-3336 • Classic

The Draw: A Mediterranean bistro goes Clubland-slick with late hours.

The Scene: With sexy lighting playing against the polished woods and the curving chair backs of a classic bistro interior, Bistro 333 draws hordes of hungry night crawlers. They feast on a menu of creative pastas and risottos, along with steak and seafood, in an intimate setting. This is a space made for partiers in search of elegant and satisfying sustenance. *Sun-Thu 11:30am-11:30pm, Fri-Sat 11:30am-4am. $$$* ≡

Hot Tip: The nightclub upstairs is open until 3am if you feel the need to work off some of those carbs.

7 West Cafe

7 Charles St. W., Bloor/Yorkville, 416-928-9041 • Classic

The Draw: This charming, artsy, and romantic cafe in a restored semi-detached Victorian draws patrons any hour, day or night.

The Scene: A kitchen that's open 24/7 can attract all sorts. Here you can expect a hip crowd with a solid quotient of club refugees in the wee hours. Twinkling lights and antique mirrors accent bare brick walls and wood furnishings, which are all the right ingredients for inspired late-night bites from a casual menu of pasta, pizza, and panini. Add a patio deck in the summer, and it's the perfect solution to hunger pangs with an uptown gloss. *Daily 24 hours. $* ≡

Hot Tip: The panini are both quickly served and superb no matter what the hour.

Sneaky Dee's

431 College St. W., Little Italy, 416-603-3090 • Hip

The Draw: Tex-Mex in the middle of the night—what more can you ask for, pardner?

The Scene: Students, bar hoppers, and 30-something night owls, all with a slightly alternative bent, stop in at this colorful spot to nosh on pub-influenced classics that include crowd favorites like nachos, burritos, and wings. *Mon-Tue 11am-3am, Wed-Thu 11am-4am, Fri 11am-4:30am, Sat 9am-4:30am, Sun 9am-3am.* ≡

Hot Tip: Drop by earlier in the evening to enjoy edgier live music performances on the venue's stage.

Best

Live Music

#46–48: Toronto's live music scene comes in all shapes and sizes, from small spaces for local singer-songwriters to the vast venues for touring acts. Here's the three that can be relied on to deliver an outstanding evening: great music and a crowd that loves to party.

Jeff Healey's Roadhouse

56 Blue Jays Way, Entertainment District, 416-593-2626 • Classic

The Draw: Blind blues-guitar legend opens bar dedicated to delivering that live rock 'n' roll experience: Crowds follow.

The Scene: The décor is classic rock cave, complete with funky, if murky, lighting, distressed walls, and minimalist, utilitarian furnishings—but it's the music that matters here, and what better foil for the best of live blues and rock from a hometown legend? Expect a downtown crowd of music lovers and plenty of music-industry professionals. *Daily 5pm-closing.* C≡

Hot Tip: Jeff himself takes to the stage Thursday nights for his special brand of blues, and on Saturdays plays with his own Jazz Kings in a free matinee.

Mod Club Theatre

722 College St. W., Little Italy, 416-588-4663 • Hip

The Draw: Owned by former glam-rocker Mark Holmes, this club is where the hottest new bands and DJs perform.

The Scene: A full-service entertainment complex and bar, including a state-of-the-art sound and light system, a full wall-size screen for video and film screenings, and enough cred and cool to bring the hipsters out in droves: What more can you want? *Daily 9pm-3am. Check concert listings for details.* C≡

Hot Tip: Saturday nights you'll find most of the crowd dressed up in Brit-pop cool of go-go boots and minis and long fake eyelashes, so come prepared.

Phoenix Concert Theatre

410 Sherbourne St., St. Lawrence, 416-323-1251 • Hip

The Draw: A legend in the Toronto entertainment scene, the Phoenix delivers 18,000 square feet of funky and original spaces devoted to music and much more.

The Scene: The Stones and Metallica have played on the main stage here, where the main floor features a 50-foot marble bar and a huge dance floor outfitted with the latest in sound and light. Le Loft overlooks the scene below with its own bar. The Parlour has pool tables to test your mettle. Look for fashion shows, arts events, live concerts, and the best DJs in town. *Opening hours depend on who's playing. Check the website (libertygroup.com/phoenix/phoenix.html) for current listings.* C≡

Hot Tip: There's sure to be a rockin' crowd Saturday nights, when famed alternative-rock radio station 102.1 FM broadcasts live on air.

Best

Martinis

#49–51: Mixologists are now a standard in the club life of this city and fierce competition to provide unique combinations has certainly raised the bar. These hot spots are trendsetters, consistently coming up with the latest, greatest, newest libation.

Flow Restaurant + Lounge*

133 Yorkville Ave., Bloor/Yorkville, 416-925-2143 • Hot & Cool

The Draw: At this sleek and stylish lounge, you'll find an upscale clientele getting the evening off to a festive start.

The Scene: You'll know why it's called Flow from the moment you walk in—the water flows everywhere here, beginning in the bubbly glass railings as you descend the stairs from the lounge to the restaurant area. The scene is typical Yorkville, upscale and fashionable, and the 30-something crowd enjoys kicking back the cocktails. The exotic drink list designed for high-end tippling is matched by an exotic menu of fusion cuisine. *Mon-Thu 5-11pm, Fri-Sat 5pm-2am.* ⊟

Hot Tip: Order the Lava Guava martini with tequila, fresh guava, and lime.

Martini Lounge

Pantages Hotel, 200 Victoria St., Downtown/Yonge, 416-362-1777 • Hot & Cool

The Draw: The fabulous martini menu, sleek space, and elegant vibe draw a great-looking international crowd.

The Scene: The stylish post-work drinking crowd mingles seamlessly with upscale visitors that include A-list celebs and the local who's-who that drop in for pre-theater and post-show drinks. HGTV's *The Designer Guys* have given the space a contemporary make-over dominated by a sleek double-sided fireplace that sets off the main room from the quieter "library," an extension of the lounge more suited to intimate conversation. *Sun-Wed 4-11pm, Thu-Sat 4pm-1am.* ⊟

Hot Tip: Come on Friday or Saturday night (8pm-midnight) for live jazz.

Rain*

19 Mercer St., Entertainment District, 416-599-7246 • Hot & Cool

The Draw: This Asian-fusion restaurant/lounge creates a sexy vibe with its seductive décor, including waterfall walls, drawing an A-list clientele.

The Scene: One of Toronto's perennial hot spots, Rain consistently draws crowds to its austere, water-themed space. Rain is a feast for the senses, complete with 15-foot waterfalls, a backlit frosted-glass bar, and bamboo elements to divide the space. Although the drink list is Asian-inspired, the martini is the drink of choice. The equally inventive menu of Asian fare is served on slate, river rocks, and Japanese pottery. *Mon-Wed 5:30-10pm, Thu-Sat 5:30-11pm.* ⊟

Hot Tip: If you want to combine dinner with your drinks, make your reservation well in advance—waiting lists of up to a month aren't uncommon here.

Meet Markets

#52–54: Downtown Toronto has a healthy population of single professionals, both young and old. Not too surprising, then, that a social scene with venues that help the beautiful people find each other has taken over the area.

C-Lounge

456 Wellington St. W., Entertainment District, 416-260-9393 • Hot & Cool

The Draw: The C-Lounge is a pure contemporary fashion statement in warm neutrals and dark leathers, with a stylish crowd to match.

The Scene: The leather couches are separated by airy drapes, and the sexy staff are dressed to kill. A fab ladies' room and two Aveda stylists in a spa area accessible to both the ladies and the guys prove this is clubbing gone ultra-posh. The scene is young, fashionable, and looking to hook up, with the odd celeb and pro-sports figure adding to the glam mood. Low lights and intimate seating make it the perfect place for serious flirting. Two large windows look out at the patio, complete with a wading pool; in good weather, you can lounge in comfort by the candlelit water. *Mon-Wed, Sat 10pm-2am, Thu 5pm-2am, Fri 9:30pm-2am.* C ≡

Hot Tip: The outdoor patios makes this a warm-weather favorite.

Crocodile Rock

240 Adelaide St. W., Entertainment District, 416-599-9751 • Classic

The Draw: Downtowners out for a good time keep this jovial spot hopping every night of the week.

The Scene: It's noisy and yes, all green, but you'll find a relaxed, good-time ambience in this crocodile-themed bar. Join the crowd of fun-loving professionals for a guaranteed night of good old-fashioned partying to a classic-rock soundtrack. *Tue-Fri 4pm-2am, Sat 7pm-2am.* C ≡

Hot Tip: Thursdays are popular, when appetizers are half-price and the pool tables are free all night long.

West Lounge

510 King St. W., Entertainment District, 416-361-9004 • Hot & Cool

The Draw: This stylish club with an exclusive atmosphere draws hordes of beautiful people.

The Scene: An address that doesn't actually exist leads to a sign and a doorway leading downstairs, where you have to pass inspection before you're allowed in. This is the perfect place to find others as beautiful as yourself, with a crowd of supermodel types and men on the prowl. *Wed-Sat 10pm-2am.* C ≡

Hot Tip: Thursdays are big here, when the spirited crowd dances to retro and old-school rock and nibbles on free hors d'oeuvres.

Best

Nouvelle Asian Restaurants

#55–57: Toronto's Asian population has been growing by leaps and bounds for decades. From the East-meets-West fusion cuisine, to the zen-like interiors and globally minded guests, these hot spots showcase some of Asia's finest contributions to the city's trendy restaurant scene.

Blowfish Restaurant + Sake Bar*

668 King St. W., Entertainment District, 416-860-0606 • Hot & Cool

The Draw: Architecturally impossible sushi, delicious sharing plates of French-influenced Asian cuisine, and a jet-set martini list make this place a hit.

The Scene: Is it a chic lounge with a great menu, or a hyper-stylish restaurant with a clubby vibe? Elegant food, well-executed cocktails, and a high-wattage décor mean that Blowfish's universally gorgeous patrons flow effortlessly between the restaurant and club realms. *Mon-Sat 5pm-2am.* $$ B≡

Hot Tip: Order a bottle of junmai daiginjo "divine droplets." The boutique sake is the only one in the world prepared in sub-zero temperatures and in conditions of 90 percent humidity, giving it a uniquely fresh and clean taste.

Doku 15

Cosmopolitan Hotel, 8 Colborne St., Downtown/Yonge, 416-368-3658 • Hot & Cool

The Draw: New-wave Asian cuisine is served in a stunning contemporary design space—and the gorgeous crowds are flocking.

The Scene: Even if it wasn't located in one of the city's hottest boutique hotels, the fashion-conscious locals and visiting celebrities would still drop by for G.Q. Pan's yin-and-yang creations. Factor in a vibrant lounge scene and some of Toronto's best DJs, and the see-and-be-seen factor skyrockets. *Mon-Wed 5-10:30pm, Thu-Sat 5-11:30pm; bar until late.* $$ B≡

Hot Tip: Order the chef's signature green-tea tiramisu.

Monsoon*

100 Simcoe St., Entertainment District, 416-979-7172 • Hot & Cool

The Draw: Starkly handsome Asian-inspired décor and fusion masterpieces draw the chic downtown set.

The Scene: The décor makes a dramatic statement in glowing red and gold, black and wood, and the suits love to sink into the leather couches in the warmly lit lounge. The scene is young and stylish, the crowd sophisticated urbanites. White linens and glowing wall treatments set an elegant mood in the dining room where exotic Japanese fusion is served on gorgeous plates of colored glass, accompanied by an extensive wine list. *Mon-Thu 5-9pm, Fri-Sat 5-11pm; bar until late.* $$ B◻≡

Hot Tip: Join the lively after-work crowd that flocks here Thursdays and Fridays.

Of-the-Moment Dining

#58–60: The newest wave of Toronto eateries fuse the triple threat—trendy décor, a chef with a pedigree, and a fashionable crowd.

Kultura

169 King St. E., Entertainment District, 416-363-9000 • Hot & Cool

The Draw: The beautiful fusion dishes and equally good-looking crowd draws in foodies and fashionistas alike.

The Scene: Both the diners—some of the trendiest and most glamorous in the city—and the mouthwatering transglobal menu are sure to seduce you. Factor in the sophisticated historical-meets-contemporary décor, and you have an instant hot spot where style, substance, and even romance meld into one. *Mon-Thu 5:30-10:30pm, Fri-Sat 5:30-11pm; bar until late.* $$ ▣ ⬚ ≡

Hot Tip: Sommelier Kim Cyr is one of the city's most respected. Put yourself in her capable hands.

Maro

135 Liberty St., Entertainment District, 416-588-2888 • Hot & Cool

The Draw: Experience the yin and yang of Toronto's stylish dining scene; every slick Western dish comes paired with an exotic Asian counterpart.

The Scene: It's an upscale party. The massive space provides plenty of opportunities for young professionals and the clubby-dining set to mingle, whether that means sipping champagne by one of the three long bars, lounging fireside, or surveying the gorgeous crowd from a raised dining booth. *Thu-Sat 4-9pm; bar until late.* $$ ≡

Hot Tip: Ask for a booth when you reserve.

Trevor Kitchen and Bar*

38 Wellington St. E., St. Lawrence, 416-941-9410 • Hot & Cool

The Draw: Trevor has mastered the pitch-perfect fine-dining experience.

The Scene: *Rarified* is the best description—from unlikely wine pairings, to chef Trevor's top-to-bottom attention to detail and his disdain for elitist dining, this is an uncommon dining experience that's attracting an uncommonly sophisticated and cool crowd. The local who's-who and visiting glitterati have anointed Trevor as the latest it spot. *Tue-Wed 4-10pm, Thu-Sat 4-11:30pm; bar until late.* $$$ ▣ ≡

Hot Tip: Anti-elitist doesn't mean come as you are; this is a dress-up place that attracts a dress-up crowd.

Best Only-in-Toronto Museums

#61–63: Canada's largest city boasts a number of unique and significant museums and galleries. Head to these powerhouse institutions for unexpected glimpses into Toronto's vast arts and culture scene.

Bata Shoe Museum
327 Bloor St. W., Bloor/Yorkville, 416-979-7799 • Hot & Cool

The Draw: This glittery and fascinating collection of shoes through the ages is both great fun and surprisingly informative.

The Scene: The building itself is a work of art, designed on five levels to resemble a shoebox. Some exhibits look at the strictly decorative aspects of shoes, while others put them in a historical and social context. Intriguing facts—and numerous celebrity shoes—abound. *Tue-Wed 10am-5pm, Thu 10am-8pm, Fri-Sat 10am-5pm, Sun noon-5pm.* $

Hot Tip: Check the website (batashoemuseum.ca) for special events, especially Thursday evenings for live music, demonstrations, and more.

Corkin Gallery
55 Mill St., Building 1, Distillery District, 416-979-1980 • Hot & Cool

The Draw: This gallery combines contemporary rotating exhibits with a permanent collection of historic photography.

The Scene: With five exhibition areas, Jane Corkin mixes three centuries of artistic influence. Housed in one of the renovated buildings of the Distillery District, the industrial spaces have white walls accented by exposed brick and stainless steel reinforcements. Exhibitions focus on contemporary themes such as the environment and mass media, and showcase Canadian and international talents. *Tue-Sat 10am-6pm, Sun noon-5pm.*

Hot Tip: Make sure to visit the hidden second-level exhibit space, which you can only tell is there if you look around the corner and see the stairs up to it.

Gardiner Museum of Ceramic Art
111 Queen's Park, University of Toronto, Bloor/Yorkville, 416-586-8080 • Hot & Cool

The Draw: This is the world's only museum devoted entirely to ceramic art, where the motto is "clay comes to life in fire."

The Scene: The museum's permanent collection features 2,700 pieces from Europe, Asia, and the Americas. Major exhibits look at ceramic traditions in both a historic and contemporary context, and have included traveling shows of masters like Picasso. An education program offers classes, and the shop has been a favorite of Torontonians since its opening in 1984. *Sat-Thu 10am-6pm, Fri 10am-9pm.* $

Hot Tip: The Gardiner sometimes offers great off-site tours such as a day in wine country. Check the website (gardinermuseum.on.ca) for details.

Best

Power Lunches

#64–66: In Toronto, power lunches have as much to do with style as with business. Sure, you'll find your share of red-tie-wearing deal-makers looking to close their next big deal—but you'll also find plenty of spots where trendier creative professionals choose to chat business in edgier surroundings.

Il Posto

148 Yorkville Ave. (Hazelton Ave.), Bloor/Yorkville, 416-968-0469 • Classic

The Draw: Top-notch Italian fare is served in a discreet and sophisticated setting.

The Scene: When the who's-who of Canadian business wants to do lunch, they schedule a two-hour minimum at this well-established spot. The reservation list could easily be roll call for the top lawyers, bankers, and politicos in the city. *Mon-Sat 11:30am-3pm and 5:30-11pm, Sun 5:30-11pm.* $$$ =

Hot Tip: Meals here are leisurely affairs. This isn't the place to come for a quick bite before heading back to the conference room, but instead the sort of place to celebrate a job well done.

Jamie Kennedy at the Gardiner

111 Queen's Park, University of Toronto, Bloor/Yorkville, 416-362-1957 • Hot & Cool

The Draw: Jamie Kennedy's simple yet elegantly refined seasonal fare is a standout in a city of top chefs.

The Scene: Place one of the city's brightest chefs in a sunlit contemporary room only steps from tony Yorkville and it's no surprise that the lifestyle shoppers, deal-makers, and elegant lunchers have responded. This is one meal that you'll want to dress up for—even in the afternoon. *Sat-Thu 11:30am-2:30pm, Fri 11:30am-2:30pm and 5:30-8:30pm.* $$ –

Hot Tip: Order a crowd-pleasing "Hopper." The Sri Lankan, aromatic coconut and flour crêpe with curried wild shrimp is a sensory feast.

Pangaea

1221 Bay St. N., Bloor/Yorkville, 416-920-2323 • Classic

The Draw: The upscale Mediterranean ambience and extensive wine list set a refined note for business proceedings.

The Scene: Gold-colored walls accented in aqua blue rise high above the wood-plank floors to create a warm backdrop for the fashionable business crowd. Tucked in a nondescript office complex, Pangaea has become a popular oasis of light and fine food, with an inventive Mediterranean–pan-Asian menu. Well-spaced tables and attentive service make this conducive to important business gatherings. *Mon-Sat 11:30am-11:30pm.* $$$ =

Hot Tip: With a *Wine Spectator* Award of Excellence for 2005 and 2006, the informed servers can help you choose the right bottle to impress.

Restaurant-Lounges

#67–69: These bars do double duty, luring those in need of a cocktail before and after their meal.

Li'ly Resto-Lounge*

656 College St., Little Italy, 416-536-5384 • Hot & Cool

The Draw: An attractive and spirited crowd is lured in by the suave nightly DJ beats and menu listing 20 speciality martinis.

The Scene: Located in the middle of the popular College Street strip, this exuberant Italian eatery offers an extensive selection of wine and cocktails, making it a great destination pre- or post-dinner. DJ mixes of dance and rock faves add to the festive atmosphere. If you want to nosh, many of the modern Italian options are available in small portions or for sharing. *Tue-Sun 6pm-2am.* $$ B =

Hot Tip: Make a reservation to ensure you get to sit in the lounge's prime real estate, one of the highly coveted booths.

One Up Resto Lounge*

130 Dundas St. W., 2nd Fl., Chinatown, 416-340-6349 • Classic

The Draw: Impeccable service lures the Blackberry set for after-work martinis.

The Scene: Power brokers and business types head to this resto-lounge where the decor is inspired by Chinatown and the menu is influenced by French and Italian cuisine. From the crostini to the steamed mussels, the palate tempters make One Up a popular gathering place for brokers, lawyers, and businesspeople who want a little nosh with their scotch, wine, or mixed drinks. *Mon-Thu 11am-3:30pm and 4:30-10pm, Fri 11am-3:30pm and 4:30pm-1:30am, Sat 4:30pm-1:30am.* $$$ B =

Hot Tip: Reserve one of three private dining areas for lunch or dinner meetings.

Rivoli*

332 Queen St. W., Queen Street, 416-596-1908 • Hip

The Draw: This popular spot offers great tunes from the house DJ and a perfect spot to hear about your next favorite band.

The Scene: Sandwiched between the elegant, somewhat funky black dining room and the back performance space, the bar area is filled with musicians and artists in between gigs and exhibitions. From '80s Brit pop to current hip-hop faves, the DJ's choices keep the crowd lively and the bartender busy with requests for local micro-brewery beers, veggie Laotian spring rolls, or Siam Wookie balls from the pan-Asian menu. *Sun-Thu 11:30am-midnight, Fri-Sat 11:30am-1am.* $$ =

Hot Tip: Arrive before 7pm if you want the option to get last-minute tickets to a performance or a table for dinner.

Best

Romantic Rendezvous

#70-72: A truly romantic dining destination is more than just good food or fine service or a lovely setting. While it is hopefully all of those things, it is also about creating a warm ambience that simultaneously makes diners feel special and puts them at ease.

Brassaii

461 King St. W., Entertainment District, 416-598-4730 • Hot & Cool

The Draw: The contemporary décor and seductive lighting create a seductive backdrop for a leisurely, intimate evening.

The Scene: From the stylish wrought-iron gate street entrance through the court-yard patio to the spacious dining room, this bistro sets the scene for romance. The young and fashionable love the dining room's long leather banquettes, high ceilings, and stainless-steel accents with floor-to-ceiling windows. After supper, the inviting lounge area heats up with attractive 30-something couples. *Mon-Fri 8:30am-10:30pm, Sat 10am-11pm, Sun 10am-2pm.* $$$ B =

Hot Tip: Reserve a table in the intimate back corner to be able to view the stars through the floor-to-ceiling windows.

Rosewater Supper Club*

19 Toronto St., St. Lawrence, 416-214-5888 • Classic

The Draw: A flawless historic renovation provides a distinctive backdrop for this fine-dining experience.

The Scene: Boasting dining rooms with 22-foot ceilings, sumptuous upholstery, and hand-painted cornice moldings, the Rosewater is a step back into Victorian-era romance and glamour. There are lounges at different levels, and live jazz plays in the Front Lounge. *Mon-Fri 11:30am-1:30pm and 5:30-10pm, Sat 5:30-10pm.* $$$ B =

Hot Tip: To best check out the scene, ask for seating on the mezzanine. For more intimacy, ask for the lower level.

Truffles

Four Seasons Hotel Toronto, 21 Avenue Rd., Bloor/Yorkville, 416-928-7331 • Classic

The Draw: It's the only restaurant in Canada to earn the CAA/AAA five-diamond award 11 years in a row. Bring her here and she'll know you mean business.

The Scene: Wrought-iron gates usher you into a rarefied atmosphere of serious-ly over-the-top pampering. Truffles is Toronto's favorite spot for special occa-sions, and you'll find your fellow diners as impeccably turned out as the high-ly acclaimed continental cuisine. With service that's attentive to a fault, this is truly the perfect spot to impress. *Tue-Sat 6-10pm.* $$$$ =

Hot Tip: Start your meal with the irresistible spaghettini with truffle foam.

e Bars

ıe to the fickle tendencies of the trendy and gorgeous, when a ̣̣̣̣̣ has to up the ante of the existing nightlife offerings. How to get the official ̣̣̣̣ester stamp of approval? High cover charges and European DJs of the moment are key to luring the young and the beautiful.

Foundation Room
19 Church St., St. Lawrence, 416-364-8368 • Hot & Cool

The Draw: A sensory escape to Marrakesh is yours in this exotic space.

The Scene: Even when the temperatures outside turn sub-zero, Foundation Room offers a bright slice of North African sunshine in the form of delicious colors and funky occident-meets-orient beats. It's strictly casual-cool as the youthful crowd sips cocktails and sinks into the countless pillows. It's Toronto's version of Casablanca. *Tue-Thu 6pm-2am, Fri-Sat 6pm-3am.* ≡

Hot Tip: Arrive on Thursdays before 10pm to guarantee yourself a spot in the casbah where you can order a refreshing pomegranate martini.

Lobby*
192 Bloor St. W., Bloor/Yorkville, 416-929-7169 • Hot & Cool

The Draw: While a petite menu offers trendy items, the real draw is the long martini list and the chance to mingle with a designer crowd.

The Scene: A glass front looks onto the street, and behind the velvet ropes await discerning door staff—if you make it past them, models and the label-conscious who follow them are found ensconced on the white upholstered banquettes. A long bar and dazzling crystal chandelier dominate the dining room in the back. *Tue-Sat 6pm-2am.* ≡

Hot Tip: Oddly enough, Lobby also does a great afternoon tea.

Rockwood
31 Mercer St., Entertainment District, 416-979-7373 • Hot & Cool

The Draw: Arguably Toronto's most handsome lounge space, Rockwood draws some of the city's best-looking crowds.

The Scene: The beautiful and the power-wielding sip sophisticated cocktails and bathe in the ambience inspired by the Canadian outdoors: rock, wood, and grass adorn the three floors. A mature clubby vibe attracts deep-pocketed types who splash out for VIP service. *Mon and Thu-Sat 10pm-3am; Grass May-October, weather permitting.* ©≡

Hot Tip: The rooftop patio Grass is a great spot to chill out under the stars—come after 10pm to miss the post-work rush.

Seafood Restaurants

#76–78: No matter how far inland they live, Canadians have a great love of seafood. In Toronto, it results in a wealth of restaurants that specialize in the bounty of the ocean, with delectable seafood flown in daily from both coasts.

Joso's
202 Davenport Rd., Bloor/Yorkville, 416-925-1903 • Classic

The Draw: It's fresh seafood presented with flair for a designer crowd.

The Scene: Dinner is part spectacle and part performance art. It may have been the bustling see-and-be-seen patio looking out at the chic boutiques of Yorkville that first drew the Hollywood stars, wealthy locals, and savvy travelers, but it's the mouthwatering seafood and stunning presentation that keep the place humming year after year. *Mon-Fri 11:30am-2pm and 5:30-10:30pm, Sat 5:30-10:30pm.* $$$ =

Hot Tip: Reservations are a must—call early to get one of the 14 seats on the street-side patio.

Pure Spirits Oyster House & Grill
55 Mill St., Distillery District, 416-361-5859 • Hot & Cool

The Draw: This oyster bar and fresh seafood joint is one of the best places to enjoy the Distillery District's buzzing scene.

The Scene: The historical Distillery District is enjoying a renaissance, and Pure Spirits is right at the heart of it. Crowds flock here for the lively atmosphere, fine seafood, and great outdoor patio. Funky light fixtures and big windows let in lots of natural light—the look is contemporary and draws upscale locals and in-the-know travelers. *Sun-Thu 11am-10pm, Fri-Sat 11am-11pm.* $$$ B =

Hot Tip: During the summer months, Pure Spirits' outdoor patio enjoys a virtually constant stream of live jazz and other events.

Starfish Oyster Bed & Grill
100 Adelaide St. E., St. Lawrence, 416-366-7827 • Classic

The Draw: The bright New York–style bistro ambience enhances the seafood that's bought fresh daily and served in charming surroundings overlooking the handsome St. James Cathedral.

The Scene: An elegant black sign over the shiny glass front of this restored historic building announces this gourmet seafood eatery. The professional down-towners who have transformed this neighborhood from a once-shabby area into condo heaven love this intimate bistro. Oysters come in several varieties, as do other delicacies of the sea. For landlubbers, there are non-seafood options as well. *Mon-Fri noon-3pm and 5-11pm, Sat 5-11pm.* $$$ B =

Hot Tip: For an all-out mollusk orgy, try the 100 Malpeque small choice oysters with a magnum of Heidsieck champagne.

Best

Sexy Lounges

#79–81: Discerning revelers who are looking for love and romance can bring a paramour or find one at these lounges that offer a potent combination of seductive ambience and luscious libations.

Budo Liquid Theatre

137 Peter St., Entertainment District, 416-593-1550 • Hot & Cool

The Draw: Budo boasts three floors of Asian-inspired style and beautiful people to provide the theater.

The Scene: The contemporary zen lounge has a minimalist feel, highlighted by Japanese poetry and art, and a 35-foot waterfall. Grab one of the signature fruit martinis and sink into a white chair on the rooftop patio for a leisurely evening amid a handsome crowd. This is one of Clubland's hot spots for the upscale 30-something crowd looking for an over-the-top good time. *Fri-Sat 9:30pm-3am, some Tuesdays.* ⒞≣

Hot Tip: Come early on a Saturday to get a coveted spot on the intimate patio.

Habitat Lounge

735 Queen St. W., Queen Street, 416-860-1551 • Hip

The Draw: This contemporary high-style restaurant-lounge has masses of Queen West cred.

The Scene: A small bar lines the wall on one side, as a crowd of creative professionals—Toronto parlance for the designers, ad people, and film and television types who've taken over the West End—lounge artfully on the white couches. Farther back, fusion cuisine is served on leather banquettes to still more beautiful people, and at the very back, another small bar glows red over the chic cocktail crowd. This is designer lounging at its best. *Tue-Sat 6pm-late.* ≣

Hot Tip: Thursday nights, a DJ takes over the sound system with electronic grooves.

Therapy Ultra Lounge

203 Richmond St. W., Entertainment District, 416-977-3089 • Hot & Cool

The Draw: You'll find all the right ingredients for a premium club experience—stylish décor, inventive cocktails, and fashionable types in the mood to party.

The Scene: The dark room throbs with the beats from a state-of-the-art sound system while the lights glow, warmly enhancing the sultry mood. The cocktail list plays tongue-in-cheek homage to therapeutic greats, with drinks like the Dr. Phil, featuring Finlandia cranberry vodka, melon liqueur, amaretto, and cranberry juice. There's a menu of Asian fusion, but the super-fashionable 30-something crowd comes here mainly to see and be seen on the overstuffed couches. *Thu-Sun 8pm-2am.* ⒞≣

Hot Tip: Come here Friday evenings to mingle with the fashionable downtowners who start their weekend here with an after-work cocktail.

Best

Spas

#82–84: Male or female, everyone is indulging in the spa experience these days. Toronto's spa scene offers a wide selection of treatments and options, with more establishments springing up all the time.

Body Blitz Spa: Health by Water
471 Adelaide St. W., Entertainment District, 416-364-0400 • Hot & Cool

The Draw: Tired of acres of soothing white walls? Trickling New Age water fountains? Pale-wood fixtures designed to soothe the soul? Looking for something a little cooler than all that? This spa is just the place.

The Scene: Treatment rooms have exposed brick and subdued design elements, giving a much-needed urban-minded update to the traditional spa décor. Scenesters, young professionals, and 30-something "it" girls drop in to recharge after—or before—a weekend of serious lounging and dancing. *Mon-Thu 10am-8pm, Fri 10am-9pm, Sat 10am-8pm, Sun 10am-6pm.* $$$$

Hot Tip: Try the Water Circuit. It's an alternating course of hot and cold plunges that includes time in the popular Sea Salt and Hot Tea Pools.

Pantages Spa and Wellness Center
Pantages Hotel Suites, 200 Victoria St., Downtown/Yonge, 416-367-1888 • Hot & Cool

The Draw: The traditional ayurvedic treatments are the best in the city.

The Scene: The Pantages' treatments take into account a person's entire personality—mind, body, and spirit. Signature treatments feature hydrotherapy, including a full-body Vichy shower, and couples facilities. This chic spa will pamper you with its wide range of services—from traditional Swedish and hot-stone massages to the exotic Deep Sea Body Cleanse and the Emerald Green Clay detoxifying body toner. Be sure to sample a drink from the aqua bar. *Sun-Mon 10am-6pm, Tue-Sat 9am-10pm.* $$$$

Hot Tip: Botox and other medical services are provided on site by staff doctors.

Stillwater Spa
Park Hyatt Toronto, 4 Avenue Rd., Bloor/Yorkville, 416-926-2389 • Classic

The Draw: This elegant and established spa for the well-heeled and in-the-know is the perfect way to relieve the stress of a full day of shopping.

The Scene: You'll find an air of pedigreed refinement here amid the pale fixtures and soft sounds of naturally running water. Seasoned attendants make your experience one of renewal. Aqua therapies are their specialty, and water can be incorporated into massage and other treatments. Wealthy Torontonians have been flocking here for ages. *Mon-Fri 9am-10pm, Sat 8am-10pm, Sun 10am-6pm.* $$$$

Hot Tip: Contact the spa concierge to ask about a lunch menu created by the Park Hyatt's executive chef, then relax by the fireplace and enjoy.

Summer Patios

#85–87: They say that there are two seasons in Toronto—winter and patio season. You'll find hardy Torontonians out on the patio somewhere even when temperatures hover around the freezing mark.

Lusso

207 Queen's Quay W., Harbourfront, 416-848-0005 • Classic

The Draw: A lively crowd of locals and out-of-towners kicks back on this vast patio beside the sparkling blue waters of Lake Ontario in the summertime.

The Scene: Located in the historic Queen's Quay Terminal, this is lakeside-patio living gone high style. The views of the great outdoors are enhanced by marble tables, high-backed booths, and even candlelight on the upper level. The menu is light and fresh and hits the spot when you're dining al fresco. *May-late Sep Mon-Fri 8:30am-2am, Sat-Sun 1pm-2am.*

Hot Tip: Try one of the luscious martinis especially designed for Lusso.

Roof Lounge

Park Hyatt Toronto, 4 Avenue Rd., 18th Fl., Bloor/Yorkville, 416-924-5471
• Classic

The Draw: A perennial favorite, this friendly hotel lounge has a terrific view of the city from the rooftop patio.

The Scene: Expert mixologist Joe Gomes has been dancing his way around the bar at this swanky watering hole for over 45 years. Well-heeled travelers and generations of locals have come for the refined yet congenial ambience, the fab cocktails, and the city view. *Daily noon-1am.*

Hot Tip: With a wood-burning fireplace, this spot can work even in chilly weather.

Sky Bar

132 Queen's Quay E., Harbourfront, 416-869-0045 • Hot & Cool

The Draw: The summer patio scene is for an exclusively high-end clientele, where al fresco is strictly upmarket.

The Scene: Torontonians get relatively few warm summer nights, so they must make the most of them. Part of the massive Guvernment Complex, Sky Bar has all you could ever want on a balmy evening. A distinctly upscale crowd congregates here during the summer months to sip fabulous cocktails and admire the gorgeous view—and each other. A beefy bouncer guards the stairs to the view you won't be able to get enough of, especially after dark when the lights make even the traffic look pretty. On weekends, the DJs and dancing crowd show up dressed to the nines and looking to make the most of a summer's evening. *May-Oct Sat 10pm-5am.*

Hot Tip: Thursdays are fashion-industry nights when the girls strut their stuff.

Best Views

#88–90: Toronto's natural setting on the shores of Lake Ontario is truly beautiful, though you'd be hard-pressed to see the lake from street level. Several landmark restaurants allow you to enhance the visual feast with a literal one on your plate.

CN Tower

301 Front St. W., Harbourfront, 416-868-6937 • Classic

The Draw: It's the world's tallest freestanding structure, isn't that enough?

The Scene: In a mere 58 seconds, you've traveled in a glass elevator at a speed of 15 mph straight up to a lookout level at 1,136 feet. Could there be a better view not only of metropolitan Toronto but of the countryside beyond, and out onto Lake Ontario? Only from the Sky Pod, farther up at 1,465 feet and offering views 100 miles out, or straight down through the Glass Floor. *Daily 9am-10pm. $$*

Hot Tip: Even if you have other plans for dinner, stop by 360 to savor a bottle from the vast 10,000-bottle wine cellar.

Panorama

55 Bloor St. W., 51st Fl., Bloor/Yorkville, 416-967-0000 • Hot & Cool

The Draw: With its stunning view of Toronto and well beyond, this restaurant-lounge provides a dramatic setting for a special occasion.

The Scene: In the summer, upscale locals flock to the popular rooftop patio, all decked out with teak seating, to sip from a long list of martinis and cocktails and enjoy casual nibbles. The décor is minimalist and sleek, a fine backdrop for the mesmerizing view. Yes, you'll find tourists here, but the more, the merrier! *Daily 5pm-2am. =*

Hot Tip: This is also a great spot for brunch.

Scaramouche

1 Benvenuto Pl., Uptown, 416-961-8011 • Classic

The Draw: Glassed-in elegance and high style atop a lofty tower lays the city at your feet.

The Scene: For more than two decades, Scaramouche has maintained an irreproachable reputation for fine dining. But it really sets itself apart from the competition with its stellar location perched high above the city with a sparkling view of the urban skyline and the lake beyond. The banks of windows make the most of it, and you're certain to enjoy one of the finer meals in the city in this chic setting. And save room for the desserts, made in-house and a local legend. *Mon-Sat 5:30-9:30pm. $$$ =*

Hot Tip: Ask for an intimate table facing west to watch the sunset.

Best Ways to Enjoy a Sunny Day

#91–93: Toronto has a relatively short summer. So when the weather's favorable, Torontonians go outside in droves. These are the places locals flock to when they want to make the most of the glorious sunshine.

The Beaches

The Beaches • Classic

The Draw: Pebbly beaches on the blue waters of Lake Ontario make for perfect leisurely summer days.

The Scene: Torontonians have saved some shoreline for urban beaches where locals can go in the summer. Beginning at the lakeside bistro near Lakeshore and Coxwell, you can explore the beaches and blue waters of the lake heading east. Past the water treatment plant, the bluffs begin; at their base are beaches that extend a mile or two along the lakeshore to Scarborough Bluffs Park.

Hot Tip: If hunger or restlessness strikes, slip up to Queen Street East to explore eclectic shops and restaurants.

High Park

1873 Bloor St. W., Parkdale • Hip

The Draw: Stroll or take in the arts at Toronto's biggest inner-city park, which covers nearly 400 acres on the city's western waterfront.

The Scene: High Park is an urban retreat of tended greenery and trees, complete with a lake and swans. You can stroll for hours along the trails, and casual refreshments are available at a kiosk. From late June until Labor Day, you can catch Shakespeare performances by CanStage (canstage.com). The same venue also hosts the annual Scream in High Park, a literary reading series that runs from late June until early July (thescream.ca).

Hot Tip: The wealthy Toronto couple who founded High Park lived at Colborne Lodge. Today, the Regency-era villa is open for viewing. Call in advance for tour times (416-392-6916).

Toronto Islands

Bay St. & Queen's Quay, Harbourfront, 416-392-8193 • Classic

The Draw: Locals and tourists alike take the ferry over to enjoy beaches and a laid-back island experience in sight of the CN Tower.

The Scene: Hop aboard a ferry and switch gears. Toronto Islanders have always had a distinctly counterculture reputation. These days the Islands are home to amusement parks, mellow beaches (including a clothing-optional stretch at Hanlan's Point), B&Bs, art galleries, restaurants, and curio shops. *Ferry rides approx. 30 min., check schedules online (torontoisland.org) for details.* $

Hot Tip: Feeling energetic? Take the ferry to Ward's Island and rent a bike or a boat at the dock.

Ways to Escape a Rainy Day

#94–96: Torontonians are a hardy lot, and they love to go out no matter what the weather. But when Mother Nature is less than welcoming, the city offers myriad ways to escape indoors.

Allan Gardens Conservatory

19 Horticultural Ave., St. Lawrence, 416-392-7288 • Classic

The Draw: These classy indoor gardens are the perfect antidote when you need a little color and cheer on a gray winter's day.

The Scene: Of the greenhouses, surely the most beautiful is the central one, with a high-domed cathedral roof to showcase a vast collection of tropical plants. Savor the collection of amaryllis, along with gorgeous plantings of flowering hibiscus, cacti, and delicate orchids. The greenhouses are set up to mimic several different environments (from tropical to arid). *Daily 10am-5pm.*

Hot Tip: Take a quick taxi ride to Sutton Place for a late afternoon drink.

Royal Ontario Museum

100 Queen's Park, Bloor/Yorkville, 416-586-5549 • Classic

The Draw: Canada's largest museum, the ROM is full of intriguing exhibits of all kinds.

The Scene: A captivating retreat from the cold, the ROM hosts shows that are certain to entertain, surprise, and impress with stunning visuals. A rich collection of tens of thousands of artifacts makes the permanent collection a feast for the senses. Be sure to check out the world-class traveling international shows. *Hours vary; call or check website for information (rom.on.ca).* $

Hot Tip: Every Friday from 4:30pm to 9:30pm, admission to the permanent collections is free, and includes event programming such as lectures, music, dance, and films.

Tea Room

Windsor Arms Hotel, 18 St. Thomas St., Bloor/Yorkville, 416-971-9666 • Classic

The Draw: It's the ultimate in old-world refinement and a fashionable ode to a quite civilized tradition.

The Scene: Join the fashionable, as well as neighborhood regulars who've been coming forever, to enjoy this ritual. Perch on the overstuffed upholstery as you sample a traditional afternoon tea that features a selection of loose-leaf teas, fresh scones with preserves and Devon cream, sandwiches, and petits fours. Built in 1927, the Tea Room is an officially designated historic property, and has always projected a certain upper-class charm. *High tea daily at 1:30pm and 3:30pm.* $$$ –

Hot Tip: Ask to be seated in one of the velvet loveseats by the fireplace.

Best

West Queen West Art Spaces

#97–99: There are lots of places for art and design in Toronto, but West Queen West deserves its own mention. This über-stylish area is packed with the hippest galleries and shops in town, and is a must for those who love to be on the cutting edge.

Made Design
867 Dundas St. W., West Queen West, 416-607-6384 • Hot & Cool

The Draw: Browse—and buy—the hottest in homegrown design items.

The Scene: Toronto's contemporary-design-savvy young professionals drop in to shop for one-of-a-kind must-have items, hobnob with designers, stay one step ahead of the glossy design mags, and browse the small space in which Canadian artists are displayed. *Tue-Fri 11am-7pm, Sat 11am-6pm, Mon by appointment only.*

Hot Tip: The gallery's owners have an intimate relationship with the designers they represent; should that beautiful table not fit your space, just ask. Chances are they can have a custom-made version produced.

Mercer Union Centre for Contemporary Visual Art
37 Lisgar St., West Queen West, 416-536-1519 • Hip

The Draw: Rubbing shoulders with one of the city's most seasoned contemporary arts crowds is reason enough to visit.

The Scene: Savvy gallery-goers meet the artists and browse their exhibitions hoping to find the next big thing. Evening lectures and pre-exhibition bashes add a party vibe to the scene. *Tue-Sat 11am-6pm.*

Hot Tip: Check the website in advance to find a well-attended, one-off art-themed event (mercerunion.org).

Museum of Contemporary Canadian Art (MOCCA)
952 Queen St. W., West Queen West, 416-395-0067 • Hip

The Draw: This is creative—if avant-garde—Canada at its showcase best.

The Scene: Curious locals and international visitors check out Canada's most significant collection of homegrown contemporary art. A permanent collection of powerhouse works complements vibrant exhibitions and an exciting events calendar, making this the epicenter of West Queen West's fabled art-driven resurrection. *Tue-Sun 11am-6pm.*

Hot Tip: Check the website for upcoming exhibition openings and special events like lectures and film presentations (mocca.toronto.on.ca).

EXPERIENCE
TORONTO

Dive into the Toronto of your choice with one of three themed itineraries: *Hot & Cool* (p.50), *Hip* (p.80), and *Classic* (p.108). Each is designed to heighten your fun-seeking experience by putting you in the right place at the right time—the best restaurants, nightlife, and attractions, and even the best days to go. While the itineraries, each followed by detailed descriptions of our top choices, reflect our favorite picks, a few additional noteworthy options are included in the listings.

Hot & Cool Toronto

Toronto's got a sleek and stylish side that's ready to show you a sizzling good time. You'll find a wide array of buzzing A-list hot spots to choose from, along with chic restaurants, exclusive nightclubs, posh hotels, and top-tier attractions. They're all packed into this three-day itinerary. So throw on your dancing shoes, order a martini, and get ready to lounge, drink, dance, and party til dawn.

Note: Venues in bold are described in detail in the listings that follow the itinerary. Venues followed by an asterisk (*) are those we recommend as both a restaurant and a destination bar.

Hot & Cool Toronto:
The Perfect Plan (3 Nights and Days)

Perfect Plan Highlights

Thursday

Afternoon	Distillery District, Corkin Gallery, Balzac's Café
Pre-dinner	Pure Spirits, Martini Lounge, Monsoon*
Dinner	Trevor Kitchen*, Blowfish*, Tomi-Kro
Nighttime	Cheval, BaBaLuu, Flow
Late-night	West Lounge, Li'ly Resto-Lounge*

Friday

Morning	Bata Shoe Museum, Artinsite
Lunch	Jamie Kennedy, Sassafraz*
Afternoon	Gardiner Museum
Pre-dinner	Holt's, One*, Rain*
Dinner	Susur, Kultura, One*
Nighttime	Budo, C-Lounge
Late-night	2 Cats Cocktail

Saturday

Morning	Eagles Golf, Pantages Spa
Lunch	Brassaii, KiWe Kitchen
Afternoon	Yorkville Shopping
Pre-dinner	Crush Wine Bar,
Dinner	Colborne Lane, Maro, Doku 15
Nighttime	Rockwood, Sky Bar
Late-night	Ultra Supper Club*, Seven, Fly

Hotel: **Cosmopolitan Hotel Toronto**

Thursday

2pm: Take a cab to the Distillery District, one of the city's trendiest neighborhoods. This newly revitalized area contains the world's largest collection of restored Victorian industrial architecture, and is home to more than 20 art galleries, numerous artist studios, stylish boutiques, and some of the city's best newest restaurants, a few featuring live jazz and blues. On summer weekends, it's a hotbed of activity, with music festivals and a Sunday farmer's market, and local artisans display art, jewelry, and crafts in kiosks along the cobblestone streets. Check out the latest trends in photographic art at the **Corkin Gallery**. Then stop in at the industrial-chic **Balzac's Café** for a relaxed cappuccino surrounded by the gallery owners.

5:30pm: Grab a patio seat at **Pure Spirits** and enjoy a half-dozen oysters on the half-shell. Or return to downtown to hook up with the stylish business types who frequent the trendy **Monsoon***. At the **Martini Lounge** located inside the Pantages

Hotel, the house specialty is celeb-spotting while sipping one of the sublime concoctions from the expert mixologists.

8pm Dinner: Don't be dismayed by the understated look of **Trevor Kitchen and Bar***—it's one of the hottest tickets in town and draws a tony crowd. For something a bit more raucous, drop into **Blowfish Restaurant + Sake Bar*** where hyper-trendy, new wave sushi meets refined European cuisine. Dress your best—you'll be mingling with a gorgeous crowd. Or for a mellower but equally memorable evening, head to the relaxed dining room at the well-loved hot spot **Tomi-Kro**.

11pm: Head to **Cheval** for hot DJ beats and indulge in bottle service with the spirited professional crowd. Yorkville is lined with exclusive nightclubs these days, but a few really stand out. You'll find lots of flashy Latin salsa and merengue moves on the crowded dance floor at **BaBaLuu**, while **Flow Restaurant + Lounge*** is known for drawing a polished and festive crowd looking for late-night fun and cool cocktails.

1am: Keep the spirits flowing by heading to King Street's **West Lounge** to hang out with the model and model-wannabe crowd. Then walk to **Li'ly Resto-Lounge*** for martinis with a

funky designer crowd seeking a more relaxed vibe.

Friday

10am: Enjoy room service in your hotel. Then step out to visit the unique fashionista-favorite **Bata Shoe Museum**, the only museum in the world dedicated to the fabulous foot accessory. Or to have a local expert give you an insider's overview of the city's neighborhoods and galleries, book a tour—well in advance—with **Artinsite**.

1pm Lunch: Jamie Kennedy at the Gardiner is a light-filled space frequented by the beautiful and powerful elite, who are obsessed with Kennedy's unique mix of locally sourced seasonal ingredients and wines.Or head to the perennially in vogue **Sassafraz*** for a French-inspired lunch offering surrounded by upscale locals and visiting celebs.

3pm: After lunch, you're perfectly situated for a tour of the recently renovated and newly chic **Gardiner Museum of Ceramic Art**, the continent's only venue devoted exclusively to clay.

6pm: Cab it back to Yonge & Bloor and stop into the **Holt's Café** for a glass of wine or cocktail among the city's elite fashionistas and stylists, or find a spot on the patio at Hazelton Hotel's **One***, where the young and eligible mingle and people-watch. **Rain*** is an excellent spot for drinks with Bay Street's young business execs.

8pm Dinner: Featuring sensational pan-Asian food from one of the world's premier chefs, **Susur** is a culinary extravaganza, though you'd better reserve well in advance. If you can't snag a reservation there, join trendy young things at **Kultura** to feast on an acclaimed international menu. Those who just enjoyed a drink at **One*** should head inside to the dining room to indulge in a flawlessly executed dinner in a sumptuous setting at the restaurant.

11pm: Cab it to Clubland, where **Budo Liquid Theatre**'s rooftop patio is always hopping when the weather's good. A little farther west, the **C-Lounge** offers posh lounging and a buzzing poolside deck.

1am: Join other trendsetters for martinis at **2 Cats Cocktail Lounge**; with so many patrons sipping cosmopolitans, you'll feel like you're in a *Sex and the City* episode. To check out the hot gay (but hetero-friendly) scene, hop up to the Gay Village to the stylish **Fuzion Resto-Lounge & Garden***.

2am: For energetic 20- and 30-somethings, **Afterlife Nightclub** hosts the hottest Friday night in town. Looking for something a little more chilled for late

night? The **Foundation Room**'s Moroccan-themed lounge scene might be just the thing. Be sure to order one of their fabulous pomegranate martinis.

 Saturday

9am: Those interested in golf should head out first thing to Maple, about a half hour's drive north, where the **Eagles Nest Golf Club** is located. If you want a golf fix, but don't want to head out of the city, make a reservation to use the putting green on the rooftop of the Hôtel Le Germain.

10am: Non-golfers should sleep off that late night of clubbing, and recover in gracious comfort at **Jamie Kennedy Wine Bar and Restaurant**, which is well known for its restorative brunch featuring exceptional organic and locally grown offerings.

11am: For a bit of gloriously self-indulgent pampering, head to **Pantages Spa and Wellness Center** at the Pantages hotel.

1:30pm Lunch: Make your way to the inviting patio at **Brassaii** in the warm months or settle into one of the leather banquettes inside beside the floor-to-ceiling windows to admire the views of downtown while tucking into flawless French bistro fare. Alternatively, make your way to the sleek and sultry **KiWe Kitchen** to indulge in delicious

Mediterranean-influenced creations in a refined atmosphere.

3pm: The time has come to tackle the fabulous **Yorkville Shopping District**, which covers both sides of Bloor from Yonge Street to Avenue Road. A block north, Hazelton Lanes offers a wide range of tempting goods.

5:30pm: Recover from your shopping expedition among well-heeled sophisticates having a glass of vino at **Crush Wine Bar** in the Entertainment District.

8pm Dinner: At red-hot **Colborne Lane**, chef Claudio Aprile is bringing his take on molecular gastronomy to the fashionista crowd. If you want a unique combination of Euro-Asian selections surrounded by a sparkly crowd, **Maro** will fit the bill. Or rub shoulders with a celebrity-thick crowd at buzzing **Doku 15**. The Asian hot spot is known for patrons and servers who are as eye-catching as the fusion bites.

11pm: Tonight offers a variety of clubbing options in the aptly named Entertainment District. **Rockwood** is a super-sleek haunt frequented by the chic cocktail set. Or join the crowds at **Therapy Ultra Lounge** and order a Dr. Phil martini. If the weather's fine, you'll want to make haste and head to the lake for a stunning view from

close up: get thee to the patio at the see-and-be-seen **Sky Bar**.

1am: After midnight, the **Ultra Supper Club*** turns into a swank dance party, while **Seven Lounge** lets you indulge in the seven deadly sins with its young designer revelers.

3am: For the boys, **Fly Nightclub** pumps out the beats until breakfast time.

Hot & Cool Toronto:
The Key Neighborhoods

Bloor/Yorkville This area is so full of international luxury brand boutiques and haute eateries that it's difficult to imagine that in the 1960s it was Toronto's answer to Haight-Ashbury, and artists like Joni Mitchell and Neil Young played its coffeehouses. This is Toronto's most upscale shopping and dining district and celebrity-spotting opportunities abound.

Distillery District The largest and best-preserved collection of Victorian industrial architecture in North America was once home to the Gooderham and Worts Distillery, the largest in the British empire. Recently the 13-acre industrial complex's 40 buildings have been converted into a pedestrian-only hotbed of culture and arts. Expect chic galleries, vibrant theaters, upscale boutiques, and fine restaurants.

Entertainment District Theaters, concert halls, and performing arts spaces earned this area its name, but lately it's the hot lounges and the increasingly chic restaurant row that provide the evening's top draw.

St. Lawrence Just east of downtown, and still home to the city's largest market, a wealth of former warehouses and industrial buildings provides the foundation for a restaurant and nightlife scene that has come to include some of Toronto's most noteworthy culinary destinations.

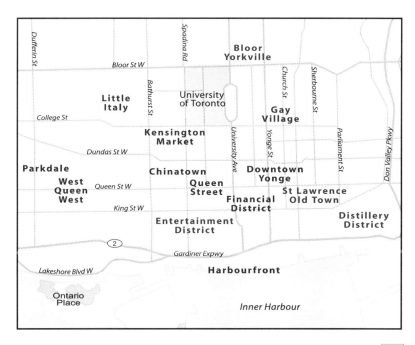

Hot & Cool Toronto:
The Shopping Blocks

Bloor Street West

From Armani to Zegna, the "Mink Mile" boasts an incredible array of exclusive international boutique brands.

Harry Rosen Canadian menswear institution offering a timeless in-house line as well as pieces from Zegna, Armani, J.Lindeberg, and other hot brands. 82 Bloor St. W. (Bay St.), 416-972-0556

Holt Renfrew The Toronto equivalent of Saks. Beauty products, fashions, and a chic cafe under one large roof. 50 Bloor St. W. (Bay St.), 416-922-2333

Lululemon Athletica Ultra-trendy, high-end, designed-in-Canada yoga-meets-street wear. 130 Bloor St. W. (Avenue Rd), 416-964-9544

Noir Men's and women's fashion lines from ultra-exclusive brands like Viktor & Rolf, Yamamoto, and Vivienne Westwood. 151 Bloor St. W. (Avenue Rd.), Unit 100, 416-962-6647

Distillery District

The historic Gooderham and Worts Distillery was recently reborn as an industrial-chic gallery, dining, and boutique shopping district chock-full of one-of-a-kind finds.

Lileo A stylish superstore carrying exclusive fashions, books, gifts, and grooming products from the world's best trendy and underground brands. 55 Mill St. (Building 35), 416-413-1410

Sandra Ainsley Gallery A massive gallery representing major contemporary Canadian and internationally recognized artists working in glass and mixed media. 55 Mill St. (Building 32), 416-214-9490

Soma Chocolate Maker Sinfully decadent chocolate treats, like limited-edition batches of artisan chocolate bars made from heirloom cacao beans. 55 Mill St. (Building 78, Unit 102), 416-815-7662

Thompson Landry Gallery An industrial-chic gallery showcasing both the great masters of Quebec art as well that province's internationally acclaimed contemporary artists. 55 Mill St. (Building 5, Unit 102), 416-364-4955

Yorkville

Rub shoulders with well-heeled locals and A-listers in these fabulous boutiques.

Anti-Hero Upscale men's boutique for rebels with deep pockets and impeccable style. 113 Yorkville Ave. (Old York Lane), 416-924-6121

The Guild Shop Beautiful jewelry, ceramics, textiles, handblown glass, and wooden objects. 118 Cumberland St. (Bellair St.), 416-921-1721

Uncle Otis Exclusive sophisticated urban streetwear from hard-to-find ultra-trendy brands. 26 Bellair St. (Yorkville Ave.), 416-920-2281

Hot & Cool Toronto:
The Hotels

Cosmopolitan Hotel Toronto • Downtown/Yonge • Trendy (97 Rms)
The Cosmopolitan is all about urban zen—maybe to the point of feng shui frenzy: Guests get gemstones on their pillows in lieu of chocolates at turndown; the layout is by Sylvia Noble (energy consultant to stars including Arnold Schwarzenegger and Ron Howard) and includes a handpicked street address and a precise number of swinging doors on each floor; and the hotel's unique "Gemstone Essence" Shizen amenities pay homage to the number eight (an important number in feng shui) by—you guessed it—aiming to soothe your eight chakras. But with only five suites per level and an eye-catching contemporary décor, it's no surprise that this spot has become a style-setter favorite. Don't worry if the whole scene sounds a little hippie-chic for your urban tastes. The Cosmopolitan delivers the goods on high design and modern creature comforts, too. Each of the 95 suites boasts floor-to-ceiling windows, a private balcony taking in either city skyline or Lake Ontario views, custom-designed furniture, and 400-thread-count Egyptian cotton linens. Pay-per-use wireless internet, Sony Dream Machines, air purifiers, and complimentary local calls are standard, and the hotel rooms are divided into two categories. Each floor contains a superior suite—think studio apartment—while the majority of rooms are in the deluxe category and offer two flat-screen televisions, a kitchenette, and an ensuite washer-dryer. Ask for a premium lake-view suite to enjoy the best views of nearby Lake Ontario. Elsewhere in the hotel, the pan-Asian fusion theme extends to dining and lounging, complete with sake-tinis in Doku 15, one of the city's hottest dining-lounging spaces, and at Shizen Spa and Solarium, where holistic Eastern philosophy teams up with classic spa treatments, providing guests with luxurious on-site pampering. And just in case you feel a bit guilty about all the self-indulgence, the Cosmopolitan gives back to the environment in the form of eco-conscious lighting, water, and heating, and the chauffeur-driven hybrid vehicles that make up the hotel's stable of runabouts. $$$ 8 Colborne St. (Yonge St.), 416-350-2000 / 800-958-3488, cosmotoronto.com

Four Seasons Toronto • Bloor/Yorkville • Timeless (380 Rms)
From the outside, it looks like just another concrete downtown high-rise, but within, it's a world of posh pampering with a staff renowned for setting new standards in service. Everyone in town knows that the concierge at the Four Seasons can get you whatever you need, accustomed as the hotel is to catering to a well-heeled clientele heavy on rock stars and Hollywood royalty. Expect no less than the best—the finest linens, most sumptuous furnishings, most exquisite attention to detail. Spacious suites cocoon guests in old-world luxury, while the Yorkville Suites, with lake or city views, are individually furnished and include original works of art. Superior rooms are located on the corners of the building and offer a walk-out balcony and—on the higher floors—panoramic city views. Amenities include a heated indoor-outdoor pool with a sundeck and 24-hour fitness facilities with state-of-the-art equipment and spa services. The highly rated Truffles, one of Toronto's top destination restaurants, is here.

Conveniently located in the heart of Yorkville, this is the perfect place to stay if you're in town for the many shopping opportunities. $$$$ 21 Avenue Rd. (Bloor St.), 416-964-0411 / 800-332-3442, fourseasons.com/toronto

Hazelton Hotel • Bloor/Yorkville • Trendy (77 Rms)

The long-awaited Hazelton sits at a key crossroads in Yorkville, steps from Bloor Street shopping, a variety of upscale restaurants, art galleries, and lounges. Designed by Yabu Pushelberg, the hotel's trendy brown and gray décor is found throughout the serenely elegant lobby, One Restaurant, the Hazel boutique, Hazelton Spa and Health Club, and the three floors of hotel rooms. Standard room features include king-size beds, Italian-made bed linens, Bulgari toiletries, WiFi, heated floors, plasma TVs, and a unique mixture of wenge paneling, cut-velvet club chairs, faux crocodile leather chairs, marble accents, and stone lamps. Ask for a room overlooking Yorkville Avenue. Go for broke in the luxe Presidential Suite. A mix of 1930s Art Deco and 21st-century technology and accessed via a private elevator, the 4,000-square-foot suite features three bed-rooms, four bathrooms, eight flat-panel TVs, two balconies, a wine cellar, and a seven-foot-long fireplace. The Hazelton Spa provides standard massage therapy and aesthetic treatments, while the 24-hour-health club has everything you could possibly need, including a lap pool. Already the talk of the town, the 25-seat Silver Screening Room was christened by the film elite during the 2007 Toronto International Film Festival and will be the lure for any in-town Hollywood royalty to showcase their latest blockbuster. $$$$ 118 Yorkville Ave. (Avenue Rd.), 416-963-6300 / 866-473-6300, thehazeltonhotel.com

Hôtel Le Germain • Entertainment District • Trendy (122 Rms)

Hôtel Le Germain opened to much fanfare in 2003, and has largely lived up to its stellar reputation. High-end design and an equally high standard of service characterize Toronto's first boutique hotel. The feel is contemporary but warm, with lots of wood accents and textural features, like thick sculptural drapery. All of it serves as a perfect backdrop for the impeccably dressed guests, composed of supermodels, celebrities, and other chic, discerning travelers. Standard rooms come with down-filled duvets, Frette linens, and Aveda toiletries. Ask for a spacious deluxe king room with a lake view. The library just off the lobby boasts a cozy open-hearth fire, a cappuccino bar, and high-speed Internet access, and there are state-of-the-art fitness facilities and a massage room on site. The stylish eatery Chez Victor adjoins the lobby. Golf aficionados should check out the rooftop putting green. $$$$ 30 Mercer St. (Blue Jays Way), 416-345-9500 / 866-345-9501, germaintoronto.com

Pantages Hotel Suites • Downtown/Yonge • Trendy (111 Rms)

The latest addition to Toronto's new but increasingly competitive boutique hotel market, the Pantages has its own unique approach to contemporary lux-ury. Every one of the 111 rooms here is a suite, and each features Egyptian linens, a rain forest showerhead and flat-screen television, and an attractive European kitchen, complete with a wide range of gourmet snacks. Deluxe suites are all different, and some are up to 530 square feet in area, and are decorated in contemporary style with warm neutral colors and dark woods. The guiding principle of design here is to ensure the traveler's well-being and to promote a healthy lifestyle. Quartz crystals are left on the pillow in lieu of chocolate. The Serenity floor offers a completely unique experience with floors scented to release the fresh aroma of the ocean. Inspired by a zen lifestyle, the 14 rooms on this floor feature Jacuzzi tubs, air purifiers, water fountains, yoga mats, and a 24-hour in-room meditation channel. There are top-notch fitness facilities, and a 9,000-square-foot spa complete with water bar. This is an impressive contemporary renovation of what was formerly a historic theater, where the refined upscale traveler can enjoy an astonishingly serene hotel experience in the heart of the city. $$$$ 200 Victoria St. (Shuter St.), 416-362-1777 / 866-852-1777, pantageshotel.com

The SoHo Metropolitan • Entertainment District • Trendy (92 Rms)
Featuring gleaming Art Deco style with luxurious appointments, the SoHo Met has spared no expense to make this a destination hotel, and if illustrious clientele are any measure of success, the investment's been sound. The gleaming brown mottled wood, a signature feature of the hotel's design that extends from the elevator to the guest rooms, is imported from Africa. Luxury rooms begin at about 600 square feet, and all include king-size beds, Frette linens, natural down duvets, complimentary wireless Internet, Molton Brown amenities, marble bathrooms, and heated floors. Ask for the spacious corner room located just above Sen5es Bakery. Ask for a room facing Wellington if you're interested in views of the landmark CN Tower and Rogers Centre, otherwise ask for a room facing Blue Jays Way; they're the largest of the non-suite options. For real luxury, go where Metallica and Britney Spears have gone, and opt for the 4,000-square-foot, three-story penthouse, complete with its own elevator, three plasma screen televisions, five bathrooms, and a roof-level balcony with gourmet barbecue and eight-person jacuzzi. It's no secret why this hotel has quickly become a favorite of artists at the very high end of the scale. Hotel amenities include a fabulous Art Deco pool and hot tub, an exercise room, and a full-service spa and salon. $$$$ 318 Wellington St. W. (Blue Jays Way), 416-599-8800 / 866-764-6638, sohomet.com

Hot & Cool Toronto:
The Restaurants

Balzac's Café • Distillery District • Cafe
Canadians are seldom far from a good cup of coffee, but Balzac's has done a particularly outstanding job of perfecting the cafe experience. Part of the historic Distillery District complex, Balzac's is housed in an airy, high-ceilinged space with exposed wooden beams and a gorgeous antique mirror behind the coffee bar. Bright young things expertly serve up your brew of choice (including fair-trade coffees) while you take in the spectacular antique chandelier. Then head up the stairs to sip in relaxed comfort along with the gallery owners and artists who occupy the studios nearby. This is the perfect place to take a break after browsing the shops and galleries. *Mon-Fri 7am-7pm, Sat-Sun 8am-7pm.* $ ≡ 55 Mill St. (Parliament St.), 416-207-1709, balzacscoffee.com

Blowfish Restaurant + Sake Bar* • Entertainment District • Fusion
Best Nouvelle Asian Restaurants The eponymous poisonous fish of foodie lore doesn't make an appearance on the Japanese-French fusion menu at Blowfish, but nobody's complaining. Chef Pan's sashimi is flawless, his hand rolls are edible art, and his uniquely inspired French fare is both inventive and delicious. Seared Cognac marinated tiger shrimp scented with san bau, lemon leaves, and truffle cream sauce add an upscale Parisian twist to the usual sushi mix. The sake menu explains the subtle nuances of the Japanese drink, appealing to newcomers and seasoned-sake veterans alike, and adding a late-night lounge vibe. Add all that to a sophisticated, buzzing vibe (complete with DJs, high ceilings, and a minimalist-chic decor) and you've got one of the hottest spots in town. *Mon-Sat 5pm-2am.* $$ B≡ 668 King St. W. (Bathurst St.), 416-860-0606, blowfishrestaurant.com

Brassaii • Entertainment District • International
Best Romantic Rendezvous Brassaii is all about style, delivered with an artistic twist. You enter through a wrought-iron gate into a courtyard patio that's a summer favorite and where you'll share your meal with life-sized metal sculptures of hounds. Set back from the street, the dining rooms beyond are handsome and modern, filled with natural light from large black-framed windows. The young and fashionable love the dining room's long leather banquettes, filling them from breakfast through dinner. After supper, the lounge area, appointed with brick walls painted white, and black leather couches, heats up with a stylish and attractive 30-something crowd. Add a brushed-stainless bar, and the corner of King and Spadina is suddenly a mecca of cool for any meal of the day. Breakfast features fresh fare like lemon blueberry pancakes, while dinner is French bistro meets comfort food. *Mon-Fri 8:30am-10:30pm, Sat 10am-11pm, Sun 10am-2pm.* $$$ B≡ 461 King St. W. (Spadina Ave.), 416-598-4730, brassaii.com

Colborne Lane • St. Lawrence • International
Best Hot Chefs The brainchild of one of Toronto's hottest restaurateurs and one of the city's flashiest chefs created a buzz long before the grand opening. Now that it's established, Colborne Lane roars. Claudio Aprile is the first local chef to venture into the exotic realm of gastronomy-meets–science experiment cuisine. Up-to-the-minute trends like foams, sous vide, micro-portions made for sharing,

and soups assembled at the table make appearances in dishes like a tea-smoked squab breast served with a spiced quince crepe, foie gras, and two chocolate sauces—one with hibiscus. The contemporary-chic sensibility translates into the industrial chic design scheme where a highly polished bar, burnished tables, and exposed brick walls adorned with period mirrors and designer lighting fixtures set the mood for hard-core foodies and adventurous style setters. *Tue-Wed 5:30-10:30pm, Thu-Sat 5:30-11pm.* $$$ B🍴≡ 45 Colborne St. (Leader Ln.), 416-368-9009, colbornelane.com

Crush Wine Bar • Entertainment District • French

A big, airy dining room awash in natural light gives this popular wine bar a sophisticated look. Crush attracts a well-groomed and well-heeled crowd of locals and visiting celebs in the know, and is said to be a favorite haunt of internationally acclaimed author Margaret Atwood. High-backed chairs, exposed brick, and lots of wooden accents warm the room. An upscale French bistro menu offers the likes of vichyssoise and poached salmon—all beautifully presented. Of course the wine list is extensive, and the staff both attentive and knowledgeable. Reservations are always recommended, and you may want to come early to sip a glass or two at the room-length bar before settling in for your meal. *Mon-Fri 11:30am-3pm and 5-10:30pm, Sat 5-10:30pm.* $$$ B≡ 455 King St. W. (Spadina Ave.), 416-977-1234, crushwinebar.com

Doku 15 • Downtown/Yonge • Asian

Best Nouvelle Asian Restaurants Doku 15 couldn't be anything but hot. The beautiful pan-Asian menu and contemporary-chic décor compete for attention with servers and guests who might have been scouted on the world's fashion runways. Celebrities like Kate Hudson—who threw a Film Festival bash here—are known to drop in for sashimi and dim sum as well as a selection of of picture-perfect, mouthwatering surprises like stir-fried sake monkfish with arugula and a black bean sauce, and Angus beef and foie gras wonton soup. Bare poured-concrete walls, designer lighting, muted seats, and long dark tables set the perfect scene. *Mon-Wed 5-10:30pm, Thu-Sat 5-11:30pm; bar until late.* $$ B≡ Cosmopolitan Hotel, 8 Colborne St. (Yonge St.), 416-368-3658, doku15.com

Fuzion Resto-Lounge & Garden* • Gay Village • Fusion

Best Gay Scenes Situated in a renovated multi-story Victorian, this elegant spot lures diners who want to enjoy the creations of Patrick Wiese. Formerly Oprah's chef, he draws daily inspiration from local market offerings. The inventive dinner menu offers rare delights such as wild boar bacon and quail egg with frisée, cornflake-crusted scallops with red cabbage and okra, or roasted sea bream with organic lentils, honey mushrooms, and kale. Late night, the upstairs lounge and house DJ playing soulful house music lures the label-conscious hetero and gay crowd with the myriad of wine and cocktail offerings, while those wanting more privacy can retire to the velvet-draped VIP area to enjoy bottle service. In summer, the garden, with its waterfall and fish pond, is a romantic spot, while the street-front Victorian courtyard lures the bold and beautiful. *Tue-Wed 5pm-11pm, Thu-Sun 5pm-2am.* $$$ B≡ 580 Church St. (Wellesley St.), 416-944-9888, fuzionexperience.com

Holt's Café • Bloor/Yorkville • International

Holt's Café provides a welcome respite from the excesses of fashion of its department store location. All dressed up in whites with shiny surfaces and bright lights with a wide bank of windows overlooking Yorkville, the Cafe sports a starkly minimalist look. A dauntingly fashionable set lunches on soup and salad, and Holt's specialty, tartines. These open-faced sandwiches are made with bread imported from the Poilâne bakery in Paris three times weekly. Perfect for an elegant bite between shopping sprees, Holt's is a favorite with fashionistas of all ages. *Mon-Wed, Sat 10am-6pm, Thu-Fri 10am-8pm, Sun noon-6pm.* $$ ▤ 50 Bloor St. W. (Bay St.), 416-922-2333, holtrenfrew.com

Jamie Kennedy at the Gardiner • Bloor/Yorkville • Canadian

Best Power Lunches Located in the recently renovated Gardiner Museum for Ceramic Arts, Jamie Kennedy's uptown restaurant is a celebration of the seasonal palate, focusing on locally sourced and organic ingredients from the bounty of southern Ontario. Known city-wide for his Yukon gold fries with lemon and mayonnaise, Kennedy further enlivens the palette with chicken liver pâté with flax and walnut tuiles or a roast rib of beef sandwich with remoulade garnishes. Each dish has an accompanying wine suggestion from the established Niagara Peninsula or the upstart Prince Edward County wine regions. The results are a raging success, luring slow-food lovers of all ages. The modern décor belies the typical museum interior, with its liberal use of glass so you can gaze upon the newly finished crystal at the Royal Ontario Museum from inside—or better yet, the outside patio. Ask for the window seats facing west and definitely make reservations for lunch and the popular Friday night dinner. *Mon-Thu 11:30am-2:30pm, Fri 11:30am-2:30pm and 6-8:30pm.* $$ ▤ Gardiner Museum, 111 Queen's Park (Bloor St.), 416-362-1957, jkkitchens.com

Jamie Kennedy Wine Bar and Restaurant • St. Lawrence • Canadian

Best Brunches Chef Jamie Kennedy's focus is on the food. The spare design is functional—wood tables and chairs—while an open concept kitchen showcases the food preparation. The walls are lined with mason jars filled with Ontario produce such as apricots, beets, and peppers. The menu items are meant to be shared and feature a combination of locally sourced ingredients. Roasted tomato soup, smoked pickerel and trout, and the infamous Yukon gold frites with lemon mayonnaise are must-haves. Each menu item has a suggested ale or wine selection, and the spiced plum and pecan cake with ginger anglaise sauce will end the meal on a high note. If you want to fit in, don't dress up. Don't be dismayed by the brusque service—the food is worth it. Definitely call ahead for a reservation. *Tue-Sat 11:30am-11pm, Sun 11am-3pm.* $$$$ ▤ 9 Church St. (Front St.), 416-362-1957, jkkitchens.com

KiWe Kitchen • Entertainment District • Fusion

From the restaurant's name—a nod to Toronto's most vibrant dining and dancing neighborhood—to the design décor, DJs, and fashionable crowd, KiWe is a microcosm of pervasively stylish King West. Blown-glass balls hang from the ceiling—think budget Dale Chihuly—and crimson-accented chairs play off the predominantly off-white space, creating a polished atmosphere. Stylish 30-somethings vie for tables in the casual cafe-style area in the front of house, as well as in the more formal dining space in the back, though the same menu of updated Mediterranean cuisine is served in both. *Tue-Wed noon-3pm and 6-10pm, Thu-Fri noon-3pm and 6-10:30pm, Sat 6-10:30pm; bar until late.* $$$ ▤ 587 King St. W. (Portland St.), 416-203-0551, kiwekitchen.com

Kultura • Entertainment District • International

Best Of-the-Moment Dining Kultura banks on a simple equation: Stylish room + delicious fusion cuisine = instant hot spot. High ceilings and a fireplace give it the feel of a trendy loft. Exposed brick and a mural depicting a stand of birch trees hint at the Canadian outdoors. The rest of the gorgeous scene is positively global. The menu of sharing plates reads like an atlas and features a rotating cast of items like Jamaican chicken risotto, duck prosciutto, and toasted lobster ravioli. The young and attractive crowd also shows up on Sundays to dine on brunch items like the breakfast soufflé of spinach, ricotta, and smoked salmon and French toast, served here with almond brittle and cinnamon roast apple caramel. *Mon-Thu 5:30-10:30pm, Fri-Sat 5:30-11pm; bar until late.* $$ ⓑ⊡≡ 169 King St. E. (Lower Jarvis St.), 416-363-9000, kulturarestaurant.com

Lee • Entertainment District • Fusion

Best Always-Trendy Tables Lee is the other brainchild of superstar chef Susur Lee, located next door to his ultra–high-end restaurant, Susur. With Lee, the master lets down his hair just a little—as do the up-to-the-minute stylish patrons. The ambience is still upscale, but it's a bit funkier and decorated in warmer colors. Pink Lucite tables contrast with copper screens and warm orange walls, all of it visible from the street through a plate-glass window. Lee's reputation in Toronto is stellar, and his legion of fans has followed him to the once-dreary stretch of King Street that now houses this almost constantly buzzing dining room. The fusion menu takes inspiration from the continental side and is priced to bring his creations to the foodie masses. A menu based around small plates includes sensations such as caramelized cod and rich coconut soup with lime and mint. *Mon-Sat 5:30-11:15pm.* $$ ≡ 603 King St. W. (Bathurst St.), 416-504-7867, susur.com

Li'ly Resto-Lounge* • Little Italy • Italian

Best Restaurant-Lounges An upscale-casual 20- and 30-something crowd holds court in what is one of bustling Little Italy's most happening resto-lounges. Pastas like gnocchi with king oyster mushrooms and brandy cream, and meats like a simple but elegant breaded, bone-in veal chop, show the influence of Italia. Late-night DJs, a long wine list offering many selections by the glass, and a roster of nearly 20 delicious martinis ensure that the lounge scene continues long after the dinner crowd has moved on. *Tue-Sun 6pm-2am.* $$ ⓑ≡ 656 College St. (Grace St.), 416-532-0419, lilylounge.com

Lobby* • Bloor/Yorkville • Fusion

A popular cocktail spot with a worthwhile Asian-fusion menu and late-night lounge scene. *See Hot & Cool Nightlife (p.69) for details. Tue-Sat 6pm-2am.* $$ ⓑ≡ 192 Bloor St. W. (Avenue Rd.), 416-929-7169, lobbyrestaurant.com

Maro • Entertainment District • Fusion

Best Of-the-Moment Dining More than just another pretty hybrid dine-lounge-dance spot, Maro backs up the modern-Asian look with substance. The massive, multi-level space features rich red hues, dark wooden accents, and boudoir-chic glossy back bars, but the main attraction is David Adjey's globally minded cuisine with an East-meets-West vibe. It's strictly cutting-edge trendy; every main dish comes in pairs, with one half honoring European culinary traditions and the other bowing to the finest of Asia. Great sight lines play to the senses of the see-and-be-seen crowds, but if you want to stand out from the masses, be sure to request one of the raised booths. *Thu-Sat 4-9pm; bar until late.* $$ ≡ 135 Liberty St. (Fraser Ave.), 416-588-2888, maro.ca

Monsoon* • Entertainment District • Asian (G)

Best Nouvelle Asian Restaurants Monsoon glows with a hot tropical feel. Join the trendy, fashionable downtown crowds with a drink in the cozy lounge area, which is dominated by a long wooden bar lined with glasses and gleaming bottles. Sink into the black leather upholstery and enjoy the busy happy-hour ambience of this popular hot spot before heading in for dinner. The dining room—think Asian meets modern—is elegantly understated in white linens and black lacquer chairs and features a pan-Asian menu that sparkles with flavorful creativity, as evidenced by offerings like crab cakes with cucumber namasa and coconut aïoli. *Mon-Thu 11:30am-2:30pm and 5-9pm, Fri 11:30am-2:30pm and 5-11pm, Sat 5-11pm; bar until late.* $$ ⊞◻= 100 Simcoe St. (Peter St.), 416-979-7172, monsoonrestaurant.ca

One* • Bloor/Yorkville • French (G)

Chef Mark McEwan's third restaurant in the city, One has a spacious bar-lounge area, a sumptuous dining room, and a vast patio that curves around the hotel's southeast corner. Designed by Yabu Pushelberg, the restaurant/bar is faithful to the Hazelton's sleek design, mixing wood floors, smoked glass, mirror paneling, cowhide, and striped onyx in shades of cream, chocolate brown, pale gray, and charcoal. McEwan offers palate tempters such as fresh oysters, pickled sardines or sea trout to start, barbecued-rib ravioli, and main courses that include grilled beef tenderloin with foie gras, duck confit with black plums, and grilled tuna with a Moroccan rub. Finish with a Quebec cheese or the vanilla coconut panna cotta. The patio and bar area attracts wealthy wannabes while the dining room is for foodies, older locals, and people on business accounts. *Daily 11:30am-midnight.* $$$ = Hazelton Hotel, 118 Yorkville Ave. (Avenue Rd.) 416-963-6300, thehazeltonhotel.com

Perigee • Distillery District • International

A media darling and favorite from the moment it opened its doors in 2004, Perigee is one of Toronto's trendiest restaurants. But come prepared for a leisurely evening—dinner at Perigee is theater, and the results can take up to four hours. Chef Pat Riley prepares your meal from a kitchen that dominates the dining room, to the delight of the well-dressed upscale diners and Food Television Network junkies alike. Here you dine omakase. Originally a term used in Japanese cuisine, the omakase concept—meaning to put yourself in the chef's hands—is applied to classic continental fare at Perigee. Diners specify five, six, or seven courses, and identify whatever items the chef is to avoid, and sit back to see what surprises appear. Dinner becomes a relaxed, improvised experience as diners watch their courses take shape. Perigee's physical appeal is true to its Distillery District location and features exposed brick, wooden beams, and solid wood furnishings. Seating at Perigee is limited, so reservations are essential. Ask for a table by the window for the best views both inside and out. *Tue-Sat 5:30-9pm.* $$$$ = 55 Mill St. (Parliament St.), 416-364-1397, perigeerestaurant.com

Pure Spirits Oyster House & Grill • Distillery District • Seafood

Best Seafood Restaurants Pure Spirits is a particularly handsome restoration of the original Gooderham Distillery's shipping room, with the exposed brick and dark wooden beams used to modern and glamorous effect against black leather and stainless steel. The crowd is well dressed, a mixture of theater-goers, artsy locals, and a few tourists, and they keep things buzzing at the dinner hour on weekends. A long bar on one side flanks cozy tables and black leather booths, with windows that look out onto a cobblestone patio. In the summer the crowds come in droves to sit on the patio from the afternoon right into the evening, absorbing the District's historic appeal along with a full lineup of live jazz. The menu doesn't disappoint. Appetizer choices include a trio of seafood tartare and Irish whisky–cured smoked salmon Napoleon, with main dishes like whole fish, ahi tuna, and salmon, along with pork tenderloin and strip loin. *Sun-Thu 11am-10pm, Fri-Sat 11am-11pm.* $$$ ⓑ ≣ 55 Mill St. (Parliament St.), 416-361-5859, purespirits.ca

Rain* • Entertainment District • Asian

This is a contemporary Southeast Asian design spot boasting two 15-foot waterfalls, a glowing bar, and photogenic, architecturally inspired bites. *See Hot & Cool Nightlife (p.71) for details. Mon-Wed 5:30-10pm, Thu-Sat 5:30-11pm.* $$$ ⓑ ⓓ = 19 Mercer St. (Blue Jays Way), 416-599-7246, rainrestaurant.ca

Sassafraz* • Bloor/Yorkville • French

Busy day and night, Sassafraz has long seduced local and international fans with its sun-filled dining room and patio. Now after a yearlong renovation, Sassafraz has brought its elegance up a notch with sleek, modern décor, luring visiting celebs, the wealthy elite, and local fashionistas. With a newly installed rooftop patio for private parties, this Yorkville mainstay maintains its status as a beloved hot spot of the neighborhood. French-inspired palate tempters include roasted cauliflower with paprika oil soup, seared scallops with beluga lentils, and maple-glazed sablefish. The roaringly popular weekend brunch consists of traditional offerings backed up by live jazz. *Daily 11am-2am.* $$$ ⓑ = 100 Cumberland St. (Bellair St.), 416-964-2222, sassafraz.ca

Sen5es Restaurant & Lounge* • Entertainment District • International

Best Fine Dining Sen5es is certainly an apt name for this handsome establishment, where all your senses are sure to be engaged before the evening is over. The dining room is elegant and muted, and retains the warm glow of the adjoining lounge area. The menu of continental fusion changes based on seasonally fresh ingredients, and is complemented by an extensive wine list. With the inviting lounge just steps away, consider extending your experience with an aperitif or a nightcap. *Tue-Sat 6-10pm; bar and bistro daily 4pm-1am.* $$$ ⓑ = SoHo Metropolitan, 318 Wellington St. W. (Blue Jays Way), 416-935-0400, senses.ca

Susur • Entertainment District • Fusion (G)

Best Hot Chefs Susur Lee, a true fusion superstar, is one of the world's premier chefs. A visit to Susur is sure to convince you that the master is at the top of his game. The neutral setting is a calming backdrop for a meal that is high drama from start to finish. The dining room is consistently packed with disciples—both famous and merely deep-pocketed and gorgeous—waiting for his exquisite and elaborate culinary and visual creations, like habanero-stuffed polenta croquette and fava beans in Thai bisque, or rib-eye of bison in black truffle sauce. It's so decadently flavorful, so artistically presented, it can almost create sensory overload. For a complete experience, place yourself in the chef's hands and order a tasting menu you'll never forget. Susur is one of the city's most talked-about restaurants, so reserve as soon as you know you're coming to town. *Tue-Thu 6-10pm, Fri-Sat 6-10:30pm.* $$$$ = 601 King St. W. (Bathurst St.), 416-603-2205, susur.com

Tomi-Kro • Leslieville/Riverside • Fusion

Everything a foodie would demand from Toronto's most exclusive restaurants can be found at Tomi-Kro for a fraction of the price and with much less attitude. Inventive and delicious dishes, thoughtfully paired wines, and skilled, proud servers who have an obvious passion for food have rightfully earned Tomi-Kro a legion of devotees. The eastern-influenced fusion menu changes often, and is as likely to surprise with noteworthy updates like five-spice Muscovy duck as it is with unique creations like the house favorite, lightly fried lobster maki balls. Newcomers and regulars alike receive a warm welcome, and are instantly made to feel part of a casually stylish, 30-something, artistic family. *Mon-Sat 6-10pm.* $$ B≡ 1214 Queen St. E. (Leslie St.), 416-463-6677

Trevor Kitchen and Bar* • St. Lawrence • Continental

Best Of-the-Moment Dining Chef and owner Trevor Wilkinson touts his highly regarded eponymous restaurant as offering an "anti-elitist fine dining experience," and though this subterranean restaurant attracts a glowing crowd of foodies, fashion-istas, and general A-listers, he manages to avoid trendster conventions. The main dining room and candlelit bar, featuring two lounges, celebrate the building's her-itage, while modern touches like original artwork and stainless-steel tables designed by Trevor himself perk up the otherwise sober space. Limited-production wines pro-vide the perfect accompaniment to Wilkinson's seasonal menus, which include items like port braised beef cheeks and an Ahi-steak frites. *Tue-Wed 4-10pm, Thu-Sat 4-11:30pm; bar until late.* $$$ B≡ 38 Wellington St. E. (Leader Ln.), 416-941-9410, trevorkitchenandbar.com

Ultra Supper Club* • Entertainment District • International

This dinner-lounge spot with an industrial-influenced décor has an updated gentle-men's club menu of meats and seafood. *See Hot & Cool Nightlife (p.72) for details. Mon-Wed 5:30pm-midnight, Thu-Sat 5:30pm-2am.* $$$ ≡ 314 Queen St. W. (Soho St.), 416-263-0330, ultrasupperclub.com

Hot & Cool Toronto:
The Nightlife

Afterlife Nightclub • Entertainment District • Dance Club

Best Dance Clubs This is one of Toronto's perennial Friday-night hot spots, where the club kids in their 20s come for loud, crowded, raucous fun. The Afterlife has three stylish floors for rowdy patrons, all here to dance the night away and lounge on the fashionable couches. Pale neon-blue lighting glows in the dimly lit danceteria as the dance floor heats up to house, R&B, and electronica. This is a guaranteed party atmosphere, and quite a happening meet market. There's no dress code, but call ahead to get on the guest list and escape those long lines. *Fri-Sat 10pm-3am.* ⓒ≡ 250 Adelaide St. W. (Duncan St.), 416-593-6126, afterlifenightclub.com

Blowfish Restaurant + Sake Bar* • Entertainment District • Bar

A French-meets-sushi restaurant with a gorgeous décor and patrons and a martini list to match. *See Hot & Cool Restaurants (p.60) for details. Mon-Sat 5pm-2am.* ≡ 668 King St. W. (Bathurst St.), 416-860-0606, blowfishrestaurant.com

Budo Liquid Theatre • Entertainment District • Lounge

Best Sexy Lounges Amid the frenetic pace of Clubland at night, Budo Liquid Theatre offers a more calming, zen-inspired lounge vibe. Ultra-fashionable clubbers pack the place, perching on the comfy couches. A waterfall soothes with its trickling sounds and sparkling visuals, and warm spotlighting glows against the wooden fixtures. There are more private VIP areas on each of the two floors inside, so be sure to ask about bottle service. It's the ultimate in see-and-be-seen lounging, and known as a place to meet like-minded, equally fabulous folk. Summers, the rooftop patio, boasting a large Buddha head and candlelight, comes alive with an elegant crowd. *Fri-Sat 9:30pm-3am, some Tuesdays.* ⓒ≡ 137 Peter St. (Richmond St. W.), 416-593-1550, budolt.com

C-Lounge • Entertainment District • Lounge

Best Meet Markets For swank clubbing at its finest, the C-Lounge is a hot spot for the 25-and-over crowd. From the valet parking to Aveda hair and makeup artists on call in the ladies' room, C-Lounge sweats the details, and the good-looking and well-dressed crowd laps it up. Sheer curtains divide a room that glows with warm lighting. A polished crowd reclines on leather couches. Summer brings a courtyard patio with a pool, drapery, and potted trees on the deck, and Lounge Thursdays feature complementary hors d'oeuvres and a DJ from 5pm to 9pm. On Fridays and Saturdays, the place really heats up after 10pm. There's a dress code, so come prepared to pass the door staff's inspection. *Mon-Wed, Sat 10pm-2am, Thu 5pm-2am, Fri 9:30pm-2am.* ⓒ≡ 456 Wellington St. W. (Draper St.), 416-260-9393, libertygroup.com

Century Room • Entertainment District • Lounge

Exposed brick walls, naturally aged hardwood floors, and high ceilings are hardly rare on Toronto's lounge scene, but if God is in the details, Century Room is a design-lounge fan's heaven. Bisazza-tiled bathrooms with LCD monitors, chic pink lighting, chocolate hardwoods, and gorgeous sofas and chaises amount to one of the city's most elite and eye-catching lounging spaces. Visiting A-listers jockey with a young and gorgeous local who's who for space at one of 14 booths offering bottle service and exclusive bathrooms. *Tue, Fri-Sat 9pm-2am.* C≡ 580 King St. W. (Portland St.), 416-203-2226, centuryroom.com

Cheval • Entertainment District • Lounge

Once a stable for the Royal Canadian Mounted Police, this lounge space named for the French word for horse avoids equine décor clichés and keeps things strictly urban and up to date. Cowhide-covered stools, a sunken lounge space, multi-hued mood lighting, DJs who play at a level that allows conversation, and an extensive martini list attract a slick, dressed-to-impress, young professional crowd. Bottle service is available, and the bartenders are skilled, but beer drinkers beware—options are limited. *Thu-Sun 10pm-2:30am.* C≡ 606 King St. W. (Portland St.), 416-363-4933, chevalbar.com

Circa • Entertainment District • Nightclub

At four stories and 55,000 square feet, this latest edition to downtown's club district is the city's most-talked-about club. Created by NYC club king Peter Gatien, this dance club is the new destination of choice for the label-conscious crowd. The entrance hall features rotating local art exhibitions, a dance floor for 1,000 guests, and a private entrance for celebs who want to bypass the red carpet. The unisex Washroom Bar, inspired by hospital décor, has its own DJ booth. The second-floor Sensacell bar area lights up when touched, and the Fathom 22 bar is a sexy modern take on nautical style. The elite reserve the VIP Cube for an intimate space above the dance floor, while those who are DJ-obsessed ask for the DJ VIP area. On Friday and Saturday nights, the beats shift from Euro electronica to old-school hip-hop with the dance floor swelling to capacity with young 20-somethings by midnight. *Fri-Sat 8pm-3am.* C≡ 126 John St. (Richmond St. W.), 416-979-0044, circatoronto.com

Flow Restaurant + Lounge* • Bloor/Yorkville • Lounge

Best Martinis A restaurant-lounge oozing high style and good taste, Flow is the ultimate Yorkville haunt. The design is set by clean lines and warm earth tones of brown and taupe, spiced up with colored murals and striped upholstery. The sophisticated lounge is a perennial hot spot teeming with a young but polished A-list crowd. Flow is equally popular as a restaurant, with a menu featuring an eclectic range of dishes, from pasta to pan-Asian fusion to an excellent osso bucco. *Mon-Thu 5-11pm, Fri-Sat 5pm-2am.* ≡ 133 Yorkville Ave. (Hazelton Ave.), 416-925-2143, flowrestaurant.com

Fly Nightclub • Gay Village • Dance Club

Best Gay Scenes Fly is arguably Toronto's premier gay-male dance club, where the beats are fast and furious and the staff is super hot. It's a hot spot for visiting Hollywood royalty, and the place where the dance club scenes in *Queer as Folk* are filmed. Three floors of style await your pleasure, with quieter conversation-friendly alcoves tucked around the dance floors that vibrate with good-looking revelers. The crowd is mixed but welcoming and straight-friendly. It's the place to go when you literally want to dance the night away. *Fri 10pm-3am, Sat 10pm-7am.* C≡ 8 Gloucester St. (Yonge St.), 416-410-5426, flynightclub.com

Foundation Room • St. Lawrence • Lounge

Best Scene Bars By reinterpreting bohemian-chic and taking lounging back to its North African roots, the Foundation Room offers a sensory feast. Acres of red and gold fabric, a rich marble bar, and ornately carved furniture, mirrors, and tin lamps that look as though they've been plucked from the Marrakesh bazaar, serve to create one of the city's most warm and colorful spaces. A DJ rocks this little slice of the casbah by spinning house tunes along with groovy Arabic numbers. A small menu of North African–inspired tapas completes the atmosphere. *Tue-Thu 6pm-2am, Fri-Sat 6pm-3am.* ≡ 19 Church St. (Front St.), 416-364-8368, foundationroom.ca

Fuzion Resto-Lounge & Garden* • Gay Village • Restaurant-Lounge

Best Gay Scenes Late night, the upstairs lounge and house DJ playing soulful house music lures the label-conscious hetero and gay crowd with the myriad of wine and cocktail offerings, while those wanting more privacy can retire to the velvet-draped VIP area to enjoy bottle service. *Tue-Wed 5pm-11pm, Thu-Sun 5pm-2am.* ≡ 580 Church St. (Wellesley St.), 416-944-9888, fuzionexperience.com

Gallery • Harbourfront • Dance Club

Best Dance Clubs Hidden within the Guvernment lurks Gallery, a 2,000-square-foot underground dance club that's packed Saturday nights and the occasional Friday. The sounds of the latest house and electronica tracks from Europe keep the main arena busy with the young and fashionable until the wee hours. Expect to be fully searched by the stringent bodyguards, but once inside, relax for a brief moment on the quilted banquettes that surround the dance floor before joining the swaying throngs. Designed by popular club designers Munge Leunge Design Associates, the club has a '70s vibe thanks to extensive use of mirrors and wallpaper. The DJs are the crème de la crème of the club scene. Deko-ze and Sydney Blu are regulars. *Fri-Sat 10pm-3am.* ⊂≡ 132 Queen's Quay E. (Jarvis St.), 416-869-1462, theguvernment.ca

Light • Entertainment District • Lounge

Design-style touches like a long black marble-and-glass bar, white wood paneling, a curving white leather bench, a large crystal chandelier, and a raised dance floor have helped make Light a popular destination with Toronto's 20-something clubbers looking for downtown sophistication. Bottle service that includes a dedicated host-waitress and complimentary bottled water and espressos when things are wrapping up adds appeal. *Fri-Sat 10pm-3am.* ⊂≡ 134 Peter St. (Richmond St. W.), 416-597-9547, lightlounge.ca

Li'ly Resto-Lounge* • Little Italy • Lounge

A large list of martinis and wines by the glass keep the room buzzing at this eye-catching spot. *See Hot & Cool Restaurants (p.63) for details. Tue-Sun 6pm-2am.* ≡ 656 College St. (Grace St.), 416-532-0419, lilylounge.com

Lobby* • Bloor/Yorkville • Bar

Best Scene Bars If you're looking for Toronto's "in" spot, look no further. White couches and white drapes are a perfect foil for the chic and well-heeled crowd. Riding the city's craze for clubs disguised as the lobby of a boutique hotel, Lobby does it with Yorkville style. Come early to enjoy champagne, later in the evening to enjoy the music and the buzzing bar scene. There is a pleasing Asian-fusion menu offered in the dining area, featuring items like soy-lacquered black cod and a Kobe sirloin burger. Be prepared to pass the scrutiny of door staff. *Tue-Sat 6pm-2am.* ⊟ 192 Bloor St. W. (Avenue Rd.), 416-929-7169, lobbyrestaurant.com

Martini Lounge • Downtown/Yonge • Lounge

Best Martinis A fabulous contemporary update by Precipice Studios, the trio of designers better known as TV's *The Designer Guys*, has injected this hotel lobby bar with vibrancy and style. A glowing onyx bar, a double-sided fireplace, low slung seating, and a long marble planter mean that this lounge-spot, popular with a beautiful crowd, draws some lustful glances of its own. Tipplers in the main space can enjoy glimpses of the hotel lobby action and can spy visiting celebrities bunking down at the hotel, while those wanting something more low-key can retire to "the library," a separate, more chilled-out space, defined by an 18-foot-high bookshelf. *Sun-Wed 4-11pm, Thu-Sat 4pm-1am; live jazz Fri-Sat 8pm-midnight.* ⊟ Pantages Hotel, 200 Victoria St. (Shuter St.), 416-362-1777, pantageshotel.com

Monsoon* • Entertainment District • Lounge

Sandblasted pine and Japanese accents give a zen feel to this dining and lounging hot spot. *See Hot & Cool Restaurants (p.64) for details. Mon-Thu 11:30am-2:30pm and 5-9pm, Fri 11:30am-2:30pm and 5-11pm, Sat 5-11pm; bar until late.* ⊟ 100 Simcoe St. (Peter St.), 416-979-7172, monsoonrestaurant.ca

One* • Bloor/Yorkville • Restaurant/Bar

Yorkville's latest hot spot is a paparazzo's dream with the celebs and fashionistas. Grab a seat on the see-and-be-seen patio and enjoy the buzzing scene. *See Hot & Cool Restaurants (p.64) for details. Daily 11:30am-midnight.* ⊟ Hazelton Hotel, 118 Yorkville Ave. (Avenue Rd.), 416-963-6300, thehazeltonhotel.com

Opal Jazz Lounge • Entertainment District • Jazz Club

Best Jazz Clubs Miles Davis's image adorns the back wall of this intimate jazz enclave on edgy Queen Street West. Red walls, ebonized wood floors, and moody black-and-white photographs of classic and modern jazz players add flair to the bar, performance area, and dining area. The menu consists of French cuisine influenced by the season and changes daily. Opal showcases local Canadian musicians such as Peter Hill, Steve Koven, and Brian Dickinson and also hosts a sprinkling of international talent. Music begins at 8pm, with the 40-plus crowd swelling the lounge for the middle set at 9:30pm each night. *Tue-Sat 5:30pm-late* C⊟ 472 Queen St. W. (Augusta Ave.), 416-646-6725, opaljazzlounge.com

Panorama • Bloor/Yorkville • Lounge

Best Views Of course you've come for the view. The city spreads out around you from the corner of Yonge and Bloor, and is intriguing by day and sparkling with city lights after dark. But the real reason to come here is for the cocktails—voted the best in town by the readers of a Toronto daily newspaper, and proving an appeal that's more than skin deep. The city's highest summer patio is softly lit and romantic, and furnished in plantation teak. The main room inside has floor-to-ceiling windows and minimalist but comfortable contemporary furniture. You'll find an eclectic menu of favorites like cheese fondue, pizzas, and rich desserts to complement those fabulous drinks. With such a sexy ambience, it's no surprise that Panorama is a favorite romantic date spot. The summer patio scene is lively but not raucous. Panorama draws a sophisticated clientele year-round. *Daily 5pm-2am.* ⊟ 55 Bloor St. W., 51st Fl. (Bay St.), 416-967-0000, panoramalounge.com

Pravda Vodka Bar • St. Lawrence • Bar

A glass front looks out on Wellington Street, and inside the sparkle continues with lacquered furnishings and a long gleaming bar. Vodka is indeed king at this chic downtown spot that has over 40 varieties. The cocktail set are smitten with this upscale bar that looks to bring a little bit of Russia to Toronto. Alongside the vodka, naturally, comes caviar, along with other Russian specialties. The eccentric chandeliers and white furnishings set against black lacquer tables and chairs are a playfully posh take on Russian themes. It's the perfect setting for a late nightcap. *Mon-Wed 5pm-1am, Thu-Sat 5pm-3am.* = 36 Wellington St. E. (Victoria St.), 416-306-2433, pravdavodkabar.ca

Rain* • Entertainment District • Bar

Best Martinis While it's no longer at the very top of the "it" list of Toronto restaurants, Rain still packs in a crowd of celebs and stylish locals who come to drink, dine, and see and be seen among the other trendy elite. The room, located in what was formerly a women's prison, is stunning, with a design inspired by Southeast Asia and dominated by two 15-foot waterfalls. Come for cocktails at the glowing bar that's lit from within, or make an evening of it and enjoy a pan-Asian fusion meal among the beautiful people. *Mon-Wed 5:30-10pm, Thu-Sat 5:30-11pm.* = 19 Mercer St. (Blue Jays Way), 416-599-7246, rainrestaurant.ca

Rockwood • Entertainment District • Lounge/Nightclub

Best Scene Bars Each of this beautiful club's namesake elements, rock and wood, has its own showcase space. Entry-level "Rock" is a paradise for tactile party-goers, with a sloping ceiling, onyx tables, Swarovski accents, and rough elements seemingly hewn from bedrock. "Wood" receives equal attention in the form of a burled walnut bar, woodblock stools, ceiling-to-floor wood accents, a requisite hardwood dance floor, and monochromatic silk-screen images of a forest. And the crowd? It's hyper-stylish 30-somethings throughout. Martini Mondays feature celebrity bartenders, DJs, and drinks that are priced to move. *Mon and Thu-Sat 10pm-3am; Grass May-October, weather permitting.* ℂ≡ 31 Mercer St. (John St.), 416-979-7373, rockwoodclub.com

Sassafraz* • Bloor/Yorkville • Restaurant/Bar

This restaurant is a Yorkville institution, and its bar caters to the rich and famous at all hours of the day and night. *See Hot & Cool Restaurants (p.65) for details. Daily 11am-2am.* = 100 Cumberland St. (Bellair St.), 416-964-2222, sassafraz.ca

Seven Lounge • Downtown • Lounge

Winning a "best of Canada" design competition gave this lounge, named for the seven deadly sins, instant cool cachet. The interior could be described as "spaceship-chic" and boasts low white sofas and tables dramatically lit in lime and purple, and acres of stainless steel and glass. The rooftop lounge features red walls, grey tiling, white trim, floor-to-ceiling windows that offer panoramic city views, a barbecue pit, and a retractable roof. Sound too good to be true? It sometimes is; the young crowd takes second billing to the venue, so scan the lineup to see if it looks like your tribe before paying to enter. *Thu-Sat 9:30pm-3am.* ℂ≡ 224 Richmond St. W. (Simcoe St.) 416-599-9797, sevenlounge.ca

Sky Bar • Harbourfront • Lounge

Best Summer Patios Prada meets Gucci at Toronto's swankiest roof patio, which is part of the huge Guvernment entertainment complex on the Harbourfront, and which stays open from spring until late fall. With the lake twinkling flirtatiously under the stars and chic patrons sipping designer martinis amid the slick white furnishings, this is the place where upscale revelers make the most of the good weather. Thursdays, when a DJ comes to play groovy tunes, are very popular. A door staff guards the entrance to this rooftop paradise, so dress to fit in with a designer crowd. *May-Oct Sat 10pm-5am.* C⬛ 132 Queen's Quay E. (Lower Jarvis St.), 416-869-0045, theguvernment.com

Therapy Ultra Lounge • Entertainment District • Lounge

Best Sexy Lounges Stylish singles come here to meet the same, making the scene while sipping on creatively mixed cocktails. A mix of corporate downtowners and glamorous types, Therapy's crowd is all grown up, but still young enough to let loose. Tiled columns, glowing red lights, and stainless-steel fixtures punctuate the darkened room of the lounge, and upstairs there's a dance floor. A bar glows invitingly, attracting designer-clad patrons who sample from the tongue-in-cheek drink list that includes the Dr. Phil Martini. Therapy is known for some of the friendliest staff around. Weekends, the place is packed with beautiful people from 10pm on. There's a style code, so be sure to dress your best. *Thu-Sun 8pm-2am.* C⬛ 203 Richmond St. W. (Bedford St.), 416-977-3089, therapylounge.com

Trevor Kitchen and Bar* • St. Lawrence • Bar

A sober but high-wattage bar with two lounges serving great food. *See Hot & Cool Restaurants (p.66) for details. Tue-Sat 4pm-late.* ⬛ 38 Wellington St. E. (Leader Ln.), 416-941-9410, trevorkitchenandbar.com

2 Cats Cocktail Lounge • Entertainment District • Lounge

2 Cats is swanky and stylish, just like the upscale crowds who love to sink into the low leather couches or perch at the long bar. This is a perfect spot to order a cosmo, where you can check out the other well-dressed patrons in their natural habitat. The design is contemporary, with clean lines and polished wood floors. The extensive cocktail menu changes on a regular basis. The fabulous 30-ish crowd has made this one of their favorite after-midnight haunts on the weekends. *Thu-Sat 9pm-2am.* ⬛ 569 King St. W. (Portland St.), 416-204-6261, 2cats.ca

Ultra Supper Club* • Entertainment District • Lounge

This club has gone all out to win the fickle hearts of Toronto hipsters, and it's paid off in spades with the crowds of beautiful people in velvet-rope lineups. Gold sheers define the space, which is punctuated by exposed brickwork, shiny white tables, and black chairs, and enhanced by glowing mood lighting. Sink back into the overstuffed booths, elevated on a platform for maximum see-and-be-seen status. An artful fusion menu is characterized by pure flavors and fresh ingredients. After midnight, they move the tables out of the way, and the place morphs into a hot dance club for a well-dressed crowd ranging from black-clad 20-somethings to the well-preserved and young at heart. DJs play old-school to electronica, although word is that the scenesters only flock to the dance floor for vintage Prince. Make reservations for a late dinner to avoid the lines. *Mon-Wed 5:30pm-midnight, Thu-Sat 5:30pm-2am.* C⬛ 314 Queen St. W. (Soho St.), 416-263-0330, ultrasupperclub.com

West Lounge • Entertainment District • Lounge

Best Meet Markets From the moment you reach the spot where 510 King St. W. should be—if in fact it did exist—getting inside the West Lounge is half the adventure. Follow the sign and go down the alley, and if you've dressed up and make nice with the door staff, there's a chance you'll get past the velvet rope to this über-cool underground three-room nightspot. This is where the beautiful people come to play mating games; models, other fashionistas, and men in Armani mingle and mix in high style. Classy vibes mix with that famous center-of-the-universe attitude for a totally Toronto club experience. The décor is offbeat, featuring richly colored faux-marble walls and glass panes that drip with translucent optical film. Come late for the hot after-midnight scene. *Wed-Sat 10pm-2am.* C = 510 King St. W. (Bathurst St.), 416-361-9004, westlounge.com

Hot & Cool Toronto:
The Attractions

Art Gallery of Ontario • Chinatown • Art Gallery
The eighth-largest art museum in North America, the AGO houses a renowned collection of over 36,000 pieces representing over 1,000 years of art history. As a well-respected world-class venue, it plays host to blockbuster traveling exhibitions of masters like Modigliani and the French Impressionists. True to its public mandate, the AGO includes a significant cross-section of Canadian art throughout history, along with collections of European art, prints, and drawings, and contemporary art. From the spring of 2005 until 2008, the AGO will undergo a significant retrofit, including a renovated exterior designed by famed architect Frank Gehry. *NOTE: It is closed through Fall 2008. Check website for current information.* $ 317 Dundas St. W. (McCaul St.), 416-979-6648, ago.net

Artinsite • Various Locations • Tour
Best Guided Tours For a real taste of the Toronto arts community, take a tour with the experts. Tours designed and led by Betty Ann Jordan, arts writer and columnist with chic *Toronto Life* magazine, take you right inside the studios and galleries that make the local arts scene hum. Neighborhood walks open your eyes to hidden treasures like all the funky new galleries on Queen Street West, or the private art collection at the Ydessa Hendeles Art Foundation. In addition, Johnson will introduce you to some of the city's top artists and art dealers. *Check the website for scheduled tours, and ask about custom and special-interest walks.* $$ 416-979-5704, artinsite.com

Bata Shoe Museum • Bloor/Yorkville • Museum
Best Only-in-Toronto Museums If you've always associated the word *museum* with stuffy educational exhibits, let the Bata change your mind. Asked to come up with a jewel to showcase Toronto socialite Sonja Bata's huge collection of shoes, architect Raymond Moriyama created a five-story structure inspired by the idea of a shoebox. Permanent and changing exhibitions include shoes of the stars and elements of pure design, as well as collections that highlight the fascinating social history of shoes. You don't have to be a fashionista to appreciate the design, nor do you need to be curious about Shaq's shoe size to enjoy what this chic little museum has to offer. Attention to detail and helpful staff make for an interesting experience in very attractive surroundings. *Tue-Wed 10am-5pm, Thu 10am-8pm, Fri-Sat 10am-5pm, Sun noon–5pm.* $ 327 Bloor St. W. (St. George St.), 416-979-7799, batashoemuseum.ca

Body Blitz Spa: Health by Water • Entertainment District • Spa
Best Spas The simple exterior reveals a spacious 11,000-square-foot high-ceiling combination of wood and glass that is a women-only retreat. Adding an urban twist to simple spa décor, the change rooms, showers, steam and sauna area are all modern and minimalist with a nod to Japanese aesthetic in the 38-foot saltwater pool area. Downtown professionals escaping their busy lives are happy to try the water circuit, which prescribes a rotation between the warm sea-salt pool, hot green tea pool, cold plunging pool, aromatherapy steam room and infrared

sauna. Those spa lovers accustomed to traditional treatments should consider the Blitz body scrub and combine it with shiatsu or aromatherapy massage to quickly revitalize in less than two hours. *Mon-Thu 10am-8pm, Fri 10am-9pm, Sat 10am-8pm, Sun 10am-6pm.* $$$$ 471 Adelaide St. W. (Portland St.), 416-364-0400, bodyblitzspa.com

CHUM/Citytv Building • Entertainment District • Tour
Best Guided Tours With unique open-concept studios, the CHUM/Citytv building is one of the most identifiable media centers in Canada. The CHUM/Citytv empire is home to an independent media network of local and cable specialty channels. The open-concept studio design means that newscasts offer a view of all the technical and other staff that keep the station humming. Music video station MuchMusic interviews the stars at street level while crowds of squealing fans congregate on the sidewalk. Tours of the studios and other facilities are gratis and offered throughout the afternoons—call ahead for times and details. *Tours offered afternoons Mon-Fri. Call ahead for details.* $ 299 Queen St. W. (John St.), 416-591-5757

Corkin Gallery • Distillery District • Art Gallery
Best Only-in-Toronto Museums Well known in the city as one of the key curators of contemporary photography, Jane Corkin moved her gallery to inhabit one of the uniquely historical spaces of the Distillery District. This multi-level gallery has five exhibition spaces (including a hidden space on the second floor), and blends permanent displays as well as touring exhibitions. Corkin's selection of modern masters from around the globe as well as up-and-coming photographers shows off a wide but well-selected range of photography, focusing on subjects from environmentalism and popular media to abstraction and landscape. *Tue-Sat 10am-6pm, Sun noon-5pm.* 55 Mill St. (Parliament St.), 416-979-1980, corkingallery.com

Distillery District • Distillery District • Site
If you've seen the film *Chicago*, you may just recognize the Distillery District locations used extensively in the Oscar-winning movie. The Gooderham & Worts Distillery opened in 1832 at this locale east of downtown and for a time was the largest distillery in the British Empire. In the early 21st century, entrepreneurs saw a future of a different kind for the deteriorating neighborhood, and invested in a renovation of the area that turned it into Toronto's newest center for the arts. Between frequent location shoots, the District is known for outdoor jazz in the summer, and houses over 20 commercial galleries, artist studios, and workshops. At Pikto (pikto.ca), a gallery devoted to the photographic arts, you can sip cappuccino on a couch while you browse photography books and magazines. In fact, the enterprise has been such a success that the whole neighborhood is now on the rise as a result, and the sidewalks are always buzzing. *Hours depend on the venue.* 55 Mill St. (Parliament St.), thedistillerydistrict.com

Eagles Nest Golf Club • Maple • Golf Course
This challenging 18-hole golf course about a half hour's drive north of the city was designed by renowned architect Doug Carrick. Featuring rugged sand dunes and sod-wall bunkers and grasses, this highly rated public course has a par of 72 and is known for tough greens. Set in green rolling hills, Eagles Nest is popular with the new, modern golfer. And after a stimulating round of links-style

golf, head to the 36,000-square-foot waterside clubhouse facilities to rehash the game over drinks or dinner. *Daily tee times 7am-5pm.* $$$$ 10000 Dufferin St. (Major McKenzie Dr.), 905-417-2300, eaglesnestgolf.com

Gardiner Museum of Ceramic Art • Bloor/Yorkville • Museum

Best Only-in-Toronto Museums Not only does this recently revamped spot house some impressive pieces of art, but the building itself is one of the best examples of modern architecture in the city. The permanent collection includes over 2,700 pieces that document the history and sheer versatility of ceramics as an art form, concentrating on works from the ancient Americas, Italian Renaissance pieces, 17th-century English pottery, and 18th-century European porcelain—in fact, it's the largest ceramics collection on the continent. Traveling exhibits have included the ceramic art of Picasso, among many others. In addition, the museum has its own pottery studio with classes open to the public and on Friday afternoons it offers both free admission and a series of films and lectures. It also has a don't-miss gift shop. *Sat-Thu 10am-6pm, Fri 10am-9pm.* $ 111 Queen's Park (Bloor St.), University of Toronto, 416-586-8080, gardinermuseum.on.ca

Got Style • Entertainment District • Shop

A unique combination of boutique and spa, Got Style offers up one-stop shopping for the perfect suit, your next favorite T-shirt, the best pair of jeans, and a hairstyle to match for the modern man. Business and casual apparel, shoes, grooming supplies, and accessories from designer and up-and-coming labels are found in this full-service men's club. Owners Melissa Austria and Seamus Clarke provide an upscale environment with leather club chairs throughout to allow a spot to contemplate what shirt to buy and several flat-screen TVs with the current game on to ensure you don't miss the score. *Mon-Wed 11am-7pm, Thu-Fri 11am-9pm, Sat 11am-7pm, Sun noon-5pm.* 489 King St. W. (Spadina Ave.), 416-260-9696 (store), 416-260-0020 (spa), gsmen.com

King Street East • Furniture District • Shopping

In recent years, this area of King Street East has become a mecca for furniture and home accessory showrooms, but you won't find any tacky flowered upholstery or DIY cheapies here. No fewer than a dozen major retailers showcase high-end designer furniture on this strip of King, making it worth a trip for window-shopping and browsing for new ideas. Furniture is elevated to the level of pure design at Up Country (214 King St. E., upcountry.ca), and check out the ultra-mod Zanzibar bar stools at Abitare Design (234 King St. E., abitaredesign.com), which are pretty unusual, but quite comfortable and available in a range of glowing colors. Whether you use it as a shopping opportunity or gallery experience, it's a fine way to spend an afternoon. King Street East between Jarvis and Parliament

Made Design • West Queen West • Shopping

Best West Queen West Art Spaces More than a sleek-chic design store, Made is a showroom for Canada's established and up-and-coming contemporary industrial designers, craftspeople, architects, and artists. Owners Shaun Moore and Julie Nicholson scour the country for the best of form and function, and present discerning shoppers with a comprehensive collection of innovative home accessories, textiles, ceramics, glass, furniture, lighting, and even jewelry. A small gallery space showcases rotating exhibitions of design and contemporary arts, and a small event calendar boasts occasional lectures and opening parties. *Tue-Fri 11am-7pm, Sat 11am-6pm, Mon by appointment only.* 867 Dundas St. W. (Manning Ave.), 416-607-6384, madedesign.ca

Ministry of the Interior • Queen Street • Shop

Located in a former autobody shop in a transitional area just north of Queen Street West, this contemporary décor shop features selections from around the globe, including modern furniture, lighting, linens, wall coverings, glassware, and accessories from designers such as Areaware, Tse Tse, Dwell, BD Barcelona, Marimekko, and David Trubridge. Owner Jason MacIsaac's former career in film as a set designer influences the layout in this cement-and-glass space that is one part showroom and one part design gallery. *Tue-Sat 10am-6pm, Sun noon-5pm.* 80 Ossington Ave. (Queen St. W.) 416-533-6684, ministryoftheinterior.net

Museum of Television • Queen Street • Museum

Recently relocated to the east end of Queen Street, this ode to television is a result of the personal collection of local media impresario Moses Znaimer, who founded CityTV. While its impact on our lives has been huge and much discussed, the television receiver as furniture, with a history of its own, has never received this kind of studied treatment before. Permanent and changing exhibits look not only at the history of the television set, but at other 20th-century cultural curiosities such as vintage cars in Latin America. Quirky and eye-opening displays will ensure that you'll never take your television set for granted again. Call ahead for details. $ 550 Queen St. E. (River St.), 416-599-7339, mztv.com

The Oasis Wellness Centre and Spa • Distillery District • Spa

At over 23,000 square feet, Oasis is Canada's largest day spa, and though size isn't everything, Oasis delivers as if it is. First-time visitors will immediately be struck by the heritage-meets-contemporary design that incorporates a sloping ceiling rising to 25 feet at its highest, as well as 63 treatment centers. Massages, in a variety of styles, countless body wraps, and a bewildering array of aesthetic treatments, including male-specific ones, make up the bulk of the individual treatments, while those looking for a well-rounded afternoon of indulgence can select from a variety of combination packages. *Mon-Thu 10am-7pm, Fri-Sat 10am-9pm, Sun 11am-6pm.* $$$$ 55 Mill St. (Parliament St.), 416-364-2626, experienceoasis.ca

Pantages Spa and Wellness Center • Downtown/Yonge • Spa

Best Spas For an over-the-top spa experience, a full 9,000 square feet of tranquil and stylish pampering await at the Pantages. Twelve treatment rooms offer a place to refresh and revitalize, catering to both male and female clientele, with facilities and special packages for couples. Treatments follow Ayurvedic principles, a 5,000-year-old system of health management developed in India. Have a full-body Vichy shower or massage, or have the aqua sommelier help you choose from over 100 varieties of bottled water. Many exclusive products and services are available, including hot-stone massage and Kona-coffee-and-vanilla body treatments. *Sun-Mon 10am-6pm, Tue-Sat 9am-10pm.* $$$$ Pantages Hotel Suites, 200 Victoria St. (Shuter St.), 416-367-1888, pantagesspa.com

Rogers Centre Tour • Entertainment District • Tour

It's billed as "The World's Greatest Entertainment Center." Take the tour and judge for yourself. The 11.5-acre facility has an interior volume, with the roof shut, of 56.5 million cubic feet, and is home field to MLB's Toronto Blue Jays and the Canadian Football League's Toronto Argonauts. It's also a 50,000-plus-seat venue for acts like U2 and Britney Spears. The roof separates into four sections that open in a circular motion, raising the height of the roof to 282 feet, or 31 stories. The tour takes approximately one hour, and allows an insider's look at this massive facility, including a museum area with memorabilia from past shows, a video about its construction, and access to areas typically off limits to the public, such as the playing field, private boxes, and team dressing rooms. *Call well in advance to book your tour, since availability will depend on the facility's busy schedule.* $ 1 Blue Jays Way (Front St. W.), 416-341-2770, rogerscentre.com

Rudsak • Queen Street • Shop

This Montreal-based leather company recently opened an outpost in Toronto, its first outside of Quebec. Known for its supple streamlined leather garments and accessories for men and women, Rudsak is sported by those who want au courant Canadian fashion design with a sleek Euro influence. Designer Evik Asatoorian's inspiration comes from his customer base of musicians, actors, and fashionistas. *Tue-Sat 10am-6pm, Sun noon-5pm.* 315 Queen St. W. (John St.), 416-595-9661, rudsak.com

Satori Urban Wellness • Bloor/Yorkville• Spa

This wellness center offers a blend of Western and Eastern therapies, appealing to 30-something professionals seeking treatments that are more than skin deep. A broad range of options is available. Massage therapy, zen shiatsu, reiki, nutrition counseling, osteopathy, homeopathy, and acupuncture round out your wellness goals. The lavender chocolate body scrub and half-hour massage leaves your skin soft as that of a newborn and is a great stress reliever to boot. *Mon-Fri 10am-9pm, Sat 10am-7pm, Sun noon-5pm.* $$$ 33 Hazelton Ave. (Scollard St.), 416-972-9355, satoriwellness.com

Textile Museum of Canada • Chinatown • Museum

In a nondescript high-rise in an out-of-the-way corner just off Chinatown, the Textile Museum is announced by a garage door painted as a jewel-toned tapestry. Once inside, you'll follow a charmingly quirky staircase, painted at ground level in a melon color that brightens to golden yellow as you go up the stairs. Four levels of temporary and permanent displays feature textile-based creations as well as their history and cultural context—sumptuous hand-knotted carpets in rich and brilliant colors, intricate laces and linens, tapestries and quilts. The permanent collection includes more than 10,000 textile pieces that span almost 2,000 years of history and 190 regions across the globe. A gift shop offers exquisite silk and handwoven scarves and purses, books, and other items. You can wander through on your own, or join a guided tour on Sundays. *Thu-Tue 11am-5pm, Wed 11am-8pm.* $ 55 Centre Ave. (Dundas St. W.), 416-599-5321, textilemuseum.ca

The Yorkville Club • Bloor/Yorkville • Health Club

The Dalai Lama might beg to differ, but the Yorkville Club presents a fine argument—that you don't have to renounce creature comforts, worldly possessions–or even chic style—to pursue physical and emotional well-being, The owners of the Yorkville Club have spared no expense in making the design-savvy 24,000-square-foot fitness mecca feel like a home away from home for the martini and lounging crowd. To help blur the distinction between gym and trendy lounge space, and to distinguish the club from the competition, guests receive perks like private flat-screen televisions on all aerobics equipment, wireless internet, full concierge services, and valet parking. A range of spa-type aesthetic treatments and classes in seven styles of yoga take the pursuit of wellness beyond the weight room. *Mon-Fri 5:30am-11pm, Sat-Sun 8am-8pm.* $$
Hazelton Lanes, 87 Avenue Rd. (Elgin Ave.), 416-961-8400, theyorkvilleclub.com

Yorkville Shopping District • Bloor/Yorkville • Shopping

In the 1970s, Yorkville was the favorite haunt of hippies and anti-establishment types. Like the hippies who grew up and cleaned up their act, the neighborhood's done the same. Popular with visitors and native Torontonians alike, the Bloor/Yorkville area is now home to Canada's most expensive shopping district. Hazelton Lanes offers a range of designer boutiques, and the flagship Holt Renfrew department store harkens from Bloor with a selection of designer wares said to be unrivaled in North America. Come ready to shop until you drop—you'll find everything from the standard upscale brands like Chanel and Gucci to smaller independent boutiques, art galleries, and antique shops. Around Bloor & Avenue Rds.

Hip Toronto

Toronto's West End has long been the epicenter of hip. It's a magnet for artists, designers, and creative types of all disciplines, creating a community of downtown dwellers who have the reputation of living—and playing—on the cutting edge of every trend. It's no accident that West Queen West, where you'll find most of the city's art galleries, is also home to some of the best clubs and lounges, the most inventive little restaurants, and the most stylish cafes. So prepare to steep yourself in some serious attitude, funky art, and great tunes in the city's most eclectic and happening spaces.

Note: Venues in bold are described in detail in the listings that follow the itinerary. Venues followed by an asterisk (*) are those we recommend as both a restaurant and a destination bar.

1. Blowfish Restaurant + Sake
   Bar (p.60)

2. Cosmopolitan Hotel (p.57)

3. Balzac's Café (p.60)

4. KiWe Kitchen (p.62)

HOT & COOL

5

6

7

8

5. Ultra Supper Club (p.72)

6. Doku 15 (p.61)

7. Hôtel Le Germain breakfast room (p.58)

8. Flow Restaurant + Lounge (p.68)

HOT & COOL

1. Drake Lounge (p.98)

2. Velvet Underground (p.102)

3. Czehoski (p.91)

4. Museum of Contemporary Canadian Art
   (p.105)

HIP

5. Esplanade Bier Markt (p.91)

6. Moksha Yoga Downtown (p.105)

7. Camera Bar and Media Gallery (p.103)

8. The Gladstone Hotel (p.98)

HIP

1. Canoe Restaurant & Bar (p.122)

2. Hockey Hall of Fame (p.140)

3. The InterContinental Toronto Centre (p.115)

4. Tea Room, Windsor Arms Hotel (p.132)

CLASSIC

5

6

7

8

5. Spadina Museum (p.141)

6. Starfish Oyster Bed & Grill (p.131)

7. Gallery Grill (p.124)

8. The Fairmont Royal York lobby (p.115)

CLASSIC

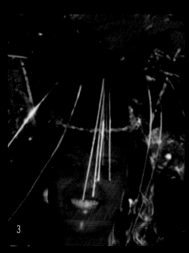

1. Leaving: Niagara Falls (p.188)
2. Prime Time: Caribana Parade (p.154)
3. Prime Time: Caribana Parade (p.154)

Hip Toronto:
The Perfect Plan (3 Nights and Days)

Perfect Plan Highlights

Thursday

Afternoon	West Queen West, Mercer Centre, MOCCA
Pre-dinner	Liberty Bistro/Bar, Communist's Daughter
Dinner	Drake Dining Rm., Oyster Boy, Caju
Nighttime	Drake Lounge, Gladstone, Habitat
Late-night	Stones Place, Mitzi's Sister*

Friday

Morning	Body Blitz, Moksha
Lunch	Zelda's, Futures
Afternoon	Mediatheque, 401 Richmond, Steam Whistle Brewing Co.
Pre-dinner	Beer Bistro, Rivoli*
Dinner	Swan, Byzantium*, Beaconsfield*
Nighttime	Revival*, Mod Club
Late-night	Velvet Underground, Bovine, Shanghai*

Saturday

Morning	St. Lawrence Market, Design Exchange
Lunch	Esplanade Bier Markt*
Afternoon	Harbourfront Centre, Power Plant Gallery
Pre-dinner	Cafe Diplomatico
Dinner	Czehoski*, Bar Italia, Kalendar
Nighttime	Sutra Tiki Bar, Sweaty Betty's, Cameron
Late-night	Convento Rico, This Is London

Hotel: Drake Hotel

2pm: Set out to explore West Queen West, the recently reborn neighborhood at the center of Toronto's urban arts craze. More than 20 galleries await your perusal, and the recent cultural boom has attracted countless hip cafes, vintage clothing stores, and designer boutiques. Should the weather work against you, take things indoors. First, head to the nearby **Mercer Union Centre for Contemporary Visual Art** where exhibitions will allow you to continue your journey through the city's vibrant arts scene. Stop at the **Museum of Contemporary Canadian Art** (MOCCA) tucked behind shops and galleries on Queen Street West. A sculpture of branches marks the entrance.

6pm: For an afternoon drink among creative professional types, head a few blocks south to the popular **Liberty Bistro/Bar**, or go north to Dundas Street West for a post-gallery libation at funky bar the **Communist's Daughter.**

8pm Dinner: Stroll down to the heart of Toronto's hipster scene at the Drake Hotel. This multipurpose venue is single-handedly responsible for the neighborhood's tremendous revitalization, and

HIP

this is *the* place to strike a pose if you want to hang with the city's most stylish hipsters. Sample the inventive Canadian cuisine at the **Drake Dining Room and Raw Bar**. If that's too much of a scene, pop down the street to **Oyster Boy,** where a real Maritimer serves up more than 20 varieties, along with other seafood that's scrupulously fresh. Or for an unusual culinary adventure—and most likely a few additions to your dining vocabulary—**Caju** is a sunny destination restaurant that dishes up hearty Brazilian fare.

11pm: No real hipster can leave Toronto without a visit to the **Drake Lounge**, where you'll find the martinis tasty and the scene fashionably artsy. Or mingle with the local arts community (and try your hand at karaoke) at the **Gladstone Hotel**. For upscale lounging,the amber-hued **Habitat Lounge** is a popular spot just a few blocks away.

1am: After midnight, spontaneous jams have been known to take place at the **Stones Place** (where you can occasionally even expect to find Mick himself if he's in town). Nearby **Mitzi's Sister*** is a perfect spot to catch a last set and last call.

Friday

9am: Sink into the glittery green vinyl chairs and observe an eclectic crowd of downtown locals at **Le Petit Déjeuner** as you order your morning eggs.

10am: Indulge this morning by signing up for one of a myriad of treatments at the industrial-chic—and female only—**Body Blitz**, a wildly popular urban day spa (see Hot & Cool Attractions). If you'd rather head outside, take a stroll through lovely **High Park**, one of Toronto's biggest green spaces. If you're determined to challenge yourself, stay downtown and drop in for a "hot" yoga class at **Moksha Yoga Downtown**, or get your adrenaline rush at **Joe Rockhead's** where you can have a rock-climbing adventure right in the heart of the city.

1pm Lunch: Check out **Zelda's** on Church Street in the heart of Toronto's Gay Village, where you can enjoy traditional fare in a highly social setting. Or head to the Annex neighborhood near the University of Toronto to **Futures Bakery & Cafe** for Eastern European classics and sweet treats in the relaxed dining area or on the large outdoor patio.

2pm: Consider a mid-afternoon culture injection with screenings at the **NFB Mediatheque** or head over to **401 Richmond**, which houses several small art galleries that reflect traditional to contemporary art disciplines. If it's time for a break from the arts, take a tour of Toronto's premier boutique brewery, the **Steam Whistle Brewing Company**, in the shadow of the CN Tower.

6pm: If the brewery tour has left you thirsting for a pint to call your own, head to the **Beer Bistro**, with a myriad of ale and lager offerings that reflect the latest brewing techniques from around the world. For pan-Asian appetizers and a game of pool, head to **Rivoli*** to hang out with local musicians and artists and find out what's going on in the local live music scene.

8pm Dinner: Dine on excellent updated diner fare at the retro-cool **Swan** on Queen West. For swanky steak and seafood and a long and creative martini list, hop in a cab to **Byzantium***, located on the east side. It's been serving it up in the Gay Village for years. To jump-start your evening of partying, consider dinner at the **Beaconsfield***, where, if you linger long enough over your delicious meal, DJs and live music acts will kick things up a notch.

11pm: On College Street, join the creative types at **Revival*** for a musician-friendly vibe and the odd celebrity sighting. Otherwise, check the listings for what's lined up at the **Mod Club Theatre** just down the street—it's known as one of the city's premier live venues. Alternatively, **Andy Pool Hall** offers cool cocktails, several pool tables, and tunes courtesy of the house DJ.

1am: Go down to Queen Street West where alternative types will find an instant spiritual home at the darkly gothic **Velvet Underground**, while those looking for rock ' n' roll will roll with the chick DJs at the **Bovine Sex Club**.

2:30am: Right next door to Bovine, the doors hardly ever close at the diner **Shanghai Cowgirl***, where clubbers congregate late night to refuel and swap stories over cold beers and diner fare.

Saturday

9am: Fuel up at the tongue-in-cheek **Beaver Café** and soak up the Queen West vibe alongside artists and other creative types.

10:30am: Take a leisurely walk to the **St. Lawrence Market**, which is lined with produce, meat, fish and take-out food stalls as well as locally created arts, crafts, and antiques. If snacking and shopping your way around the market doesn't entice, it's only a short walk to the Financial District and the **Design Exchange**, which chronicles the principles of 20th-century design.

1pm Lunch: The **Esplanade Bier Markt***, a cross between Belgian brasserie and slick club, is just two blocks from St. Lawrence Market. For lighter, more casual fare, go west to Queen Street's **Tequila Bookworm Café** for its healthy sandwiches, wide selection of magazines, and cutting-edge fiction offerings.

2pm: After lunch, make your way down to the **Harbourfront Centre** where contemporary art is on dis-

HIP

play in cool digs at the **Power Plant Gallery**. Still at the Harbourfront Centre, watch artists making beautiful items in ceramics, textiles, and other media, then head to Bounty Contemporary Canadian Craft Shop to purchase the fruits of their labor. Alternatively, survey the city skyline and vibrant lakefront district while walking the short distance to the **Toronto Music Garden** to lose yourself in one of the city's most unique public spaces. The Garden depicts a piece of classical music in a wholly modern landscaped space, and the self guided audio tours give a new perspective on music. Should you prefer a more leisurely option, check the Saturday matinee listings and relax with a drink and an arthouse film at the **Camera Bar and Media Gallery**.

6pm: One of art's purposes is to provoke discussion, so join the hipsters on College at the **Cafe Diplomatico** for a cappuccino and a conversation. Or stop in at Kensington's **Moonbean Coffee Company** for a fair-trade caffeine break and watch the locals shop for dinner or listen to impromptu buskers on Augusta Avenue. Pop into **Ukula** for some tunes for the iPod, a Euro music mag, or coffee served with a side of house DJ tunes.

8pm Dinner: Stay in Little Italy for—what else?—classic and updated Italian cuisine at **Bar Italia**, or innovative cafe fare at the perennially bustling little **Kalendar**. If you're in the mood for culinary acrobatics, join the foodie crowd at **Czehoski*** to dine on Nathan Isberg's adventurous Canadian dishes; he's one of the city's hottest up-and-coming chefs.

11pm: Distinctive clubbing beckons in colorful Polynesian flavors at the **Sutra Tiki Bar**. Queen Street West's **Sweaty Betty's** serves up libations to indie rockers and artists, while the **Cameron Public House** is a prime spot for an icy brew and to catch the last rock set.

1am: Catch the drag-queen show and learn a few salsa moves at **El Convento Rico** or stop by the **Phoenix Concert Theatre** to see which of the latest rock or pop touring acts is on stage.

2am: Use your charm to get through the line at **This Is London** and dance the night away to a mix of hip-hop and house.

The Morning After
Mitzi's Café and Gallery has an excellent brunch that's as popular with the west end art set as it is with young professionals.

Hip Toronto:
The Key Neighborhoods

Little Italy Toronto's Little Italy is one of the city's busiest and most colorful shopping, dining, and lounging destinations. Sure, you can find a traditional coffeeshop if you're looking for a slice of the old country, but College Street's hip boutiques, restaurants, and thriving nightlife scene are positively up to date.

Parkdale Found along the westernmost reaches of Queen Street (west of Gladstone Avenue), this once downtrodden, now working-class, and soon-to-be-gentrified neighborhood hasn't yet enjoyed the renaissance that West Queen West has, but the times, they are a-changin'. The young and artistic crowds are moving in and the restaurants, shops, and services are starting to reflect it.

Queen Street Once strictly the domain of the urban and artistic, the stretch of Queen between University Avenue and Trinity Bellwoods Park now welcomes all comers with its youthful vibe. University to Spadina Avenue means shopping for international urban clothing brands and dining and drinking at funky see-and-be-seen spots. Head west of Spadina to find one-of-a-kind boutiques full of locally designed fashions.

West Queen West Queen Street west of Trinity Bellwoods Park was until recently a tired and dilapidated neighborhood, but it's been reborn as one of North America's most happening contemporary gallery strolls. This is Toronto's hipster ground zero.

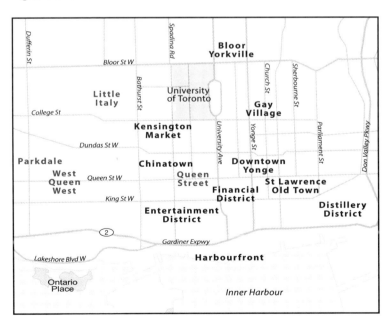

Hip Toronto:
The Shopping Blocks

Little Italy

Like the vibrant restaurants that have made Little Italy popular, the neighborhood's shops attract a young, style-conscious, always-trendy crowd.

Lilliput Hats Retro-chic headwear popular with fashionistas and visiting celebrities. 462 College St. (Bathurst St.), 416-536-5933

Soundscapes Hipster favorite music store with frequent in-store performances by local and visiting bands. 572 College St. (Manning Ave.), 416-537-1620

Ukula Collections of hard-to-find international street-wear brands, with an on-site espresso bar. 492 College St. (Palmerston Blvd.), 416-619-9282

Queen Street East

Though not as popular as the western stretch of Queen Street, Queen East offers a number of funky, unique-to-Toronto shops sure to impress.

Doll Factory by Damzels Locally designed, rock star–inspired funky fashions for women, popular with scensters and A-listers like Kirsten Dunst and Kate Hudson. 1122 Queen St. E. (Bertmount Ave.), 416-598-0509

Nathalie Roze & Co. Colorful one-off indie fashions from a local designer and a popular do-it-yourself craft and fashion workshop. 1015 Queen St. E. (Pape Ave), 416-792-1699

Thrill of the Find Vintage couture and designer pieces from lines like Fendi, Prada, and Gucci. 1172 Queen St. E. (Jones Ave.), 416-461-9313

Queen Street West

Toronto's hippest independent boutiques can be found on Queen Street West, the epicenter of Toronto's funky shopping scene.

Fleurtje In-house–designed colorful handbags share pride of place with a selection of Canadian-designed accessories for men and women. 764 Queen St. W. (Niagara St.), 416-504-5552

Fresh Collective Seasonal collections from up-and-coming Toronto fashion designers. 692 Queen St. W. (Euclid Ave.), 416-594-1313

Magic Pony Hipper-than-thou clothing, books, art, gifts, and collectibles. 694 Queen St. W. (Euclid Ave.), 416-861-1684

Peach Beserk Silk-screened dresses and accessories in a kaleidoscope of colors from a Toronto institution, designer Kingi Carpenter. 507 Queen St. W. (Spadina Ave.), 416-504-1711

Hip Toronto:
The Hotels

Drake Hotel • West Queen West • Trendy (19 Rms)
Once a dive best known for draft beer in dirty glasses, the Drake Hotel underwent a stunning multimillion-dollar renovation and reopened as the haunt of the über-hip on artsy Queen Street West. Attention to detail extends to every corner, from the dance cave to the "Crash Pads" that combine antique elements and high-end modern design with a dash of the eccentric. The 385-square-foot luxe suite features dark hardwood floors against white walls, contemporary furnishings, and a striking bathroom with a glass shower stall. The other rooms are all different and feature restored antiques, DVD and CD players, and queen-size beds. Ask for one of the three "Salon Rooms"; they're over 200 square feet and feature either plush carpeting or charcoal-colored hardwood floors, custom millwork, and vintage-chic sofas. The work of local artists is on display throughout the hotel—one of the owners is himself a working artist. The staff are young and attractive, friendly and attitude-free. Amenities include several meal options from breakfast to sushi to late night, along with a lounge and dance bar all located on site. $$$ 1150 Queen St. W. (Beaconsfield St.), 416-531-5042 / 866-372-5386, thedrakehotel.ca

Gladstone Hotel • West Queen West • Trendy (37 Rms)
Where the Drake went contemporary high style, the Gladstone has taken a different approach to renovating its once historically seedy space. The Glad retained and restored old architectural features like its big wooden beams, heavy wood bars and trim, and gorgeous baroque moldings, and spiffed them up with cool touches of contemporary luxury like stainless-steel plumbing against exposed brick. All of the guest rooms were designed by both famous and emerging artists who entered their proposals in a competition. As a result, each is unique, ranging in style from high-end to designer to Arts and Crafts. All include flat-screen TVs, Internet access, and down duvets, and are accessible by either the grand staircase or Toronto's last surviving Victorian hand-operated elevator. High white ceilings arch over wooden plank floors that gleam with TLC. Those wanting to splurge should opt for the two-story Rockstar suite; housed in the building's turret, it has 360-degree city views. The hip and artsy congregate at this veritable institution in the arts community, and especially at the bar, which is the oldest continuously operating tavern in Toronto. Three bars on three floors host entertaining events from cabaret to film screenings to fashion shows. $$$ 1214 Queen St. W. (Gladstone Ave.), 416-531-4635, gladstonehotel.ca

Madison Manor • Bloor/Yorkville • Timeless (23 Rms)
The Madison is old Yorkville with a youthful vibe; a Victorian mansion on a quiet leafy street just blocks from the monied classes shopping at Avenue and Bloor, with a patio that rocks until the wee hours in the summer. The houses that make up the Madison were built in 1892, and the Madison wears its age with good humor. Inside, the labyrinthine hallways are elegant and immaculate, with ornate polished dark-wood trim set against pale walls and dark

green carpets. The décor includes a creative blend of authentic antique fixtures—lights, furniture—and modern amenities like satellite TV and cable. Ask for a room facing Madison Avenue (rather than the patio) for a quieter stay. Room 201 is a particular favorite—a charming mini-suite with oak armoire, sitting area with gas fireplace, and stained-glass window. The pub features an antique player piano and fireplace along with the patio, and as in the rest of the Madison, the mood is young and hip, with classy antique accents. $$$ 20 Madison Ave. (Bloor St. W.), 416-922-5579 / 877-561-7048, madisonavenuepub.com

Hip Toronto:
The Restaurants

Bar Italia • Little Italy • Italian
A classic of Little Italy, this longstanding institution is responsible for first drawing the upmarket artistic crowds to this part of town. Characterized by attentive
and thoughtful service, Bar Italia offers fresh Italian cuisine with a hip College
Street vibe. Dark wood booths and paneling balanced by blue walls and sexy
lighting make it a romantic dining experience, and you can then retire to the
slick bar and lounge upstairs to continue the evening after dinner. Italian food
is popular in Toronto, but it's rare to find it prepared this well, with creations
like insalata di salmone with warm wild salmon, and entrées featuring pasta and
risotto, steak, seafood, and lamb. A long wine list complements the menu. *Daily
11am-11pm, Sat-Sun 11am-2:30pm; bar daily until 2am.* $$$ = 582 College
St. W. (Manning St.), 416-535-3621, bar-italia.ca

Bar One* • West Queen West • Italian
Bar One has a glass front that beckons you into a minimalist, chic, and inviting
space in yellow and ochre, punctuated by red stools lined up along a slinky bar.
The key to the menu is deliciously simple Italian food prepared with a twist, like
the ever-popular antipasto Bar One for two, loaded with grilled vegetables,
focaccia, and olives, among other delicacies. Along with great food comes a hip,
black-clad funky clientele that packs the place from day into night. It takes on
a sexy martini-lounge ambience with late-night eats Thursday through Saturday.
Mon-Fri 11am-2am, Sat-Sun 9am-2am. $$$ B= 924 Queen St. W. (Shaw
St.), 416-535-1655, bar-one.com

The Beaconsfield* • West Queen West • International
The Beaconsfield ups the ante on West Queen West's funky dinner scene.
Beautiful dishes like spicy mint and coconut sambal encrusted salmon, roast-
ed beet and chèvre salad, and Guinness-braised short ribs are prepared in the
open kitchen and served to a crowd drawn from the nearby art galleries. Wood
paneling, leather banquettes, and a polished bar set the mood, while late-night
DJs and the occasional live music act add authenticity to the bar-lounge vibe.
Mon-Sat 5pm-2am, Sun 11am-3pm. $$ B= 1154 Queen St. W. (Beaconsfield
Ave.), 416-516-2550, thebeaconsfield.com

Beaver Café • West Queen West • Cafe
With a tongue-in-cheek beaver-themed décor and laid-back vibe, the Beaver
Cafe is a favorite of edgy local artists and gallery owners. A bright room, friend-
ly service, and a minimalist menu of light fare are a good fit for the leisurely
cafe-style ambience. The grilled panini come especially recommended, with fill-
ings like chèvre, sun-dried tomatoes, and ham. Offerings are full of pleasant
surprises, like the tasty rustic nana (banana) bread. The Beaver is most popu-
lar at breakfast time for heaped plates of ham and eggs, house-baked pastries,
and lighter fare like granola. *Daily 9am-10pm; bar until 2am.* $ = 1192 Queen
St. W. (Northcote St.), 416-537-2768

Beer Bistro • Downtown/Yonge • French

The goal of the Bistro's owners (a beer writer and a chef) is to spread the word about the wonderful world of beer. A menu of over 100 selections (including craft brews) is classified by taste, not country or name, and includes categories like "crisp," "spicy," or "bold." A whole menu of beer-based continental bistro fare helps the brews go down. Located on a busy downtown corner in a bright, sleekly modern room, Beer Bistro is especially busy with downtown professionals at lunchtime. Its outstanding range of cold brews also makes it a fine escape from the summer heat. *Mon-Wed 11:30am-midnight, Thu-Sat 11:30am-1am, Sun 10:30am-10pm; bar until late.* $$ B≡ 18 King St. E. (Yonge St.), 416-861-9872, beerbistro.com

Byzantium* • Gay Village • International

Long considered one of the best martini bars in town, the Byzantium also boasts a fine restaurant in a stylish setting. Green walls contrast with the cushioned orange chairs of the perennially busy bar and lounge, while in the dining room, lush floral arrangements soften the formal tables and seating. The seafood is especially recommended, and the Byzantium Classic is a popular choice of Black Angus strip loin and black tiger shrimp tempura. A long wine list complements the menu, which includes sublime desserts like homemade ice cream and baked-to-order cookies. Service is both playful and efficient, and the overall vibe is upscale but friendly with that special Boystown touch. It's stylish and clubby and the patrons are too. *Daily 5:30pm-2am.* $$$ B≡ 499 Church St. (Wellesley St.), 416-922-3859

Cafe Diplomatico • Little Italy • Cafe

With a simple and casual Italian cafe menu of thin-crust pizza, pasta, and panini, "the Dip" defies trendiness, which only seems to fuel its hipster cachet. The real veteran of Little Italy has a laid-back atmosphere that has even been known to draw Sophia Loren when she's in town. The interior is nothing special—tile floors and plain white vinyl chairs—but in good weather, it's one of the most popular patios on College to watch the parade of fashionable humanity go by. Unhurried service means you can linger over your latte for hours, and even in bad weather, you'll find a scene of stylish hipsters of all ages and university students doing the same. *Daily 8am-1:30am.* $ ≡ 594 College St. W. (Clinton St.), 416-534-4637, diplomatico.ca

Caju • West Queen West • Brazilian

Best Ethnic Dining Modern and minimalist behind its glass storefront, Caju brings the exotica of Brazil to Toronto. Walls of pale blue and green complement a sleek bar and polished wood floors. Further down the long room, rows of tables and tan leather banquettes create an inviting dining area. Expect the unusual— an appetizer of grilled sardines over a corn flan and young greens, a special of grouper rolled in cassava flour, and a host of menu items that will likely expand your vocabulary. Attention to detail—from the Brazilian cherrywood floors, to the bossa nova playing in the background, to the fabulous caipirinhas (a traditional Brazilian cocktail)—make it a memorable trip south. Caju is open only for dinner and draws a young and eclectic crowd of regulars, along with foodies coming for the latest new tastes. You'll find your servers friendly and knowledgeable, the mood casual and festive. *Tue-Thu 5:30-10pm, Fri-Sat 5:30-11pm.* $$ ≡ 922 Queen St. W. (Crawford St.), 416-532-2550, caju.ca

Czehoski* • Queen Street • Canadian

Best Canadian Cuisine Chef Nathan Isberg's self described "decadent comfort food" has created one of Toronto's loudest buzzes. Truffled Brie pierogies with an apple-white wine velouté, and a wallet-busting sirloin-bison burger, exhibit a commitment to style and substance that carries over into the room's design theme. This former illegal craps den and later butcher shop has hardwood floors, original brick walls, and even a leftover butcher's block. A main floor lounge evokes the building's history, while upstairs a pub—complete with a casual menu, fireplace, and contemporary art on the walls—and a rooftop patio contribute to a lively bar scene. Weekend brunch items like chestnut flour crepes with roasted pears and cream cheese maple syrup keep the rooms filled on weekend mornings. *Daily 11:30am-10:30pm; bar until 2am nightly.* $$ B = 678 Queen St. W. (Euclid Ave.), 416-366-6787, czehoski.com

Drake Dining Room and Raw Bar* • West Queen West • Canadian

Best Canadian Cuisine Hipster hub that it is, the Drake is sure to dazzle in its stylishly offbeat and colorful dining room. This was a high-class renovation taken to the extreme, with the hotel—and its dining room—treated as fine art. Insist on a table or booth where you can lounge decadently on the chic green banquettes while you dine and take in the vibe. Executive chef Anthony Rose is one of the city's rising stars, and the fare will impress with its interpretations of Canadian cuisine that focus on applying classic techniques to local and seasonal ingredients. The results are superb, and include a raw bar with sushi, oysters, and venison tartare, small plates featuring seared scallops and barbecued octopus with creamed parsley, and large plates of cedar-baked organic salmon, all of it prepared with an exquisite attention to detail that creates a happy marriage of form and substance. Film and television types join artists and celebs for dinner in this sociable ambience. Reservations are recommended most days and essential Thursday through Sunday when the line can go out the door. But don't be daunted by the crowds—it's worth wading through the lounge to the dining room. *Mon-Tue 11am-2pm and 6-10pm, Wed-Sat 11am-2pm and 6-11pm, Sun 11am-2pm and 6-9pm.* $$ = 1150 Queen St. W. (Beaconsfield St.), 416-531-5042, thedrakehotel.ca

Esplanade Bier Markt* • St. Lawrence • Belgian

This block of the Esplanade is home to several pseudo-Celtic pubs, but unlike its neighbors, the Bier Markt draws on Belgium for its brasserie-style brew and menu offerings. The décor is slick and modern, with more traditional brasserie accents like wooden stools at the long bar and rustic wooden chairs and polished brass pillars in the dining room. The extensive beer list includes fruity dessert brews, and the menu features fresh and inventive takes on Belgian brasserie fare like a wurst sampler and gourmet poutine, steak frites, and filet mignon burger. And the mussels are divinely fresh and fragrantly spiced, accompanied by substantial quantities of sourdough bread. This upscale brew pub and dining room turns into a nightclub after dark when yuppie crowds pack the dance floor and hunky staff make sure the festivities are enjoyable. *Mon-Wed 11am-11pm, Thu-Fri 11am-midnight, Sat-Sun noon-midnight.* $$ B = 58 The Esplanade (Church St.), 416-862-7575, thebiermarkt.com

Café • Bloor/Yorkville • Bakery/Cafe

a day and featuring a protected all-season patio, Futures Bakery or is a trendy and popular spot, bustling with artistic-urban types f the day. Its divine breads are served at many of Toronto's best and here in a standard breakfast and light cafe menu. Genuinely friendly service, a leisurely pace, and patio seating make it the perfect place for people-watching, very-late-night snacking, or getting a fresh and flavorful start to the day. *Daily 7:30am-midnight.* $ ▤ 483 Bloor St. W. (Bathurst St.), 416-922-5875

Kalendar • Little Italy • International
The prettiest little cafe on the College Street strip, and one of the most romantic dinner spots in town, Kalendar has long been a local favorite. Antique chandeliers hold court over wooden floors, and there are plenty of booths and corners for quiet conversation, even though it's typically busy, busy, busy with 30-something yuppies and older hipsters alike. Though the mood is unpretentious, head-to-toe black will never go out of style at Kalendar. With its cozy ambience and hospitable feel, this is a place where you can enjoy casual cafe fare of pizza, pasta, and panini, sip cocktails, and linger over cappuccino very happily. *Mon-Wed 9:30am-10:30pm, Thu-Fri 9:30am-11pm, Sat 10:30am-11pm, Sun 10:30am-10:30pm.* $$ ▤ 546 College St. W. (Euclid St.), 416-923-4138, kalendar.com

Le Petit Déjeuner • St. Lawrence • Cafe
The electric-green booths are the first thing you'll notice about this funky eatery on newly yuppified King Street East. Here you'll be served a homestyle breakfast and lunch classics prepared simply and well, and eat with a crowd that represents a wide cross-section of urban Toronto—lawyers and construction workers, students and civil servants. Relaxed earth tones and exposed brick complement the glittering green booths. The staff are young and enthusiastic. This welcoming start or boost to the day is a hospitable and fun find, and the vibe continues with dinner service when live music sets the perfect, funky mood. *Mon-Wed 8am-6:30pm, Thu-Fri 8am-10pm, Sat 9am-3pm, Sun 10am-3pm.* $ ▤ 191 King St. E. (Frederick St.), 416-703-1560, petitdejeuner.ca

Liberty Bistro/Bar • West Queen West • Cafe
With a cafe menu of appetizers, salads, pastas, and panini, and a busy and friendly vibe, this oasis of casual charm nestled amid converted warehouses and industrial buildings is sure to win you over in no time. The ivy-covered building sports a fine people-watching patio in the summer, but buzzes year-round after work with the creative types and young professionals who work and live in this neighborhood of upscale condos and production and design studios. *Mon-Fri 11:30am-9:30pm, Sat-Sun 11am-9:30pm.* $$ ▤ 25 Liberty St. (Atlantic St.), 416-533-8828, theliberty.ca

Mitzi's Café and Gallery • Parkdale • Cafe
Best Brunches The bright purple and yellow walls, local crowd, shabby-hipster mismatched Formica tables, and even the funky artwork—which changes monthly and is for sale—are only side attractions to what is one of the city's favorite brunches. This popular spot, located on a tree-lined side street, offers an in-the-know crowd a gourmet alternative to the greasy-spoon breakfast. Expect savory items like a variety of gourmet eggs Benedict and a delicious

Stilton frittata, or sweeter dishes like pancakes or French toast covered in a mouthwatering butter pecan sauce. It's brunch only on the weekends, while weekdays see a host of soups, salads, and sandwiches added to the notable mix to make it a good lunch stop as well. *Mon-Fri 7:30am-4pm, Sat-Sun 9am-4pm.* $ ▬ 100 Sorauren Ave. (Pearson Ave.), 416-588-1234, mitzissister.com

Mitzi's Sister* • Parkdale • Pub Grub

Mitzi's latest addition to the family does for pub grub what Mitzi's Café and Gallery does for breakfast fare. A so-shabby-it's-hip décor provides the perfect backdrop for the grittier West Queen West hipsters who show up to nosh on fabulously re-imagined starters like marinated beets with warm couscous, pecan-encrusted chèvre, and Riesling-soaked Granny Smith apples, and mains that include house pastas and a lamb burger with shallots, rosemary, and garlic served on a pada bun. Nightly live music sessions create a bar atmosphere after the dinner crowds have thinned. *Mon-Fri 4pm-midnight, Sat-Sun 10am-midnight; bar until late.* $ ▬ 1554 Queen St. W. (Dowling Ave.), 416-532-2570, mitzissister.com

Moonbean Coffee Company • Kensington Market • Cafe

Enjoy a cup of java and a healthy start to the day in the midst of Kensington Market at the Moonbean. If the weather's good, take a seat on the front or back patio along with neighborhood regulars and downtowners. Here the java is of gourmet quality. Moonbean roasts its own beans, which makes for a deliciously flavorful cup. You can choose from over 50 varieties, many of them fair-trade and organic brews. Tea lovers will also find much to love here, with a wide selection to choose from. A light menu of baked goods also beckons, including samosas and bagels. The nana (banana) bread comes highly recommended. For a heartier start to the day, try the fresh bagel with egg, cheese, and vegetables. *Daily 7am-10pm.* $ ▬ 30 St. Andrews St. (Kensington St.), 416-595-0327, moonbeancoffee.com

Oyster Boy • West Queen West • Seafood

Owned by a real Maritimer, Oyster Boy mixes a variety of mollusks with Queen Street artsy-cool for a winning dining experience. Oyster Boy is all seafood, all the time, with no respite for the uninitiated and pure heaven for lovers of oysters, mussels, fish, and other delicacies from the ocean. Congenial service enhances the mood. Don't let the goofy sign and unassuming storefront deceive you—the place is packed with the usual West End hipsters, along with a few foodies drawn by glowing reviews. *Sun-Wed 5-10pm, Thu-Sat 5-11pm.* $$ ▬ 872 Queen St. W. (Crawford St.), 416-534-3432, oysterboy.ca

Queen Mother • Queen Street • Asian

Forget England. The British name and the pub-style wooden booths found inside are the only touches of Windsor. As for the rest, think King of Siam. The Queen Mum has been dishing out Thai, Vietnamese, and Laotian fare—and a handful of pub-inspired dishes like burgers—to Queen Street's young and artsy for more than 30 years, making it one of the street's stalwart eateries. In warmer months, try to score a table on the small, bustling patio at the rear of the restaurant and forget that one of Toronto's most happening street scenes is only steps away. *Sun-Thu 11:30am-11pm, Fri-Sat 11:30am-midnight.* $ ▬ 208 Queen St. W. (University Ave.), 416-598-4719, queenmothercafe.ca

Revival* • Little Italy • International
A former church turned baroque-styled hipster eatery with a Sunday jazz brunch. *See Hip Nightlife (p.100) for details. Fri-Sat 9pm-3am; other nights according to music schedule.* $$ ≡ 783 College St. W. (Shaw St.), 416-535-7888, revivalbar.com

Rivoli* • Queen Street • International
Best Restaurant-Lounges The Rivoli has long defined the groovy ambience of Queen Street West. For many years, it was known mostly for its live music and DJs, but more recently it has drawn crowds for a wider range of events—from comedy nights to literary readings to burlesque—with a more eclectic and upscale crowd in attendance. What's often overlooked, however, is the Rivoli's equally eclectic menu: It's international fusion, with pastas, risottos, and calamari all being top favorites, and includes everything from burgers to Asian dishes to Caribbean fare. The black-and-white neon bar adds to the funky vibe of this fine institution, where the suits come for a hip lunchtime respite or after-work escape, and a crowd rich in artists and musicians regularly fills the place for performances and events—and cocktails. *Sun-Thu 11:30am-midnight, Fri-Sat 11:30am-1am.* $$ ≡ 332 Queen St. W. (Peter St.), 416-596-1908, rivoli.ca

Shanghai Cowgirl* • Queen Street • International
Mix a classic diner with Queen Street hip and a quirky imagination, and you'll have Shanghai Cowgirl. The tongue-in-cheek, over-the-top-diner décor lends the place a fun and casual ambience. Since it's open from 10:30am and until 4am on weekends, fashionable hipsters flock here at all hours, especially to carry on the party in the wee hours. The varied menu of pan-global offerings includes Southern fried chicken, Asian noodle dishes, and Belgian-style mussels, among many other eclectic dishes. If you're in need of sustenance and people-watching after the clubs, the perennially hip Shanghai won't disappoint. *Sun-Thu 10:30am-midnight, Fri-Sat 10:30am-4am.* $ ≡ 538 Queen St. W. (Bathurst St.), 416-203-6623, shanghaicowgirl.com

Swan • West Queen West • Diner
Best Always-Trendy Tables The Norman Rockwell–esque décor features Formica tables, a long polished lunch counter, an old Coca-Cola cooler, and wooden booths; everything else, including a crowd made up of media types, local artists, and the generally stylish, is on the hipster leading edge. With dishes like capon in a vanilla-oatmeal crust, bacon-wrapped grilled oysters, and succulent marinated short ribs, this fashionable spot attracts a loyal following. The very popular brunch menu features the usual finds as well as a handful of more inventive dishes like Arctic char salad. *Mon-Fri noon-3:30pm and 5-10:30pm, Sat 10am-3:30pm and 5-11pm, Sun 10:30am-3:30pm and 5-10:30pm.* $$ ≡ 892 Queen St. W. (Crawford St.), 416-532-0452

Tequila Bookworm Café and Books • Queen Street • Cafe
Comfortable sofas, free wireless on weekdays, funky artwork on the walls, exposed brick, and a selection of used books and magazines—this cafe doubles as a bookstore—virtually demand lingering. Kick-start your day with an espresso and a fluffy Belgian waffle, or arrive later to dine on a selection of hearty soups, salads, and ample sandwiches. A mellow vibe extends from the patrons

to the staff (who aren't always quick), so remember to grab a magazine or book from the stacks and catch up on reading while you wait for your meal. *Sun-Thu 10am-11pm, Fri-Sat 10am-midnight.* $ ≡ 512 Queen St. W. (Denison Ave.), 416-504-7335, tequilabookworm.blogspot.com

Zelda's • Gay Village • Diner

An eccentric tongue-in-cheek décor plays up the Gay Village connection with elements of Southern bordello, Indian ashram, and trailer park, although the crowd here represents a broad cross-section of urban cool of all ages, genders, and persuasions. Theme days may feature the hunky staff dressed in drag or military outfits, and don't be surprised if your fellow diners are too—the crowd is half the fun. An open kitchen serves up tasty California-style fare with mixed influences (and a sense of humor) like the I Love Juicy Burger and Wok and Roll Spring Rolls. The dining room dominates until evening, when all attention turns to the lounge. But in good weather, the bright summer patio sees lines down the block. Even standing in line, you'll be entertained by the colorful crowd, and it's well worth the wait to take a seat and nurse a mojito late into the afternoon. *Mon-Thu 11am-11:30pm, Fri-Sat 11am-12:30am, Sun 10am-11:30pm.* $ B ≡ 542 Church St. (Wellesley St.), 416-922-2526, zeldas.ca

HIP

Hip Toronto:
The Nightlife

Andy Pool Hall • Little Italy • Lounge
Combining a retro-'60s lounge space with a traditional neighborhood pool hall, the Andy offers Toronto's hipsters a unique space to lounge, dance, and shoot stick. The colorfully decorated room features seating straight from JFK Airport's Concorde departure lounge and five red-felt–covered pool tables, ensuring you'll never wait long for your turn at the table. In-house DJs, as well as guests brought in by cooler-than-thou promoters, provide a funky backdrop to the nightly festivities. Note that select events have cover charges; call ahead or check the website for details. *Mon 6pm-2am, Tue-Fri 7pm-2am, Sat 6pm-2am.* ⓒ≣ 489 College St. W. (Bathurst St.), 416-923-5300, andypoolhall.com

Bar One* • West Queen West • Restaurant/Bar
A stylish Italian eatery with a martini-lounge vibe and late-night menu. *See Hip Restaurants (p.89) for description. Mon-Fri 11am-2am, Sat-Sun 9am-2am.* ≣ 924 Queen St. W. (Shaw St.), 416-535-1655, bar-one.com

The Beaconsfield* • West Queen West • Bar
This stylish and funky resto-lounge-bar across from the hipster-central Drake Hotel has an excellent menu and late-night DJs. *See Hip Restaurants (p.89) for details. Mon-Sat 5pm-2am, Sun 11am-3pm.* ≣ 1154 Queen St. W. (Beaconsfield Ave.), 416-516-2550, thebeaconsfield.com

Boiler House • Distillery District • Jazz Club
Boiler House is synonymous with live jazz, and that's what keeps the room jammed with savvy, artistic music lovers from all over Toronto and beyond. A long bar affords a great view of the stage, where musicians including resident music director and Grammy-nominated trumpeter and vocalist Kevin Clark,perform the standards along with more-modern selections. There's plenty of standing room for guests to enjoy a cocktail or sample a glass from the lengthy wine list. The large space is divided into a separate dining area, and cozy two-person booths make the warehouse-type space feel more intimate. For the hungry, there's a menu of updated Creole cuisine. The music starts at 7pm Wednesday through Saturday, with a jazz brunch on weekends. *Tue-Sat 5pm-late, Sun 11am-3pm.* ⓒ≣ 55 Mill St. (Parliament St.), 416-203-2121, boilerhouse.ca

Bovine Sex Club • Queen Street • Bar
Not nearly as bizarre as the name suggests, the Bovine is home to a cadre of female DJs who spin alternative music from retro to glam to punk in a bar with a Dadaist interior design conceived by local artists. In a darkened room with spots of bright colored lights, you'll be hangin' with a crowd that gives new meaning to hip. The throbbing sound system makes it impossible to chat—this is all about the music. Live cutting-edge acts take the stage some nights. There's always a lively, sexy crowd here ready to party until closing. *Daily 9pm-2am.* ⓒ≣ 542 Queen St. W. (Ryerson Ave.), 416-504-4239, bovinesexclub.com

Byzantium* • Gay Village • Lounge
Best Gay Scenes A buzzing restaurant and lounge with a predominantly gay crowd and notable martini list. *See Hip Restaurants, (p.90) for details. Daily 5:30pm-2am.* ≡ 499 Church St. (Wellesley St.), 416-922-3859

The Cameron Public House • Queen Street • Live Music
The Cameron is one of Toronto's most authentically bohemian hangouts, and even the murals adorning the pub's street front have credibility among the art-school set. Indoors, monthly rotating art exhibitions grace the walls, while live musical acts perform—sometimes simultaneously—in the two gritty but welcoming rooms. Some of Toronto's most famous bands, including the Barenaked Ladies, played here before making it big, and the bar has a reputation for booking up-and-coming talent. If local theater is more your style, check the website; the Cameron also stages plays. *Daily 4pm-2am.* ℂ≡ 408 Queen St. West (Vanauley St.), 416-703-0811, thecameron.com

The Communist's Daughter • West Queen West • Bar
This neighborhood favorite is known for a chilled-out, small-town vibe that runs from the mellow staff to the young, attitude-free crowd. An old lunch counter, a jukebox, vinyl chairs, Formica tables, and a bar-top pickled egg jar are a nod to yesteryear, but the divey scene is more up to date in an almost ironic way. The small menu is available past midnight on weekends. Live gypsy jazz provides entertainment on Saturdays, while country-folk music makes the scene on Sundays. *Mon-Fri 5pm-2am, Sat-Sun 3pm-2am.* ≡ 1149 Dundas St. W. (Ossington Ave.), 647-435-0103

The Comrade Bar • Leslieville • Bar
Envelope yourself in a unique ambience that combines 1930s French colonial décor and an Asian sensibility. Owners Nikki Andriet and Dean Fletcher were the proprietors of furniture and accessory store Leigh & James, and their distinctive aesthetic is clearly evident in the Comrade. Low curved dark-wood chairs and couches, red silk lanterns, a hammered tin ceiling, exposed brick walls, vintage accessories, and Saigon posters create a seductive atmosphere that appeals to funky 30-somethings in search of a new hot spot to flirt. Actor-bartender-owner Ryan McVittie encourages choosing old school–style cocktails like a Pink Squirrel or Café Comrade Martini, but late-night drinkers can also choose from locally brewed and selected import beers or local wines. Simultaneously cozy and sexy, this is both a great place to share stories with a small group of old friends and a good spot to entice a new lover. *Tue-Sun 5pm-closing.* ⌐ 758 Queen St. E. (Broadview), 416-778-9449

Czehoski* • Queen Street • Lounge
A stylish main-floor lounge and more casual upstairs nouvelle pub and patio complement what is one of Toronto's hottest dining rooms. *See Hip Restaurants (p.91) for details. Daily 11:30am-late.* ≡ 678 Queen St. W. (Euclid Ave.), 416-366-6787, czehoski.com

The Dakota • West Queen West • Bar/Live Music
Whether the crowd of urban hipsters flocks to this country and western–themed bar out of a love for the music or simply to make an ironic statement is moot; the place rocks. Young professionals, said hipsters, and a

few regulars who might have been plucked from small-town Ontario mingle seamlessly. What appears to be a genuine old saloon is in fact an old punk club, updated with salvaged barn elements. Mint juleps are the drink of choice, and while country music dominates, bluegrass and roots acts also make appearances, particularly at the Sunday-only One Table Bluegrass Brunch, a communal Tex-Mex inspired feast and live bluegrass session. *Mon-Sat 5pm-2am, Sun 11am-2am.* ≡ 249 Ossington Ave. (Dundas St. W.), 416-850-4579, thedakotatavern.com

Drake Lounge* • West Queen West • Lounge

The Drake is a mecca for the city's hip and creative crowd, and the cats who gather here in droves are stylishly funky—like the place itself—with a solid art-school contingent that tends toward the over-30 demographic. The mood is set by a green-and-bronze-hued room, with warm brown leather furnishings and a wood bar, and artistic wall treatments that look like a Rorschach test. A wide screen plays flicks silently above the fireplace, around which arm-chairs and a couch invite you to sit and stay a while. Order a martini and take in the groovy setting—you might even be entertained by DJs or performance art. Then head down to the throbbing dance club in the basement. Or check out some of the original art and photography the Drake exhibits each month. The young, good-looking staff are refreshingly helpful and free of attitude. Note that the lines start by 8pm on Friday and Saturday evenings, so come early for dinner in the adjoining dining room and get a free pass into the lounge ahead of the line. Weekends can be noisy in the lounge, making the year-round rooftop patio a better bet for more intimate evenings. You won't want to miss this see-and-be-seen spot for the creative classes. *Daily 6pm-2:30am.* ©≡ Drake Hotel, 1150 Queen St. W. (Beaconsfield St.), 416-531-5042, thedrakehotel.ca

El Convento Rico • Little Italy • Dance Club

El Convento Rico is known for throbbing merengue and a wild crowd of seri-ous partiers both gay and straight. The retro-glitzy décor is an ode to '70s excesses with colored lighting and lava lamps set against a wood bar, and a lounge area done in minimalist style. Expect sheer dance-club excitement and an over-the-top floor show from both the DJs and the crowd in what is called "Toronto's most mixed bar." The crowd may be diverse, but there's nothing but straight-up Latin music in all its many forms. On Saturdays, the Latino drag-queen show starts at 1am. *Thu-Sun 9pm-3am.* ©≡ 750 College St. W. (Shaw St.), 416-588-7800, elconventorico.com

Esplanade Bier Markt* • St. Lawrence • Pub

An extensive list of domestic and imported beers and microbrews appeals to hipper beer lovers of all ages. *See Hip Restaurants (p.91) for details. Mon-Wed 11am-11pm, Thu-Fri 11am-midnight, Sat-Sun noon-midnight.* ≡ 58 The Esplanade (Church St.), 416-862-7575, thebiermarkt.com

The Gladstone Hotel • West Queen West • Bar-Lounge

The Gladstone offers the latest in cool, housed in lovingly restored historic digs. There are three venues for your pleasure, including the spacious Ballroom, where events including fashion shows, burlesque and vaudeville, live music, and DJs find a home in front of a funky crowd. The Melody Bar is famous for being the city's hottest karaoke spot Thursday through Saturday nights in an attractive room that features its original 1930s Art Deco wood bar and ten-foot ceilings. The smaller and more modern Art Bar hosts poetry readings and various improv events. Join the cool crowd for a raucous night of arty partying, outfitted with—after extensive renovations—arguably the most fabulous men's public bathrooms in town. Expect lines on weekends, especially for the Melody Bar. *Also note that while the Melody Bar has no cover charge, some events in the Ballroom do.* ≡ The Gladstone Hotel, 1214 Queen St. W. (Gladstone Ave.), 416-531-4635, gladstonehotel.com

Habitat Lounge • Queen Street • Lounge

Best Sexy Lounges Come to Habitat to mingle with a downtown crowd of creative professionals who work in television and film, fashion, and the arts, along with a smattering of better-dressed corporate types. The bar glows in amber tones against darkly painted wood floors and white leather couches. The restaurant is located at the back of the room, where the white booths and black leather chairs have more seating for the martini-fueled crowd. The menu is eclectic and casual, with pastas and delicious desserts among the favorites. A smaller bar smolders at the back of the room, where an illuminated panel in fiery orangey red highlights the patrons to dramatic effect. Although it's busiest (and loudest) on weekends, the weeknight crowds are reliably solid and the setting more conducive to conversation. *Tue-Sat 6pm-late.* ≡ 735 Queen St. W. (Manning St.), 416-860-1551, habitatlounge.com

Mitzi's Sister* • Parkdale • Bar

A funky neighborhood bar with gourmet-influenced pub grub and live music nightly. *See Hip Restaurants (p.93) for details. Mon-Fri 4pm-late, Sat-Sun 10am-late.* ≡ 1554 Queen St. W. (Dowling Ave.), 416-532-2570, mitzissister.com

Mod Club Theatre • Little Italy • Live Music/Dance Club

Best Live Music The Mod Club satisfies the city's fetish for Brit-pop cool. While the decorations are early '60s-era mod, the scene, with most evenings' agendas event-driven, is new and cutting-edge. The stage is draped in red curtains at one end of the big, long room. The bar is lit up in white along one side of the room, and there's a drink list to satisfy most tastes. Most of the space is given over to the music fans who come to dance or just listen, but there's also a dramatically lit smaller lounge area with tables off to the side. Owner Mark Holmes was once a Canadian pop star as lead singer for '80s hair band Platinum Blonde. He's now known as one of the friendliest club owners in town, and his respect for and in the music industry has made this one of the city's leading live-music venues, with an emphasis on alternative rock and new music. The young, eclectic, music-savvy crowd is hospitable and dresses retro-Brit for Mod Club nights. *Daily 9pm-3am; check concert listings for details.* ⊂≡ 722 College St. W. (Crawford St.), 416-588-4663, themodclub.com

Phoenix Concert Theatre • St. Lawrence • Live Music

Best Live Music Host to international acts like the Stones, Metallica, and U2, the Phoenix has been serving up live music, live-to-air DJs, and event programming to the cool masses for decades. With a main floor that includes a dance floor, five bars—including a 50-foot marble bar, a 20-by-30-foot stage, stylish crowds, fab music, and fine drinks—there's plenty to keep you partying all night long. There's also a gallery-level loft that overlooks the main room and a parlour that is quieter and more private, complete with decorative bar and billiards. Check the listings, and join the hepcat crowds for a memorable evening. *Opening hours change depending on who's playing. Check the website for current listings.* ⓒ≡ 410 Sherbourne St. (Carlton St.), 416-323-1251, libertygroup.com/phoenix/phoenix.html

Revival* • Little Italy • Bar/Live Music

Housed in what was a Baptist church in the '60s, Revival applies the retro-church theme to its baroquely plush décor. Well-heeled over-30 hipsters lap up the cocktails and the musician-friendly ambience, where Kid Rock has been known to show up to sing a tune or two, and Justin Timberlake dropped in to jam with the Black Eyed Peas. Scarlet crushed-velvet sofas welcome the creative crowds of film, fashion, and music-industry partygoers. The mood is post-modern upscale hip with more fun than pretense in the mix. Friday is blues night. *Fri-Sat 9pm-3am, other nights according to music schedule.* ⓒ≡ 783 College St. W. (Shaw St.), 416-535-7888, revivalbar.com

Rivoli* • Queen Street • Bar/Live Music

This restaurant has a vibrant bar scene, busy summer patio, and diverse line-up of live entertainment acts ranging from spoken word performances to readings and live music. *See Hip Restaurants (p.94) for details. Sun-Thu 11:30am-midnight, Fri-Sat 11:30am-1am.* ⓒ≡ 332-334 Queen St. W. (Peter St.), 416-596-1908, rivoli.ca

Shanghai Cowgirl* • Queen Street • Lounge

Late-night restaurant with a post-clubbing party atmosphere. *See Hip Restaurants, (p.94) for description. Sun-Thu 10:30am-midnight, Fri-Sat 10:30am-4am.* ≡ 538 Queen St. W. (Bathurst St.), 416-203-6623, shanghaicowgirl.com

Sneaky Dee's • Little Italy • Live Music

Best Late-Night Eats In a city with a scarce number of late-night hot spots, Sneaky Dee's has reigned supreme for over 20 years. Housed in a two-story brick building, it offers not only a simple Tex-Mex menu and affordable cold beer, but live punk and rock music upstairs Wednesday to Saturday as well. On Sundays, Wavelength is a pay-what-you-can assortment of live music and DJ stylings. Downstairs, you'll find a casual, youthful décor of rock posters, Day of the Dead paraphernalia, and other post-college accoutrements. Local breweries reign supreme, but Mexico's Corona is found in abundance, and Tuesdays it's always hard to find a table with the well-known half-price fajitas special. Offered until 4pm, weekend brunch is a perfect antidote to a previous night's revelry with traditional breakfast items, Tex-Mex selections, and classic huevos rancheros. *Mon-Tue 11am-3am, Wed-Thu 11am-4am, Fri 11am-4:30am, Sat 9am-4:30am, Sun 9am-3am.* ≡ 431 College St. W. (Bathurst St.), 416-603-3090, sneaky-dees.com

Stones Place • Parkdale • Bar/Live Music

Smitten with the city's low-key version of hip, the Rolling Stones have opened their last few world tours by rehearsing for a few months in "tdot" (the hipster's term for Toronto), and Stones Place is vintage Toronto. Mick and the boys have even been known to show up at this Stones-themed haunt. It's all done up as a crazy Old West tavern, and covered in Stones memorabilia. Circular booths at the back feature overstuffed burgundy upholstery and a great view of the stage. Stones Place is known for the cool live bands it draws here, late-night jamming, Primpin'—a gay-oriented rap night—and a crowd as hip as its Queen Street address. The drink list ranges from basic brews to martinis. It's a favorite with local musicians, and there's sure to be a few in the crowd. *Thu-Sat 8pm-2am.* C≡ 1225 Queen St. W. (Duffren St.), 416-536-4242, stonesplace.ca

Sutra Tiki Bar • Little Italy • Bar

Up front, the lounge is billed as a classy champagne and oyster bar, the décor a mix of minimalist furnishings and old-grained woods. But in the back, toward the patio, the theme is Polynesian, complete with sand-covered floors, straw umbrellas, and awnings held in place with bamboo stalks. The tiki, featuring plenty of fruit and little umbrellas, is the latest drink of choice, now that cosmopolitans are so yesterday. Its variations come with names like Wicky Wacky Woo (coconut rum, melon liquor, and pineapple juice), and pack a heady punch. Check the listings for DJs, and share an exotic evening in Little Italy with hip College Street types of mixed ages, mostly clustered around the crowded see-and-be-seen bar. *Daily 8pm-2am.* C≡ 612 College St. W. (Clinton St.), 416-537-8755

Sweaty Betty's • West Queen West • Bar

With red walls, earth-colored tile floors, and basement rec-room furniture, this neighborhood favorite bar feels comfortable and familiar. The room contains Toronto's most venerated jukebox, and regulars are invited to mix their own CD to add to the eclectic mix that includes local bands, old-time favorites, and even '80s glam rock. Events like the monthly artist speaker series and weekly DJ heavy-metal night are part of the diverse but reliably fun and buzzing scene. Asian action films and discounted sake make for a great Sunday afternoon diversion, and a small selection of soups and sandwiches makes for some delicious cheap eats. *Daily 5pm-2am.* ≡ 13 Ossington Ave. (Queen St. W.), 416-535-6861, sweatybettysbar.com

This Is London • Entertainment District • Lounge/Dance Club

Best Celebrity Hangouts A favorite of over-30 club kids and A-listers, this is the most exclusive club in town. From the foyer with a flickering fireplace, it's downstairs for dancing or upstairs to the lounge. The décor is Brit-pop Mod, and the upscale crowd dresses for it in retro style. Theme nights set the tone for the music, so check listings to know what to expect. It's tongue-in-cheek, yet sophisticated, and Room 364—the VIP lounge—is a favorite with celebrities. Bottle service is available, and the club has the city's most stylish ladies' rooms, with two stylists on hand to recoiff and revamp your look midway through the evening. This is where the edgiest of the monied classes come to party until 3am. *Fri-Sat 10pm-3am.* C≡ 364 Richmond St. W. (Peter St.), 416-351-1100, thisislondonclub.com

HIP

Velvet Underground • Queen Street • Lounge

The venerable Velvet Underground has long seduced with alternative-rock music and a one-of-a-kind design that features found-object sculptures by local artists, pool tables, and a mix of baroque and ultra-modern décor. The crowd too, is "alternative," ranging from dyed-in-the-wool hipsters to those who exchange their weekday suits and yuppie personas for edgier after-hours duds. And when it comes to alt-fashionistas, the competition can be fierce—but great fun to watch. This lush martini lounge and dance bar with an alternative groove often hosts events during the week as well as on weekends, so check listings and come early. *Thu-Sun 10pm-3am.* Ⓒ≡ 510 Queen St. W. (Portland St.), 416-504-6688, libertygroup.com

Hip Toronto:
The Attractions

Camera Bar and Media Gallery • West Queen West • Art Cinema/Gallery
Owned by acclaimed independent filmmaker Atom Egoyan (*The Sweet Hereafter, Exotica*), the Camera Bar combines hip lounge and cafe society with an art film venue to good effect. Screenings take place in a state-of-the-art digital screening room. Then artsy crowds congregate to discuss and debate the films around a communal table or comfortable seating in the lounge area. A full bar offers a selection of wines, beers, and cocktails, and a light menu of casual cafe classics is available. Unique in Toronto, the Camera Bar was much talked about when it opened. The initial hype has passed, but the simple contemporary design, innovative screenings, and a community of hip film buffs have kept the atmosphere vibrant and fun. Check the listings for rare films and monthly screenings devoted to shorts. *Screenings Tue-Sun 7pm and 9pm; Sat shorts 5pm; check listings for details.* $ 1028 Queen St. W. (Ossington Ave.), 416-530-0011, camerabar.ca

Cinematheque Ontario • Chinatown • Art Cinema
Housed in the basement of the Art Gallery of Ontario, but operating independent of the gallery exhibits, the Cinematheque offers an ambitious program of screenings of independent and avant-garde art, vintage, and foreign films. Programs include traveling screenings, often with the artist or director in attendance. The comfortable and intimate screening room is modern in design, with two screenings nightly throughout the week and an added matinee on Saturdays that often focuses on visual art. The programs, which sometimes include lively pre- and post-screening discussions and lectures, are well attended by Toronto's creative classes. *Check listings for specific event details.* $ Art Gallery of Ontario, 317 Dundas St. W. (McCaul St.); box office: 55 Bloor St. W. (Bay St.), 416-968-3456, cinemathequeontario.ca

Design Exchange • Financial District • Museum
Best Contemporary Art and Design Spaces Billed as Canada's premier center for design and innovation, the Design Exchange is a cutting-edge museum and educational institution housed in the former home of the Toronto Stock Exchange. In addition to exhibits devoted to fashion, industrial, and household design, the museum has shows that focus on specific materials and other components, such as plastic or wheels. Curators take pains to live up to the principles they espouse, creating displays that are a treat to take in. The sleek retro '50s chairs and cloverleaf nesting tables in the permanent collection are a must-see all on their own. The DX's mandate is to promote design concepts, including accessible design for disabled persons, as well as to commemorate Canadian industrial design. In addition to worthwhile exhibits, the DX offers workshops, educational programs, competitions for design students at a national level, and a lecture series featuring the world's leading designers. *Mon-Fri 9am-5pm, Sat-Sun noon-5pm.* $ 234 Bay St. (Wellington St.), 416-363-6121, dx.org

401 Richmond • Entertainment District • Art Space

Best Contemporary Art and Design Spaces This old industrial building was revamped in 1994 by the owner-architects, who saw the building's possibilities and turned it into the hip downtown home of the arts that it is today. Follow the rabbit warren of hallways through four floors of art galleries and studios, funky fashion retailers, and arts organizations. It's home to places like Gallery 44, dedicated to modern photographic art; film festival offices; and dub poets' associations. This is an excellent opportunity to get a look at the local arts scene at street level, and perhaps even network with other creative professionals. The building includes a cafe on the ground floor and a charming rooftop garden patio with a view of the busy downtown. *Hours vary according to tenants; special events occur evenings; galleries are typically Tue-Sat noon-5pm.* 401 Richmond St. W. (Spadina Ave.), 416-595-5900, 401richmond.net

Harbourfront Centre • Harbourfront • Art Space/Park

There's always something going on at the Harbourfront Centre, whether it's shows at the York Quay galleries, a literary reading, a dance, or a theatrical performance. Offerings often focus on a central theme and typically have an international flavor; the well-attended Danish Festival, for instance, featured visual arts, dance, and films, all from Denmark. Exhibits and performances take place both indoors and outdoors, weather permitting. A craft studio and shop features cool ceramics, textile art, and other unique items. In the winter, rent skates and join the fun at the Natrel outdoor skating rink. *Tue-Thu, Sun noon-5pm, Fri-Sat noon-8pm; check listings for details on other venues and events.* $ 235 Queen's Quay W. (York St.), 416-973-4000, harbourfrontcentre.com

High Park • Parkdale • Park

Best Ways to Enjoy a Sunny Day At the southwestern edge of metropolitan Toronto, 400 acres of wooded trails and greenery await. A favorite of locals, the park includes a lake along which you can stroll and feed the swans. During the summer months, a fabulous outdoor amphitheater hosts Shakespearean drama and comedy, produced by CanStage. From late June until early July, you can catch Scream in the Park, a hip literary reading series that draws huge crowds. If you need a little break from all the fast-paced urbanity around you, High Park is a lovely retreat on a beautiful day. 1873 Bloor St. W. (High Park Ave.), city.toronto.on.ca/parks/parks_gardens/highpark.htm

Joe Rockhead's • West Queen West • Sports

Both experienced and novice rock climbers can find the right course to challenge them here, among the 21,000 square feet of indoor climbing terrains. High standards of training for staff ensure an experience that's both safe and fun. Flexible passes can include equipment rental. Reservations are recommended for lessons, although walk-ins are sometimes accommodated. Take on the challenge of a climb here, and savor a welcome respite from more-intellectual pursuits. *Mon-Fri noon-11pm, Sat-Sun 10am-7pm.* $$$ 29 Fraser Ave. (Liberty St.), 416-538-7670, joerockheads.com

Mercer Union Centre for Contemporary Visual Art • West Queen West • Art Space

Best West Queen West Art Spaces While many of West Queen West's art spaces seem to have sprung up overnight, the Mercer, an artist-run space dedicated to providing production and exhibition space to a host of Canadian and international contemporary artists, has been attracting its share of hip gallery-goers since 1979. Rotating exhibitions form the core of the event calendar, while occasional lectures and evening parties, some with DJs, also draw the art-obsessed West Queen West crowds. *Tue-Sat 11am-6pm.* 37 Lisgar St. (Queen St. W.), 416-536-1519, mercerunion.org

Moksha Yoga Downtown • West Queen West • Sports
If you can't get through the day without your yoga workout, or even if you just feel like trying something new, Moksha Yoga Down Town welcomes expert devotees and rank beginners alike. Moksha Yoga is a studio for "hot yoga," practiced at a room temperature of 99 degrees Fahrenheit (37 degrees Celsius) to allow for deep stretching and to promote detoxification. Your body gets a comprehensive workout in a studio designed to meet high environmental standards. A rotating schedule of classes is on offer seven days a week, drop-ins are always welcome, and mats can be rented for a nominal charge. Guests can also book basic spa treatments that include facials, hair removal, and a variety of massages. *Class schedule varies; call for details.* $$ 860 Richmond St. W., 3rd Fl. (Strachan St.), 416-361-3033, mokshayogadowntown.com

Museum of Contemporary Canadian Art (MOCCA) • West Queen West • Museum
Best West Queen West Art Spaces MOCCA, one of the city's newest museums, and certainly one of the hottest if you judge by the chic crowds that flock to its exhibitions, shows the very best of Canadian contemporary visual art. The permanent collection reads like a who's-who of Canada's modern art landscape, while rotating exhibitions reliably break new ground. Well-attended events like art film screenings and lectures, and a number of one-off happenings meant to complement citywide events like the Toronto International Art Fair, add to the festive vibe. *Tue-Sun 11am-6pm.* 952 Queen St. W. (Shaw St.), 416-395-0067, mocca.toronto.on.ca

National Film Board Mediatheque • Entertainment District • Film Museum
The NFB's Mediatheque is a film-viewing center located in an intriguing contemporary space overlooking the corner of John and Richmond Streets. The NFB offers over 1,200 titles for viewing. Single or double viewing stations sport comfortable leatherette recliners. Once ensconced, you can select from animated shorts and features, documentaries, news programs, dramatic shorts and features, and experimental films, all at your fingertips thanks to cutting-edge touch-screen technology. You get to enjoy the films on a private flat-screen high-definition television, with speakers in the chair's headrest. It's easy to while away the morning browsing through the astounding catalog, and friendly staff are always available to answer questions. The Mediatheque hosts groups of various kinds, so a quick call to check the schedule is recommended. *Mon-Tue 1-7pm, Wed 10am-7pm, Thu-Sat 10am-10pm, Sun noon-5pm.* $ 150 John St. (Richmond St.), 416-973-3012, nfb.ca/mediatheque

Ontario College of Art & Design • Chinatown • Art Gallery
Known for producing a wide range of working artists—some of Canada's most exciting and innovative among them—the Ontario College of Art & Design is one of Canada's premier art schools. The recent recipient of a multimillion-dollar expansion and renovation, it is now the fourth-largest institution of its kind in North America. Informal visits are possible by calling ahead or checking with

the office, and the student gallery is open during business hours for viewing the work of the next generation of up-and-coming Canadian artists. Expect the kind of cutting-edge work only art school can produce—and colored hair and body piercings in abundance among the students. *Check with the office for an informal visit.* 100 McCaul St. (Dundas St. W.), 416-977-6000, ocad.on.ca

Power Plant Gallery • Harbourfront • Art Gallery

Best Contemporary Art and Design Spaces Housed in a former trucking garage, the Power Plant is a focal point for contemporary art in the city, and hosts a full slate of exhibitions, shows, lectures, and educational programs. Part of the Harbourfront Centre for the Arts, the Power Plant consists of three rooms of adjustable gallery space. Innovative lighting systems create dramatic backdrops and highlight the exhibitions. Expect up-and-coming as well as more established contemporary artists and what is arguably this city's most up-to-the-minute art crowd. Innovation and originality are the buzzwords. *Tue-Sun noon-6pm.* $ 231 Queen's Quay W. (York St.), 416-973-4949, thepowerplant.org

St. Lawrence Market • St. Lawrence • Market

Best Historic Buildings St. Lawrence Market has been feeding Torontonians for two centuries in the spot it still occupies. While the neighborhood's going condo these days, the St. Lawrence hasn't been gentrified. It's still housed in a huge building that looks like an auction house with concrete floors and bright stalls—all scrupulously clean. Two floors beckon with traditional farmer's market fare of meats, fish, cheeses, produce, along with international crafts and clothing, and more than a few surprises. Don't miss Caviar Direct, dealing only in caviar and delectable smoked salmon, or the ever-popular Mustachio, which serves up authentic Italian sandwiches to hungry shoppers. Other vendors offer organic produce, fresh-roasted coffee, gourmet tofu, and sushi. You'll find a mixed crowd, from students to socialites, gay and straight, and every ethnicity imaginable. Don't miss the Market Gallery where small exhibitions on the art, culture, and history of the city are staged, and be sure to visit the lesser-known North Market Building on Saturdays when it hosts a farmer's market and Sundays when an antique market holds court. *Tue-Thu 8am-6pm, Fri 8am-7pm, Sat 5am-5pm.* 92 Front St. E. (Jarvis St.), 416-392-7219, stlawrencemarket.com

Steam Whistle Brewing Company • Harbourfront • Tour

Best Guided Tours In the shadow of the CN Tower, this state-of-the-art boutique brewery was started by young up-and-comers who took over the old John Street Roundhouse building in 1999. A pilsner is their signature brew; you'll find it served at most of the hottest clubs in the Entertainment District. Tours along the catwalks through the impressive works, complete with tastings, run every hour in the afternoons. *Mon-Sat noon-6pm, Sun noon-5pm; tours Mon-Sat 1pm-5pm. Call ahead in case there's a private function.* $ The Roundhouse, 255 Bremner Blvd. (Blue Jays Way), 416-362-2337, steamwhistle.ca

Toronto Music Garden • Harbourfront • Garden

Can a garden inspired by classical music ever be hip? It can be if it translates a famous piece of music into an urban garden landscape and invites you in with a 70-minute audio tour explaining the works. Designer Julie Moir Messervy has reimagined Bach's First Suite for Unaccompanied Cello in garden features, with each dance movement within the suite corresponding to a different section in the garden. The audio tour, narrated by Yo-Yo Ma and the designer, adds to the experience, as does a seasonal concert schedule. The self-guided handheld audio players can be picked up daily 10am-8pm at the Marina Quay West office, southwest of the Garden, for a rental fee of $5. 475 Queen's Quay W. (Lower Portland St.), 416-973-4000, toronto.ca/parks/musicgarden_events.htm

Toronto School of Art Gallery • Chinatown • Art Gallery
The Toronto School of Art was formed in the 1970s as an anti-establishment art school, and left-of-center politics have been part of the artistic landscape here ever since. The political discussions remain, but the school has also developed into a well-respected private institution with a wide range of visual arts programs on offer. A small student gallery here houses the work of the current and future avant-gardists, in addition to faculty exhibits, and attracts a local, art-savvy crowd. *Informal visits to the school itself are possible, call ahead to check.* 410 Adelaide St. W., 3rd Fl. (Spadina Ave.), 416-504-7910, tsa-art.ca

Ukula • Little Italy • Shop
To call Ukula a clothing shop would be to sell it short. Far short. Sure the racks are chock-full of über-cool indie brands like Tiger of Sweden and Canadian label Common Cloth, but the owners of Ukula are dedicated to showcasing independent media in all its forms and you never know what might be happening when you drop by. Fashion shows, literary readings, and performances by up-and-coming bands are everyday events, and even during quieter—read daytime—hours, an iPod listening center, a small reading lounge, a selection of global-chic magazines, and a coffee bar complete with DJ create one of this city's most spontaneous scenes. *Mon-Fri 11am-7pm, Sat 11am-6pm, Sun noon-6pm; check the website for events outside store hours.* 492 College St. (Bathurst St.), 416-619-9282, ukula.com

West Queen West • Neighborhood
What is today a thriving, upscale, artsy mecca has undergone a great deal of transformation in recent years—from its former heyday as an artists' haunt in the '70s, through falling fortunes, to the resurgence of the independent art scene in the late '90s, and fueled of late by the stunning Drake Hotel renovation that's brought in a whole new era of cool. The result is a surge of historic renovations and an interesting mix of designer and vintage clothing stores; cool modern and retro furniture; specialty shops like Queen Street Video, where 6,000 hard-to-find titles have recruited the likes of Quentin Tarantino, among others; and the art galleries and artists that have always given the street its unique flavor. You'll easily find more black clothing and hair dye per capita here than in any other neighborhood, as well as some unique shopping. But the real fun comes in the countless opportunities to hook up with the local hipsters. Queen St. W. between Bathurst and Gladstone, westqueenwest.ca

Classic Toronto

What was once a prim and proper Victorian city has been transformed by waves of newcomers who have added cosmopolitan European flair, the exotic tastes of Asia, and the rhythms of the Caribbean, among many other influences. This Classic Toronto itinerary reveals the city's many facets—from colorful neighborhoods and a well-established music scene to elegant restaurants and world-class institutions.

Note: Venues in bold are described in detail in the listings that follow the itinerary. Venues followed by an asterisk (*) are those we recommend as both a restaurant and a destination bar.

Classic Toronto:
The Perfect Plan (3 Nights and Days)

Perfect Plan Highlights

Thursday

Morning	**CN Tower, Rogers Centre, Hockey Hall**
Lunch	**George, Starfish**
Afternoon	**Toronto Islands, Queen's Quay Term., Toronto Antiques**
Pre-dinner	**Lusso, Rosewater***
Dinner	**Harbour 60, Canoe, Bymark**
Nighttime	**Healey's, Rex Hotel, Crocodile Rock,**
Late-night	**Hair of the Dog, C'est What?**

Friday

Morning	**Studio Café, Golf, Spa**
Lunch	**Corner House, Joso's**
Afternoon	**Casa Loma, Spadina**
Pre-dinner	**Tea Room, Caren's Wine**
Dinner	**Truffles, Boba North 44°**
Nighttime	**Hemingway's, Roof Lounge**
Late-night	**Avenue, 7 West Cafe**

Saturday

Morning	**Café Supreme, Beaches, ROM**
Lunch	**Bright Pearl Seafood, One Up Resto/Lounge***
Afternoon	**Kensington Market, Chinatown**
Pre-dinner	**Hemispheres, Library**
Dinner	**Splendido, Courtyard**
Nighttime	**The Docks, Live**
Late-night	**Myth, Lolita's Lust***

Hotel: **Fairmont Royal York**

Thursday

9am: Get a jump-start on the day at the **Bloor Street Diner & Bistro Express** on King and University, and watch the sharply suited Financial District types hurry by as you linger over your latte.

10am: Begin your exploration of classic Toronto with a look—a really spectacular look—at the city from above ground. A marvel of modern engineering, the world's tallest freestanding structure, and the lynchpin of the Toronto skyline, the famed **CN Tower** is a fitting way to begin your visit of the town. When you come back down to earth, head next door to tour **Rogers Centre**, the world's first completely retractable domed stadium and home to professional baseball's Blue Jays as well as the Canadian Football League's Argonauts. Walk through BCE Place, housing the soaring Allan Lambert Galleria. This elaborate light-filled walkway connecting Bay and Yonge Streets regularly features art exhibitions and offers access to the beloved **Hockey Hall of Fame**.

1pm Lunch: **George**, with its neutral-toned décor and wrought-iron accents, oozes sophistication and glamour, and is full of powerful clientele. If you're hankering for seafood, it's a few blocks down King Street East to **Starfish Oyster Bed & Grill**, a bustling New York–style spot located in a lovely park setting.

2pm: After lunch, return to the lakeside for a walk along the Harbourfront. Boat tours can whisk you off on the sparkling waters of Lake Ontario. Take one of the ferries to the **Toronto Islands** and explore the "other" Toronto of beaches and gardens and the counterculture vibe of the Islanders. If weather doesn't make a boat trip appealing, Queen's Quay Terminal offers upscale souvenir-shopping opportunities in bright and airy surroundings, while **Toronto Antiques on King** can be counted on to provide some retail therapy.

6pm: Make your way to the busy lakeside patio at **Lusso**, or duck into the romantic environs of **Rosewater Supper Club***.

8pm Dinner: For a swank steakhouse experience, there's none better than **Harbour 60**, located in the posh former home of the Harbour Commission. If you didn't get enough of the view from the CN Tower, or just want to enjoy the sparkling nighttime version, **Canoe Restaurant & Bar** awaits with superb Canadian cuisine at the top of the TD Tower. In that same office tower **Bymark** lies half-hidden in the concourse

level, a sexy slice of the Financial District distinguished by its luxurious décor and soaring views. The dining room is elegant, but the lounge provides superior people-watching opportunities—come early for a drink to catch the movers and shakers playing mating games at the bar.

10pm: Check out the live music at the eponymous **Jeff Healey's Roadhouse**, where the owner, blind blues guitarist Jeff Healey, is a local legend. If jazz is more your style, the best in Canadian and international acts play every night at the venerable **Rex Hotel Jazz & Blues Bar**. Or join the throngs of partying downtowners at **Crocodile Rock**, where classic rock is the soundtrack of choice, and you may just bump into the celebs and pro-sports figures who frequent the joint.

Midnight: Upscale pubbing and a popular patio are the order of the day at Gay Village mainstay **Hair of the Dog**. If hunger pinches in the late-night hours, the kitchen at lively pub **C'est What?** is open until 2am.

 Friday

9am: Head uptown for a stylish breakfast in artistic surroundings at the **Studio Café** in the Four Seasons.

10am: Are the greens calling? If so, it's a short drive to Oakville and the home of Tiger Woods' "shot of 2000," **Glen Abbey Golf Club**, for a round of 18 holes. Or perhaps the delayed stresses of travel leave you in need of celebrity-level pampering at the renowned **Stillwater Spa**, located nearby in the Park Hyatt.

1pm Lunch: **Corner House** has a charming patio that's open in warm weather—and highly recommendable, elegant French dishes. Or for succulent seafood that impresses even Hollywood types, consider **Joso's**, with its patio that overlooks the designer boutiques of Yorkville. Also in Yorkville, **Pangaea** welcomes a sophisticated clientele with delicious Mediterranean fare.

2pm: Explore Toronto's castle, **Casa Loma**, where imposing 19th-century grandeur rises majestically above the modern city. Or head next door to **Spadina Museum** where you can stroll the manicured grounds and check out an Edwardian townhouse whose original decorations reflect the art scene in Toronto throughout the 20th century.

3:30pm: Take a load off your feet and have high tea (last seating at 3:30) at the **Tea Room at the Windsor Arms Hotel**. It's a timeless, sophisticated affair that's been attracting Toronto's well-heeled types for decades. Alternatively, make a stop at **Caren's Wine and Cheese Bar** for a sampling of fruits of the vine.

7:30pm Dinner: Ret an evening of lu. The ultra-posh fails to seduce its its high-end contir. ...uisine and service that's second to none. Or you can choose to go fresh and colorful at the ever-popular **Boba**, where fusion gets a healthy spin in a gorgeous dining room. A short cab ride further north, to fashionable Yonge and Eglinton (called "Young and Eligible" by locals), takes you to the famous **North 44°**, a fine-dining establishment well known for its Mediterranean-inspired masterpieces.

10pm: Stay uptown to check out the nightlife scene above Bloor. **Hemingway's** has an often-packed heated rooftop patio, where the mood is friendly and the celebs have been known to come out to play. For a real piece of Toronto history, head to the **Roof Lounge** at the Park Hyatt, an upscale watering hole with a terrific view of the city.

Midnight: Relax in sophistication at the Four Seasons' **Avenue.**

2am: When you need sustenance, **7 West Cafe**, just down the street, has a kitchen that's open 24/7.

Saturday

9am: **Café Supreme** offers a view of the busy intersection at University and Wellington in the Financial District. Or, if the day is sunny and superb, take a cab to Queen Street East and the Beaches neighborhood. **The Sunset Grill** is a long-standing Beaches institution that will welcome you with a bountiful traditional breakfast.

10am: If the weather works to your advantage, go for a scenic walk along the boardwalk by the Beaches along Lake Ontario or amble Queen Street East for its myriad of shops and boutiques. Alternatively, visit the grand and imposing **Royal Ontario Museum (ROM)**, but dismiss any notions you might have about stuffiness—in Toronto, museums aim to please, fascinate, and entertain as well as educate, so catch the latest blockbuster show or browse the vast permanent collection.

1pm Lunch: **Bright Pearl Seafood** serves up authentic dim sum, or for a glamorous experience in Chinatown and some delicious continental cuisine, **One Up Resto/Lounge*** beckons.

2pm: Visit **Kensington Market**, a timelessly bohemian feast for the eyes with an eclectic array of shops, multi-ethnic stalls, and a roster of colorful locals. Or hit the pavement in nearby **Chinatown**. Though Toronto boasts no fewer than five Chinatowns, the one centered on the intersection of Spadina and Dundas is the largest and busiest.

5pm: Join the late-afternoon crowd of professionals for a drink at **Hemispheres Lounge and Bistro** at the Met. Or head to the cozy wood-paneled comfort of the **Library Bar**.

7:30pm Dinner: This evening's dinner options are especially enticing. In midtown, **Splendido** impresses with its sublime fusion menu and sunny décor. Steeped in old-world glamour, the **Courtyard Cafe** at the Windsor Arms, with its airy room, potted palms, and classic continental menu, will sweep you into a Hollywood frame of mind. Downtown, above a nightclub, is a rarefied sanctuary with a roaring fireplace, rich draperies, and delicious French fare that is called the **Fifth Grill**.

10pm: Hit **The Docks**, Toronto's massive, waterside come-one-come-all nightlife spot to drink, dance and lounge, or remain downtown to join an upscale crowd lounging and listening to sophisticated live jazz at **Live @ Courthouse**.

Midnight: Grab a cab to Greektown and make your way directly to the bar at **Myth***, or **Lolita's Lust & the Chinchilla Lounge*** for a libation.

2am: When the night wears on and hunger pangs hit, **Bistro 333** serves up Italian fare until 4am.

The Morning After
Brunch at the **Gallery Grill**, and ask for a table overlooking the Oxford and Cambridge–styled Great Hall.

Classic Toronto:
The Key Neighborhoods

Bloor/Yorkville Though this area is Toronto's most upscale and trendy address, not every eatery or shop looks to the future. Many of the most vibrant restaurants and fabulous boutiques boast charming décor and timeless collections of clothing, gifts, and art that cater to those with deep pockets and classically minded tastes. Remember to keep an eye out for visiting Hollywood royalty; the Four Seasons Hotel is a hot spot during the International Film Festival.

Downtown/Yonge Top sightseeing attractions, destination restaurants, endless shopping possibilities, and one of this city's most thriving—if brash—street scenes can be found along Yonge Street.

Financial District From power lunches to after-work drinks and bustling dining spots with billion-dollar views, the Financial District's many drinking and eating hot spots cater to Toronto's tradition-minded business and social elite.

Little Italy College Street west of Bathurst Street offers something for everyone, and visitors looking for Little Italy's classic appeal won't have to look far. Gelato shops, cappuccino bars, excellent restaurants, and unique boutiques amount to what is one of the city's liveliest stretches of pavement.

CLASSIC

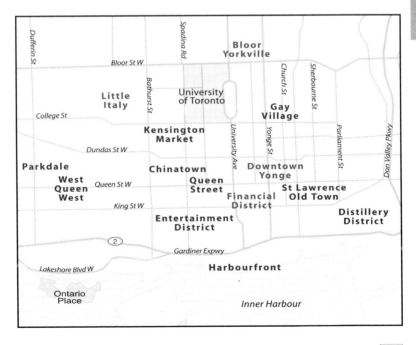

Classic Toronto:
The Shopping Blocks

The Eaton Centre

Drawing over one million eager shoppers weekly, this massive urban mall offers something for everyone and ranks as the most visited attraction in Toronto. 2 Queen St. W. (Yonge St.)

The Bay Leading, multi-level department store carrying a vast range of items including luxury fashions and beauty products. 416-861-9111

Coast Mountain Sports High-performance gear and clothing for outdoor enthusiasts of all stripes. 416-598-3785

Indigo Books and Music Large and highly popular bookstore carrying usual finds as well as gift books and items of local interest appealing to locals and visitors alike. 416-591-3622

Queen Street

While the edgier elements of Queen Street's shopping scene have moved west, the stretch of pavement between University and Spadina still draws a bustling crowd with stylish boutiques, big-name stores, and a youthful vibe.

Fluevog Shoes Canadian-designed footwear for rock stars and the generally fabulous. 242 Queen St. W. (John St.), 416-581-1420

Lush Cosmetics Handmade cosmetics and bath products. 312 Queen St. W. (Soho St.), 416-599-5874

Silver Snail A Toronto institution, this comic store has a range of collectibles and graphic novels. 367 Queen St. W. (Peter St.), 416-593-0889

Yorkville/Bloor Street West

For those with refined, classic tastes, Yorkville and Bloor Street's tony boutiques offer quality, service, and a wealth of must-have finds.

The Cashmere Shop Fine men's and women's cashmere sweaters and accessories in a rainbow of elegant colors. 24 Bellair St. (Cumberland St.), 416-925-0831

Heffel Gallery The exhibition space of Canada's leading fine-art auction house contains an impressive, rotating cast of masterpieces—all for sale, of course. 13 Hazelton Ave. (Scollard St.), 416-961-6505

Roots The flagship superstore of the famous Canadian athletic clothing and leather goods brand. 100 Bloor Street W. (Bellair St.), 416-323-3289

Stollery's Old-world gentlemen's store stocking fine classic British brands. 1 Bloor Street W. (Yonge St.), 416-922-6173

Classic Toronto:
The Hotels

Fairmont Royal York • Downtown/Yonge • Grand (1,376 Rms)
You'll bask in grand style from the moment the liveried doorman greets you. From there, walk up the marble staircase to a lobby that is all Waspy elegance, from the ornately tiled floors and the painted inlaid ceiling, to the gilt fixtures, the crest and Rose of York (one presumes) on the carpeting, and the pseudo-brocade upholstery. The staff is experienced in welcoming celebrities, heads of state, and visiting regents, though even if you aren't a monarch, expect to be treated as no less than royalty. The Fairmont View Rooms are the best non-suite rooms; they're 250 square feet in size and come with a king-size bed and harbor view. Ask about Fairmont Gold, a separate luxury-hotel-within-a-hotel on its own floor with top-of-the-line amenities that include complimentary wireless, deluxe breakfasts, daily afternoon hors d'oeuvres, fast check-in, and a dedicated concierge. For the ultimate in gilt-edged luxury, ask for one of the specialty suites. The Prime Minister Suite is 850 square feet of sumptuous furnishings, including a full kitchen and dining area, king-size bed, and private en-suite marble bathroom. All the specialty suites offer a view of the busy downtown core. There are many dining options at the Royal York, including the posh Library Bar. $$$$ 100 Front St. W. (York St.), 416-368-2511 / 800-441-1414, fairmont.com/royalyork

Hilton Toronto • Financial District • Timeless (601 Rms)
After an award-winning $25 million renovation, the Hilton Toronto boasts a sleek contemporary interior. Comfort and attentive service meet here in a convenient downtown location at the heart of the action. The lobby is sober and elegant, with a striking modern décor punctuated by huge columns. Opt for any of the Executive Level rooms where guests enjoy a complimentary continental breakfast, hors d'oeuvres, exclusive staff, complimentary wireless, shoeshine, and other gourmet snacks all day in the Executive Lounge while enjoying a panoramic view of the downtown area. Rooms ending in 01 or 03 offer excellent views of the CN Tower, Rogers Centre, and Lake Ontario, making them most popular with those in the know. If you're looking for the ultimate in prestige, consider the Crowne Suites, located on the 32nd floor with access to a wood-paneled library and living room. The largest Crowne Suite offers 1,812 square feet of elegant furnishings, a fireplace, a stunning city view, and amenities that include high-speed Internet access. There's also a pool and fitness room for your enjoyment. $$$$ 145 Richmond St. W. (University Ave.), 416-869-3456 / 800-445-8667, hilton.com

InterContinental Toronto Centre • Entertainment District • Timeless (586 Rms)
One of a wave of hotel renovations completed in the last few years, this $30 million retrofit got it right—it was an investment in pure style that sets the InterContinental distinctly apart from the rest. All the downtown hotels have their share of business-class clientele, but the InterContinental's high-end design and ideal location in the Entertainment District make it just as appealing to upscale vacationers. The vast lobby is modern and minimalist, with a bank of windows splashing natural light onto the marble floors, and all guest

rooms offer high-speed Internet access, an oversize marble bathroom, opening bay windows, and twice-daily housekeeping. Guests staying in one of the 90 Club InterContinental rooms enjoy daily luxury breakfasts, all-day tea and coffee, private check-in, exclusive staff, complimentary wireless access, and afternoon hors d'oeuvres. Ask for a room number ending in 00 as they are corner rooms with particularly notable skyline views. For all-out luxury furnished in sophisticated style, and your very own sunny lakeside patio, ask for the two-bedroom Waterview Suite. Located in the lobby, Azure Restaurant & Bar is a sophisticated and stylish bar and lounge, a favorite of local downtown professionals as well as out-of-towners. The InterContinental also has an in-house spa where you can splurge on an herbal body-glow polish or go for a traditional Ayurvedic massage. $$$ 225 Front St. W. (Simcoe St.), 416-597-1400 / 800-422-7969, torontocentre.intercontinental.com

Le Meridien King Edward Hotel • St. Lawrence • Grand (298 Rms)

This Toronto landmark has been pleasing clientele from Margaret Thatcher to Britney Spears for over a century. Le Royal Meridien King Edward Hotel celebrated its 100th anniversary in 2004 and wears its age gracefully. You'll be swept away by the grandeur of what the locals affectionately call the King Ed. From the moment you enter the foyer with its soaring ceilings, you'll understand its appeal to the international jet set. Rooms are artfully furnished in reproduction Edwardian style, complete with dark cherrywood and mahogany furniture, fine linens, and marble bathrooms. Note that the Royal Club rooms offer 355 square feet of luxury, including a king-size bed and a variety of city views. For the most posh rooms, ask for one of the Royal Suites, 1,800 square feet of luxury that includes a spacious living area. Some have a skylight or second bathroom. Amenities include a well-equipped 1,500-square-foot fitness room, a European-style spa, and the sumptuous dining room Victoria's. This is an opulent home away from home for the discerning traveler who likes comfort and is looking to avoid the generic and tour lodgings—and perhaps rub shoulders with the entertainment world's elite. $$$$ 37 King St. E. (Victoria St.), 416-863-9700 / 800-543-4300, lemeridien.com

Metropolitan Hotel • Chinatown • Timeless (422 Rms)

Located at the intersection of the Financial District and Chinatown, the Met is a classy alternative to the downtown hotels. The Met's low-key elegance and ideal location close to financial markets, theaters, museums, and all the downtown attractions have made it popular with a wide range of upscale travelers. The Metropolitan's owners are committed to delivering an exceptional experience, and they've succeeded by paying attention to the details. Standard features include Italian linens on European natural-down duvets, and high-speed Internet access. Ask for a southwest facing room to enjoy CN Tower views, or upgrade to an Executive Suite to enjoy an oversize marble bathroom with a whirlpool tub, plus a walk-in closet. The furnishings and décor in richly textured neutrals add to the tastefully understated luxury of the place. You can swim year-round in a heated indoor pool, stay in shape at the health club, and make use of complimentary wireless access in the hotel lobby. The Met's reputation for excellence extends to its restaurants. Lai Wah Heen has won international recognition for gourmet Cantonese cuisine, and Hemispheres Lounge & Bistro offers beautifully plated Asian fusion in a more casual atmosphere. $$$ 108 Chestnut St. (Dundas Ave.), 416-977-5000 / 800-668-6600, metropolitan.com/toronto

Park Hyatt Toronto • Bloor/Yorkville • Timeless (346 Rms)

The Park Hyatt is more than just another pretty face. Planted firmly at the chic corner of Avenue and Bloor, right in the heart of Yorkville, the Park Hyatt boasts grand hallways with polished wood beams that create the palatial atmosphere of a private estate. Guests staying in the South Tower enjoy views that take in the landmark CN tower, while those in the North Tower—particularly those staying on higher floors and in rooms that end in 23—have slightly more spacious rooms with great views of the Annex, a vibrant neighborhood that contains some of Toronto's most famous attractions. Standard deluxe rooms range from 300 to 400 square feet and feature marble bathrooms, plush terry bathrobes, and complimentary high-speed Internet access, along with feather beds in the South Tower rooms. For the ultimate Hyatt experience, ask for the Algonquin Suite, 2,500 square feet on the 15th floor that has a living room with a fully appointed entertainment center, a separate office, and a spectacular carved-wood four-poster bed, among many other features. And don't forget to check out the adjoining Stillwater Spa, to which wealthy Torontonians have been flocking for generations. $$$$ 4 Avenue Rd. (Bloor St. W.), 416-925-1234 / 800-633-7313, parktoronto.hyatt.com

Sutton Place • Financial District • Timeless (375 Rms)

The chairs and couches of the Sutton Place's elegant lobby are often occupied by upscale travelers who've been making this hotel a special-occasion venue for decades. Marble floors are covered with sumptuous rugs and ersatz Victorian furniture that give the room an understated European elegance. Sutton Place offers low-key luxury that has attracted all kinds of guests—from business types to vacationers, celebrities to heads of state. Original art and antiques grace all the rooms, which include 64 luxury suites that measure 540 square feet and provide a living room. Ask for a corner king room, which comes with an oversize bed and two huge windows that allow you to scope out downtown. La Grande Residence, a hotel within a hotel, is geared toward extended stays. Special amenities include 24-hour room service and twice-daily maid service, gourmet dining options, and a spacious health club. La Grande Residence suites include a living room, a full kitchen, and heated marble floors. $$$$ 955 Bay St. (Gerrard St. W.), 416-924-9221 / 866-378-8866, toronto.suttonplace.com

Westin Harbour Castle • Harbourfront • Timeless (977 Rms)

A 20-year recipient of the CAA/AAA four-diamond award, this spacious luxury hotel located right on Toronto's waterfront offers far more than just a great view. Solicitous service caters to clients in town on both business and leisure travel, and the signature Westin "Heavenly Bed" and "Heavenly Bath" are standard in all rooms. Rooms—all of which are non-smoking—are comfortably appointed in your choice of either contemporary or traditional furnishings, and if you're traveling with Fido, he gets a Heavenly Bed of his own. While all lake-view rooms offer stunning vistas, ask to stay in the South Tower and you'll forget that the city is right outside your front door. All rooms include a king-size bed, high-speed Internet access, and a spacious sitting area. Enjoy a massage at the hotel's spa as you look out over the Toronto Islands or hit the exercise rooms; they offer the same gorgeous view and provide direct access to the sundeck and tennis courts. $$$ 1 Harbour Sq. (York St.), 416-869-1600 / 800-228-3000, westin.com/harbourcastle

Windsor Arms Hotel • Bloor/Yorkville • Grand (28 Rms)

From the moment it threw open its doors a century ago, this classy haunt for the rich and famous has never been just a place to sleep, but also a chic spot to see and be seen. Sweeping grandeur greets you at the entrance—from the lobby to the gallery level, all done in neutrals and dark wood trim. You may share your stay with the stars, who love the old-world elegance that is matched with modern standards of excellence (it boasts the highest staff-to-guest ratio in Canada). Twenty-six luxury suites and two luxury rooms are available, tastefully furnished and outfitted with fine Frette linens, state-of-the-art sound systems, Jacuzzi tubs, and high-speed Internet access. The 1,500-square-foot Sultan Suites feature a king-size bed, two bathrooms, and a fireplace in the den, but ask for the one with a second fireplace in the bathroom for the ultimate in luxury. Expect celebrity-level pampering, including 24-hour butler service and room service—even a Bentley at your disposal as a limousine. Amenities include a fine spa featuring a wide range of services and a pool, as well as stylish dining and lounging options in the Courtyard Cafe, Club 22, and the Tea Room. $$$$ 18 St. Thomas St. (Bloor St. W.), 416-971-9666 / 877-999-2767, windsorarmshotel.com

Classic Toronto:
The Restaurants

Annona • Bloor/Yorkville • Continental
Named after the Roman goddess of the harvest, Annona serves a bountiful, deity-worthy feast at all hours of the day. The room, decorated in plum with gold accents, is a fitting backdrop for the local who's-who, hotel guests, and celebrities—particularly during the Toronto International Film Festival—who start their days with scrambled eggs with smoked salmon and capers, lunch on beautiful crab cakes, then return at dinner to enjoy grilled items from Joan Monfaredi's all-kosher kitchen. Those with a sweet tooth shouldn't pass on the signature caramelized pineapple tart with rum ice cream. *Mon-Fri 6:30am-11pm, Sat-Sun 7am-11pm.* $$$ = Park Hyatt Toronto, 4 Avenue Rd. (Bloor St. W.), 416-324-1567, parktoronto.hyatt.com

Auberge du Pommier • Uptown • French
Best Fine Dining Located in a historic building created from two stonecutters' cottages, the Auberge is one of Toronto's premier special-occasion dinner destinations. A whitewashed building with a black roof and French doors sets a romantic tone, and the warmly lit interior is classic white with ornate moldings and arches. Pale linens offset comfortable seating to create an overall impression of classic elegance. In the summer months, be sure to ask for seating on the garden terrace. An extensive wine list complements the French-Mediterranean cuisine, beautifully prepared with the finest ingredients. Savory choices include crispy seared tuna with spiced tartare, peppered pineapple, and petit pois salad. Classically minded locals and visitors looking for a memorably refined evening of pampered service and fine dining won't be disappointed with Auberge. *Mon-Thu 5-9pm, Fri-Sat 5:30-9:30pm.* $$$ 4150 Yonge St. (York Mills St.), 416-222-2220, oliverbonacini.com

Babur • Entertainment District • Indian
Best Ethnic Dining Much acclaimed in the local media, Babur prepares sumptuous Northern Indian food that keeps downtown crowds from all walks of life coming. An extensive menu of classics, along with tandoori, breads, and plenty of vegetarian choices, are prepared by enthusiastic chefs you can watch as they work. The friendly staff can help even those with no knowledge of Indian fare find mouthwatering fish, chicken, or meats, fiery hot or not. No matter what your choice, you'll find the food fresh and vibrant with the flavors of the subcontinent. In a long room, solid wooden dining-room chairs and white linens are saved from looking sterile by the arched white ceiling and delicate light fixtures. Strains of sitar add atmosphere without being cloying. Especially popular with professionals who work in the area, this is Indian food like you've never experienced it. *Mon-Sat 11:30am-3pm and 5-10:30pm, Sun 11:30am-3pm and 5-9:30pm.* $$ = 273 Queen St. W. (McCaul St.), 416-599-7720, babur.ca

Biagio Ristorante • St. Lawrence • Italian
Biagio aims to impress from the moment you enter. An attractive crowd of downtowners and foodies love the Old Town elegance of this historic dining room located in St. Lawrence House. Soaring ceilings and gracious moldings are balanced

by simple white linens to create a sophisticated look. Tucked in the back of the historic building and away from the street, a beautiful wrought-iron fence makes the flagstone patio one of the city's most refined spots for al fresco dining. It's a popular spot for lunch on a summer's day, hidden away from the bustle of downtown. An extensive menu of northern Italian classics has earned it a Distinguished Restaurants of North America award. It has also scored a coveted *Wine Spectator* Award of Excellence, so remember to order a glass of wine from the vintage cellar to accompany your leisurely meal. *Mon-Fri noon-2:30pm and 6-10pm, Sat 6-10pm.* $$$ ⊟ 155 King St. E. (Jarvis St.), 416-366-4040

Biff's • St. Lawrence • French

Directly across the street from the Hummingbird Centre for the Performing Arts, the refined and classy Biff's buzzes with well-dressed pre- and post-theater crowds. Floor-to-ceiling windows face busy Front Street, and that glossy veneer of sophistication continues inside with a long gleaming bar, white linens, and Art Nouveau light fixtures. The cuisine is upscale French done with imagination and artistry, the wine list is long, the service is impeccable, and the martinis are well reviewed. For a quiet drink—very quiet!—come during showtimes and have that long bar mostly to yourself, or come early and join the theatergoers for the pre-show buzz. *Mon-Fri 11:30am-2:30pm and 5-11pm, Sat 5-11pm.* $$$ ⒷΞ 4 Front St. E. (Yonge St.), 416-860-0086, oliverbonacini.com

Bistro & Bakery Thuet • Entertainment District • French

Best Hot Chefs Culinary wunderkind Marc Thuet's eponymous restaurant is a must-visit for serious foodies who value their foie gras. Crisp white linens and high-backed black leather chairs offer a simple but elegant setting that allows Thuet's dishes to take the main stage. Some, like Kobe beef bavette with shallot sauce, have a permanent place on the "Classics" menu, while others, like wood pigeon and Ontario lamb loin farcie with roasted root vegetables or chestnut-and-date crusted medallion of red deer, are seasonal opportunities not to be missed. Adventurous gourmands looking for a rarified experience can trust the Alsatian chef with the "surprise" eight-course degustation menu and accompanying wine pairings; it's a rite of passage on this city's culinary scene. *Tue-Fri 11:30am-2pm and 5:30-11pm, Sat 5:30-11pm, Sun 11am-2pm.* $$$ Ξ 609 King St. W. (Bathurst St.), 416-603-2777, thuet.ca

Bistro 990 • Financial District • French

With impeccable style and service, this perennially popular bistro serving Provençal-style cuisine remains hot by virtue of the steady stream of hungry Hollywood A-listers, savvy Financial District denizens, and others in the know. A big striped awning lends a continental flavor to this bustling celebrity-studded bistro, and low ceilings and yellow stucco contribute to the upscale European feel of the place. Offerings include succulent grilled flank steak in bordelaise sauce, corn-crusted sea bass, and desserts baked on the premises. *Mon-Fri noon-3pm and 5:30-11pm, Sat 5:30-11pm, Sun 5:30-10pm.* $$$ ⒷΞ 990 Bay St. (Wellesley St.), 416-921-9990, bistro990.ca

Bistro 333 • Entertainment District • International

Best Late-Night Eats This upscale but casual eatery caters to all comers and draws the clubbing crowds of the Entertainment District with a menu of classics and a kitchen that stays open until 4am on the weekends. There's a throbbing dance club upstairs, but Bistro 333 is where the club kids go to snack and chat in quieter surroundings. The wood-paneled room is elegant and sports a long carved-wood bar and intimate lighting—and is generally filled with a friendly crowd. The menu offers casual fare like pizza and quesadillas, several pasta selections, and entrées that include steak and seafood. The bar menu is just as long, featuring a long list of wines and martinis, including the After Dinner Martini of vodka, coffee liqueur, Southern Comfort, and crème de cacao. *Sun-Thu 11:30am-11:30pm, Fri-Sat 11:30am-4am.* $$$ ≡ 333 King St. W. (Widmer St.), 416-971-3336, clubmenage.ca

Bloor Street Diner & Bistro Express • Financial District • International
The original Bloor Street Diner & Bistro (on Bloor, natch), brought a completely unique concept to Toronto dining—French bistro combined with American diner, in both décor and menu—and a cross-section of locals came in droves the moment it opened its doors. Now, as part of a small franchise with a handful of locations citywide, the Bistro Express on King West serves hungry downtown white-collar types their fix of java, breakfast, and lunch, and offers both hearty and more delicate fare with a busy, friendly charm. Choose from breakfast classics like pancakes or eggs benedict, or ground sirloin burgers and steak frites later in the day. *Daily 7am-5pm.* $ ≡ 145 King St. W. (University Ave.), 416-928-3105, bloorstreetdiner.com

Boba • Bloor/Yorkville • International
One of Toronto's finest destination restaurants, Boba offers a mature and sophisticated dining experience to an equally sophisticated crowd. Located within a converted Victorian townhouse with high ceilings and elegant moldings, Boba is awash in color. Dining here is a refined but friendly experience. This is a favorite spot of well-to-do locals, and the owners are personable and solicitous, which just adds to Boba's charm. A décor in sumptuous red and blue colors is balanced with earthy tones, all brightened by plenty of natural light from the large windows that overlook busy Avenue Road. A healthy, offbeat menu includes exotic fare like Thai steak tartare, and linguine with smoked salmon and red onion confit. Boba is known for using only the finest ingredients. *Mon-Thu 5:45-9:30pm, Fri-Sat 5:45-10pm.* $$$$ — 90 Avenue Rd. (Elgin St.), 416-961-2622, boba.ca

Bright Pearl Seafood • Chinatown • Asian
A diverse mix of people from all over Toronto—and beyond—come to Bright Pearl to savor its fresh Cantonese cuisine. Known for its all-day dim sum, Bright Pearl offers a delightfully authentic Chinatown experience. Carts are piled high with a selection of the 80 to 100 tantalizing dim sum dishes on offer and served up by friendly and knowledgeable staff. The Peking duck comes highly recommended. Note that the seafood is still swimming in a tank you pass at the entrance. Join the crowds at this bustling Chinatown landmark to experience a taste of Toronto's international scene. *Daily 9am-10pm.* $$ ≡ 346-348 Spadina Ave. (St. Andrew St.), 416-979-3988, brightpearlseafood.com

Bymark • Financial District • Continental (G)
With a location inside the TD Bank Tower and a suitably imposing design, Bymark is a tribute to the masculine vibe of the Financial District. The sober dining room and lounge with dark leather seating toes the line between classic and modern chic and the patrons do too, making this the spot to impress bosses or colleagues from out of town. Or just come to soak up the high-powered, upscale ambience for the fun of it. Expect nothing but the best in both service and cuisine. The menu

choices feature fresh seafood and classic contemporary cooking, rounded out by an extensive wine list and served up by black-clad supermodel types. Or take your business upstairs to the bar and lounge area, a sexy, swank watering hole for movers and shakers. Ingeniously located in the courtyard of the TD Tower, Bymark allows you to sit in luxury gazing at the office towers and stars beyond, watching the hustle of the District as it unfolds around you. *Mon-Fri 11am-11pm, Sat 5-11pm.* $$$$ B≡ 66 Wellington St. W. (Bay St.), 416-777-1144, bymarkdowntown.com

C'est What? • St. Lawrence • International

Located on a busy corner in the Old Town, C'est What? is a perennially popular destination—at all hours of the day and night and with all walks of life. It's part lively pub, part restaurant with an "ethno-clectic" menu that features everything from shepherd's pie to chicken satay, and part live music venue that has seen the likes of Jewel and Wilco grace the stage. Crowds of music lovers and downtowners just looking for casual fun fill the popular pub till closing. C'est What? occupies the basement of a historic building, with a wood bar and furnishings to complete the look. The kitchen's open until 2am daily to accommodate your need for post-midnight sustenance. *Daily 11:30-2am; live music weekends; check listings.* $$ B≡ 67 Front St. E. (Church St.), 416-867-9499, cestwhat.ca

Café Supreme • Financial District • Cafe

Enjoy a gourmet coffee, latte, or cup of tea and a light breakfast alongside a good cross-section of Bay Street business types and other well-dressed downtowners in a Euro-cafe ambience. The corner of University and Wellington bustles weekday mornings with the people who keep Canada's financial engine humming. The sidewalk parade provides ample entertainment, which you can enjoy from one of Supreme's couches or perched on a windowside chair. Pleasant young staff and comfortable surroundings make this a fine way to start the day. *Mon-Fri 6:30am-5:30pm.* $ ≡ 40 University Ave. (Wellington St.), 416-585-7896, cafesupreme.ca

Canoe Restaurant & Bar* • Financial District • Canadian (G)

Best Canadian Cuisine Perched at the top of a skyscraper in Toronto's Financial District, Canoe boasts a breathtaking view that extends beyond the Toronto Islands and over Lake Ontario. Canada was opened up by fur traders in canoes, and Canoe the restaurant takes its inspiration from its iconic name by offering original takes on Canadian cuisine. This is one of Toronto's favorite power-lunch spots, and the crowd here will be rife with expense accounts. The menu uses classical methods in combination with local, seasonal, and other Canadian ingredients like B.C. sablefish, Yarmouth lobster, and Digby clams, among others, to produce exquisite creations. Come early to enjoy the view from the bar—either go with a cocktail or select a glass from the extensive wine list. The modern, minimalist design, all done in pale woods and neutral colors, incorporates a theme of Canadian wilderness, with touches like driftwood and snowshoes on the walls. The overall ambience is open and airy, and clearly dominated by the soaring views. One of the city's most civilized dining experiences, this is classic Toronto at its very best. *Mon-Wed noon-2:30pm and 5-10pm, Thu-Fri noon-2:30pm and 5-10:30pm.* $$$ B≡ 66 Wellington St. W., 54th Fl. (Bay St.), 416-364-0054, canoerestaurant.com

Caren's Wine and Cheese Bar • Bloor/Yorkville • Continental

The crowd is stylish, upscale, and uptown, typical of the posh Yorkville neighborhood. People perch at a polished bar or decorate the tables, sipping from a long wine list that includes a bottle for every taste. The menu really delivers—even the small tapas-style nibbles are carefully prepared. Especially popular are the gourmet cheese platters and cheese fondue, which are an excellent foil for the fruits of the vine. Lively and intimate, this is the spot for refined tippling with a polished Yorkville crowd. *Sun-Wed noon-11pm, Thu-Sat noon-midnight; bar until late.* $$$ B≡ 158 Cumberland St. (Avenue Rd.), 416-962-5158, carenswineandcheese.com

Centro Restaurant and Lounge* • Uptown • Italian

"Young and Eligible" is what locals call the uptown corner of Yonge and Eglinton, and even a casual observer is bound to notice the higher than average quotient of upscale young professionals here. What's also sprung up in the area is a collection of shops and restaurants that cater to this clientele. Centro pulls in not only these stylish locals, but Hollywood heavyweights like Kathleen Turner. The cool mod space features slick barstools around a polished wood bar and a two-level dining room. Dine on beautiful Italian cuisine at this glamorous spot, and select a bottle from an impressive wine list that has won it the *Wine Spectator* "Best of" Award of Excellence. *Restaurant Mon-Sat 5-11pm; lounge Wed-Sat 5pm-1am.* $$ B≡ 2472 Yonge St. (Eglinton Ave.), 416-483-2211, centro.ca

Coco Lezzone Grill and Porto Bar • Little Italy • Italian

It's always Fashion Week at Coco, favorite haunt of celebs like Teri Hatcher and U2's Edge, as well as Prada-clad locals and a few tourists too. The style is grand—columns and arches, and majestic hanging light fixtures contrasted by dark woods and rich red drapes. A menu of Italian classics, heavy on pasta and risotto, with mains of lamb, veal, Black Angus strip loin, and a good quotient of fresh seafood, is prepared with a level of artistry that fits the surroundings. The dinner rush is busy, with the noise levels growing as the night goes on. This is Toronto's high-end scene at its best, so come early for a drink at the bar to check out the stylish crowd, and wear your best so you can feel like a star yourself. *Mon-Tue 5:30-11pm, Wed-Sun noon-11pm; bar until late.* $$$ B≡ 602 College St. W. (Clinton St.), 416-535-1489, cocolezzone.com

Coppi Ristorante • Uptown • Italian

For serious fans of simple Italian cuisine, this restaurant, named in honor of World War II–era cycling star Fausto Coppi, is an oasis of tradition. Chef Michelangelo Colella's dishes like porcini risotto, snapper baked in sea salt, and grilled calf's liver celebrate subtle flavoring and have earned a loyal following of discerning Toronto diners. The rich blue and terra-cotta walls help create an old-world atmosphere and the room is always busy; particularly each October and November when they fly white truffles in from Alba and organize a showcase seasonal menu, pairing the pungent fungi with the best wines of the Piedmont region. *Mon-Fri noon-1:30pm and 5:30-9pm, Sat 5:30-9:30pm.* $$ ⊐ 3363 Yonge St. (Golfdale Rd.), 416-484-4464, coppiristorante.com

Corner House • Uptown • Continental

This tiny charmer nestled in a renovated home in the shadow of Casa Loma couldn't be farther off Toronto's hipster radar, and that's just the way the loyal crowd likes it. The memorable atmosphere—imagine a tranquil and sophisticated country cottage—ranks the Corner House among this city's most romantic places to dine, but thankfully the Corner House is more than just a pretty face. You can't go wrong with any selection from the continental menu as everything is delicious; regulars swear by chef Herbert Barnsteiner's mesmerizing, updated seafood classics, while oenephiles commend the thoughtful and surprisingly broad selection of wines. The downside? With only four small rooms to accommodate the city's most romantic foodies, you'll want to book long in advance for a special occasion. *Tue-Thu 5:30-10pm, Fri noon-2pm and 5:30-10pm, Sat 5:30-10pm.* $$ ⊟ 501 Davenport Rd. (Madison Ave.), 416-923-2604, cornerhouse.sites.toronto.com

Courtyard Cafe • Bloor/Yorkville • Continental
Housed in the celeb-rich Windsor Arms, the Courtyard Cafe has a clientele regularly sprinkled with Hollywood greats, rock stars, and supermodels. The dining room is grand in the old Hollywood tradition—think of the era of Bogart and Cagney. Anchored by round upholstered booths in the center and a sprinkling of potted palms, and brightened by Art Deco lighting fixtures and a soaring ceiling, the décor reeks of classic glamour and style. An award-winning chef prepares a fine selection of continental classics, and you'll also find a lengthy list of wine selections housed in a temperature-controlled wine cellar. The Courtyard Cafe also serves a posh buffet brunch on Sundays. *Mon 11:30am-2pm, Tue-Sat 11:30am-2pm and 5-9pm, Sun 10:30am-3:30pm.* $$$ ⊟ Windsor Arms Hotel, 18 St. Thomas St. (Bloor St. W.), 416-971-9666, windsorarmshotel.com

Crepes à Go Go • Bloor/Yorkville • French
If hunger pangs can wait till mid-morning, Crepes à Go Go will satisfy with baguettes, patisseries, and, of course, delectable crepes offered both in the form of sweet desserts and heartier savory meals. Take-out is extremely popular, and there are only four tables from which to savor the French cafe atmosphere, purportedly so authentic it's a favorite with displaced Montrealers. At least one visit is a must for francophiles and anyone with a hankering for tantalizing patisserie treats. *Mon-Thu 11am-6pm, Fri 11am-8pm, Sat 10am-8pm, Sun 11am-6pm.* $ ⊟ 18 Yorkville Ave. (Yonge St.), 416-922-6765, crepesagogo.com

The Fifth Grill • Entertainment District • French
The Fifth is a calm oasis of candlelit elegance, and a traditional but glamorous clientele dresses the part. A pianist sets the mood, and a flickering fireplace casts a glow over the dark wood paneling, softened by white sheers artfully draped over tall windows. Tasting menus are available so that you can sample an exquisite range of the conservative but flawlessly executed French fusion dishes served in these luxe surroundings. An enchanting experience from start to finish, the Fifth serves up a truly memorable meal. It's reservation only at this destination restaurant. *Wed-Sat 5-10:30pm.* $$$$ ⊟ 225 Richmond St. W. (Duncan St.), 416-979-3005, thefifthgrill.com

Gallery Grill • University of Toronto • Continental (G)
Best Brunches Housed in a venerable building on the University of Toronto campus, with tall neo-Gothic windows and soaring ceilings, this is surely one of the loveliest dining rooms in the city. Reservations are a must at this hideaway of fine dining, open only for lunch and known to academics and traditional Torontonians looking for a dose of leisurely old-world atmosphere. The menu consists of fresh updates on traditional classics like warm spinach salad and eggs-in-the-hole. The service is attentive and efficient. If you pay attention, you may even catch some juicy academic gossip from the next table over. *Mon-Fri noon-2:30pm, Sun noon-3pm.* $$ ⊟ 7 Hart House Cir., 2nd Fl. (Queen's Park), 416-978-2445, gallerygrill.com

Gamelle • Little Italy • French
Beautiful Gamelle boasts a romantic aura and invites intimate tête-à-têtes. From the rough wood floors to the open kitchen, Gamelle provides a perfect setting for couples who want to imagine that they're dining somewhere in the French country-side. This rustic bistro is a neighborhood favorite, popular with a young professional crowd as well as foodies who've read the rave reviews. To the intimate French mood, add a delectable menu that mixes tradition with innovation. *Mon 6-10pm, Tue-Wed noon-2:30pm and 6-10pm, Thu-Fri noon-2:30pm and 6-11pm, Sat 6-11pm.* $$$ ≈ 468 College St. W. (Markham St.), 416-923-6254, gamelle.com

George • St. Lawrence • International
Once an 1850s-era chocolate factory, this room has been reborn as one of Toronto's finest dining destinations. Where crisp white linens and richly hued wooden floors nod to tradition, and soft mauve chairs and elegant Art Nouveau flourishes add touches of updated style, chef Lorenzo Loseto shines. All dishes, like pecan-dusted bison rib-eye with barley risotto and foie gras mole, are presented in smaller portions sized to suit a five-course culinary extravaganza. Factor in Pam Misener, one of Toronto's top sommeliers, and you have a rarified dining experience that's perfect for very special occasions. *Mon noon-2pm, Tue-Fri noon-2pm and 5-10:30pm, Sat 5-10:30pm.* $$$ ≈ 111 Queen St. E. (Church St.), 416-863-6006, georgeonqueen.com

Globe Bistro • Greektown • Canadian (G)
Tucked in between retail shops on Danforth Avenue, this fine dining eatery is an elegant retreat from busy life. Linger in the front lounge area for a pre-dinner drink or to listen to jazz vocalist Julie Michaels. The main dining room décor is a subtle mix of neutrals, the sort of low-key background that allows diners to focus on the food and their companions. The dinner menu mixes Mediterranean influences with seasonal ingredients such as maple syrup and wild ginger poached black cod or roasted aged strip loin with coffee gnocchi. Patrons from the affluent neighborhoods of Rosedale and Forest Hill frequent the place, thanks to the impeccable service and refined atmosphere. *Mon-Fri 11:30am-2pm and 6pm-late, Sat 6pm-late, Sun 11am-2pm and 6pm-late.* $$$ ≈ 124 Danforth Ave. (Broadview), 416-466-2000, globebistro.com

Harbour 60 • Harbourfront • Steak House
Housed in the former home of the Toronto Harbour Commission, Harbour 60 is a classic steak house drawing a swanky old-school crowd. With a grand entrance and opulent dining rooms, Harbour 60 makes it easy to pretend that you've been accepted into an exclusive business club. The furnishings are palatial and feature brocaded upholstery in elegant neutral tones spiced up with royal blue and red accents. Fellow diners are well dressed. The kitchen delivers with a superbly executed menu of classics—appetizers like smoked salmon, Maryland crab cakes, and lobster bisque, mains of seafood and beluga caviar at market prices, and naturally, those divine steaks. This is the ultimate high-end steak-house experience. *Mon-Fri 11:30am-12:30am, Sat-Sun 5pm-12:30am.* $$$$ ≈ 60 Harbour St. (Bay St.), 416-777-2111, harboursixty.com

Hemispheres Lounge and Bistro • Chinatown • International
Visitors and locals alike love this bright, beautiful room. Hemispheres bustles with both business types and lunching ladies from the afternoon to the dinner hour.

Rising miles above the typical hotel restaurant-lounge in ambience and quality, Hemispheres takes its Chinatown locale as inspiration. The gorgeous black-and-white plates highlight dishes that put an East-West spin on local ingredients. Many offerings feature seafood with delicate flavorings like lemongrass. If you feel like watching Chinatown in action, ask for a table by one of the windows that face the street. After dinner, Hemispheres becomes a quiet, relaxing lounge. *Restaurant: Tue-Sat 5:30-10pm; bistro: Daily noon-11pm.* $$$ ≡ Metropolitan Hotel, 110 Chestnut St. (University Ave.), 416-599-8000, metropolitan.com/toronto/hemis/

Hot House Café • St. Lawrence • Continental
This casual, friendly downtown haunt is a big favorite with a cross-section of Toronto diners. The Hot House Cafe has overlooked the busy corner of Front and Church streets for more than a decade. Busy any night of the week with a mixed crowd of students and downtown types, the Hot House offers an extensive menu of classics, from crab cakes and a salad of deviled Brie and poached salmon to main dishes of pastas, pizzette, and veal scallopini. The polished wood floors highlight a slick bar and colorful, artsy dining area that buzzes hospitably at all hours. Live jazz provides the backdrop to the very popular Sunday brunch. Sip your Bloody Mary and watch all of Toronto walk by. *Mon-Thu 11am-11pm, Fri-Sat 11am-midnight, Sun 9:30am-11pm.* $$ ≡ 35 Church St. (Front St. E.), 416-366-7800, hothousecafe.com

Il Posto • Bloor/Yorkville • Italian
Best Power Lunches Dark wooden floors, muted walls, and high-backed black-and-gray-striped chairs might sound subdued, but this elegant Italian dining room in the heart of trendy Yorkville attracts a high-wattage crowd. Both at lunchtime and for dinner, the local business crowd and those on dates come together to dine on delicate risottos, fine pastas, and delicious items from the grill. Regulars enjoy the house favorite, spaghetti and clams, and appreciate the knowledgeable waitstaff's recommendations on wine pairings. As it's only steps from the Four Seasons Hotel, Il Posto also offers a great chance at celebrity spotting during the Film Festival. *Mon-Sat 11:30am-3pm and 5:30-11pm, Sun 5:30-11pm.* $$$ ≡ 148 Yorkville Ave. (Hazelton Ave.), 416-968-0469, ilposto.ca

Joso's • Bloor/Yorkville • Seafood (G)
Best Seafood Restaurants With fish so fresh you'll swear Toronto had moved seaside, Joso's has a reputation for excellence that goes well beyond Canadian borders. Famed Italian actor Marcello Mastroianni, in fact, found reasons to work in Toronto just to visit this Yorkville haunt, and you can regularly expect to find a crowd sprinkled with both local and international celebrities from the top of the A-list—though the food and vibe remain strictly classic. Reservations are a must most evenings, and the dining room can get noisy, but that's made up for by excellent service from staff who bring the catches of the day table-side for you to choose from. The popular and beloved summer patio overlooks the chic designer boutiques of Yorkville. *Mon-Fri 11:30am-2pm and 5:30-10:30pm, Sat 5:30-10:30pm.* $$$ ≡ 202 Davenport Rd. (Avenue Rd.), 416-925-1903, josos.com

KitKat2/Club Lucky • Entertainment District • Italian
Don't get this one confused with the original KitKat on King,.the popular casual eatery that's been packing them in for decades. With big windows and exposed brick, dark wood accents, and a gleaming, polished bar, this KitKat is more upscale, more polished, and has a separate and more casual whiskey room down-

stairs. The dining room is busy with pre-theater crowds through the dinner hour, then bustles after midnight with a hungry and diverse crowd who come for southern Italian classics served by a friendly staff. *Tue-Sat 4pm-11pm; bar until late.* $$$ B= 117 John St. (Adelaide St.), 416-977-8890, kitkattoronto.com

La Maquette • St. Lawrence • French
With the air of an estate conservatory, La Maquette is characterized by its sheer elegance. An older well-dressed clientele comes here for old-fashioned romance. La Maquette has often been voted the most romantic restaurant in town, and you'll easily see why. Marble-tiled floors highlight potted ferns and bouquets of lilies, and crystal chandeliers glitter overhead. You'll dine on fine Italian and French cuisine as you gaze through the huge banks of windows that illuminate the first floor. A grand staircase leads to a solarium beneath cathedral ceilings that overlooks St. James Cathedral and the Toronto Sculpture Garden. In the summer, a courtyard patio has the same view. *Mon-Fri 11am-11pm, Sat 5-11pm.* $$ = 111 King St. E. (Church St.), 416-366-8191, lamaquette.com

Lai Wah Heen • Chinatown • Asian
The entrepreneurs behind the Metropolitan Hotel chain have a simple philosophy—to deliver the best not only in accommodations, but to focus equal attention on the food and beverage side of the business. The result has been a number of award-winning restaurants. Lai Wah Heen starts with upscale continental service in posh surroundings and adds superb Cantonese cuisine. And it's clear it's got a successful concept at work—the Financial District types flock here for lunch. The dinner hour sees a conservative but handsomely dressed crowd of discerning locals, along with a smattering of expense-account types. Black ladder-back chairs, white linens, and a long elegant bar create a sophisticated and cosmopolitan dining room. Enjoy the latest in fine Cantonese, with its emphasis on tropical fruits and the exotic spices of the South Pacific, all of it served with continental flair. *Daily 11:30am-3pm and 5:30-10:30pm.* $$$ = Metropolitan Hotel, 108 Chestnut St., 2nd Fl. (University Ave.), 416-977-9899, metropolitan.com/lwh

Lolita's Lust & the Chinchilla Lounge* • Greektown • Greek
A restaurant with notable Greek cuisine and a vibrant lounge scene. *See Classic Nightlife (p.135) for details. Daily 6pm-2am.* $$ B= 513 Danforth Ave. (Fenwick St.), 416-465-1751, lolitaslust.ca

Michelle's Brasserie • Bloor/Yorkville • French
French cuisine goes country at Michelle's, which serves hungry shoppers and upscale trendsetters classics with a twist. Art Nouveau wrought ironwork adds to the brasserie charm. At the handsome marble bar is an extensive beer list with brews from Germany, Belgium, and France, as well as various Canadian provinces. With the kitchen open until closing at 2am, you'll find late-night Yorkville clubbers snacking on lobster and mussels, steak, prime rib, sandwiches, and tapas-style small plates. The heated garden patio is open year-round. *Sun-Mon 11:30am-10pm, Tue-Sat 11am-2am.* $$ B= 162 Cumberland Ave. (Yorkville Ave.), 416-944-1504, michellesbrasserie.ca

Myth* • Greektown • Mediterranean
A Mediterranean restaurant with a mainstream clubby late-night vibe and dance floor. *See Classic Nightlife (p.136) for details. Mon-Fri noon-11pm, Sat 5-11pm; bar until late.* $$$ B= 417 Danforth Ave. (Chester St.), 416-461-8383, myth.to

Niagara Street Cafe • Entertainment District • French

Cream walls, wooden booths, and mirrors suggest French bistro roots, but the menu, influenced by Chef Michael Caballo's stint in Madrid, looks further south. adding an unexpected Spanish flair to the typical bistro lineup. There's the ubiquitous steak—paired here with grilled veal tongue, spiced red onion petals, and celery root purée—but it's the old-world dishes like cornish hen with couscous, braised rabbit, and fried tripe with brava sauce that attract the well dressed 30-something crowd. The kitchen is dedicated to using organic dairy products, naturally raised meats, and artisan offerings where possible, upping the foodie appeal, as does the wine list and seasonal menu. *Wed-Thu 6-10pm, Fri-Sat 6-10:30pm, Sun 10:30am-3pm and 6-10pm.* $$ ≡ 169 Niagara St. (Wellington St. W.), 416-703-4222, niagarastreetcafe.com

North 44° • Uptown • Continental

North 44° is both Toronto's latitude and star chef Mark McEwan's gift to the city's fine-dining repertoire. In the wealthy and stylish neighborhood of Yonge and Eglinton, North 44° tempts sophisticated, classically minded palates with updated style. The fare is sumptuous and consistently draws well-heeled locals and the odd traveling celebrity. The menu features appetizers of seared tuna, panfried crab cakes, and white prawn risotto, mains of roasted bison tenderloin with savory rub and truffle risotto, and whole Dover sole in brown butter with caper berries. The space is warmly lit, and punctuated by faux French windows. A black-and-white exterior reflects the elegant minimalism at work in the décor. But however elegant the setting, the crowds really flock here for the superlative food. *Mon-Thu 5-10pm, Fri-Sat 5-11pm.* $$$ ≡ 2537 Yonge St. (Briarhill Ave.), 416-487-4897, north44restaurant.com

One Up Resto/Lounge* • Chinatown • Continental

Best Restaurant-Lounges The décor is an elegant take on its location on the edges of Chinatown, while the equally decorative plates offer a fresh look at continental cuisine. Financial District types love the inventive cuisine in this dining room. With dark red walls set against exposed brick, glowing lights, and black lacquered woods, and a tiled bar and glass wall that create a shimmering effect, One Up has a vibrant, sleek, and gleaming décor that matches its mood. The artfully presented fare beckons too. Start with wild mushroom crostini or seafood tartare, then graduate to pasta with lamb, seafood bouillabaisse, or duck. Stylish professionals flock to the bar and lounge area for after-work cocktails, especially the martini specials on Thursdays. Devoted fans keep the place bustling at all hours, and especially on weekends. *Mon-Thu 11am-3:30pm and 4:30-10pm, Fri 11am-3:30pm and 4:30pm-1:30am, Sat 4:30pm-1:30am.* $$ B≡ 130 Dundas St. W., 2nd Fl. (Bay St.), 416-340-6349, oneup.ca

Opus • Bloor/Yorkville • French (G)

Best Fine Dining A small, sleek, curved bar greets you upon entering Opus off a leafy Yorkville street. It's charming, but a mere prelude to the main attraction here—a seriously sexy dining room. It's all about understated Manhattan-style glamour. Taupe walls contrast with black leather seating and white linens, and the most distinctive feature is the large columns covered in gleaming wood. Diners include an international who's-who as well as discerning, fashionable, and well-heeled locals who revel in the sophisticated ambience. The menu features fine French-based fusion cuisine that changes regularly and includes high-end delicacies, and the extensive wine list has garnered Opus a *Wine Spectator* Grand Award. Splurge and order the caviar and champagne—this is definitely the best place to do it. *Daily 5:30-11:30pm.* $$$ _ 37 Prince Arthur Ave. (St. George St.), 416-921-3105, opusrestaurant.com

Oro • Financial District • International

A happy marriage of style and substance, Oro takes classical cooking to new heights with a contemporary approach and a flair for visuals both on and off the plate. Stylish downtowners and Bay Street heavies alike flock to this local favorite for the ever-changing cuisine, with influences ranging from hearty Italian to exotic Moroccan, complemented by a serious wine list. *Mon-Sat 5:30-10:30pm.* $$ = 45 Elm St. (Bay St.), 416-597-0155, ororestaurant.com

Ouzeri • Greektown • Greek

Best Ethnic Dining Both the menu and the Mediterranean vibe at this busy, classy Greektown restaurant are so authentic that you'll feel like you've stepped right into Athens. Black wrought-iron railings and a striped awning create an attractive European entrance. Come summer, crowds congregate on the patio to people-watch, sample the flavorful cuisine, and dream of the Parthenon. Start with marinated olives and feta and proceed to main dishes laden with octopus and other seafood or traditional favorites like moussaka. A plate-glass front means you can watch the stylish crowds that take over Greektown in the evening year-round. *Sun-Thu 11:30am-11pm, Fri-Sat 11:30am-midnight.* $$ = 500A Danforth Ave. (Logan St.), 416-778-0500, ouzeri.com

Pangaea • Bloor/Yorkville • Continental (G)

Best Power Lunches A sophisticated crowd regularly turns out to enjoy the stylish, civilized experience at this popular spot. Steps from the frantic bustle of Bay and Bloor, Pangaea is an airy space in warm Mediterranean hues of gold and blue, where tiny lights twinkle from a high ceiling of distressed white metal onto light wood floors. While the décor is all about inviting warmth, it's the excellence of the food that keeps this upscale eatery buzzing with stylish Yorkville shoppers in the afternoon and an uptown crowd at the dinner hour. The Mediterranean-inspired menu is heavy on seafood and pastas, along with regional exotica like caribou. *Mon-Sat 11:30am-11:30pm.* $$$ = 1221 Bay St. N. (Bloor St. W.), 416-920-2323, pangaearestaurant.com

Prego Della Piazza • Bloor/Yorkville • Italian

Prego is a handsome restaurant decorated in a masculine, Italianate style. A sophisticated bar scene complete with piano draws a well-heeled after-work crowd, while the menu of well-executed steaks and seafood keep the room buzzing late into the night. With a substantial wine list that includes many fine vintages, and a celebrity-rich summer patio that overlooks busy Bloor at Avenue Road, Prego is also a great choice for people-watching. *Mon-Sat noon-4pm and 5-11pm.* $$$ B= 150 Bloor St. W. (Avenue Rd.), 416-920-9900, pregodellapiazza.ca

Provence Delices • St. Lawrence • French

With a wine list that has earned it the *Wine Spectator* Award of Excellence since 1999, Provence has won its many traditional-minded fans with consistently high standards in both food and service. Discerning Torontonians and the odd traveler in the know flock to this warm room. White French doors lead to a summer patio, while inside crisp linens accent antique candelabras. Offerings are based on French classics and feature a sampling menu that includes baked stuffed mussels, tartine, and Malpeque oysters. Regular menu specialties include mustard flank steak, venison, and rabbit. A large selection of cheeses and wines by the glass complete your meal. Service is attentive and friendly, completing this enchanting old-world experience in Gallic-flavored fine dining. *Daily noon-2pm and 6-10pm.* $$$ ⬛ 12 Amelia St. (Parliament St.), 416-924-9901, provencerestaurant.com

Richtree • Downtown/Yonge • International
Richtree is a unique concept eatery, where fresh foods are laid out at various stations—bakery, sushi, grill, salads, and so on—and cooked to order on demand. On a busy corner, the open and airy space bustles with before- and after-work crowds hooked on the delectable foods. The food stations are efficiently arranged, and the staff are friendly and attentive in preparing your individual selections. Don't expect ordinary cafeteria offerings—they make use of only the finest ingredients, and you can see it all for yourself. Fresh fish and meats are cut to order, and a nice wine list and cocktails add to the experience. It's a colorful and flavorful option for breakfast, when the pastry chefs present their tantalizing pastries, and also ideal for a quick lunch in the heart of downtown. *Sun-Thu 7:30am-midnight, Fri-Sat 7:30am-2am.* $$$ ⬛ BCE Place, 42 Yonge St. (Front St.), 416-366-8986, richtree.ca

Rosewater Supper Club* • St. Lawrence • Fusion
Best Romantic Rendezvous In a city rife with historic renovations, this opulent retrofit of an 1852 landmark truly lives up to the superlatives—"stunning" hardly does it justice. Downtown crowds—think brokers and theatergoers—love the grand dining room with 22-foot ceilings and soaring windows. Columns and decorative moldings add to the sumptuous period design. The chefs work behind a transparent screen etched in roses, producing inventive dishes of French-global fusion. Join the chic after-work executive types in the elegant lounge for a stylish drink, especially on busy Thursdays when complimentary hors d'oeuvres draw crowds. *Mon-Fri 11:30am-1:30pm and 5:30-10pm, Sat 5:30-10pm.* $$$ ⬛ 19 Toronto St. (King St. E.), 416-214-5888, libertygroup.com

Scaramouche • Uptown • Continental (G)
Best Views Perched atop the Avenue Road hill and offering a fabulous view of the Toronto skyline, Scaramouche has long been synonymous with high-end dining. The sleek modern-classic décor belies its location in an unassuming high-rise. Toronto's reserved, well-to-do classes, along with movers and shakers looking to impress, have been making Scaramouche their restaurant of choice for years. Sophisticated, continental-inspired dishes please the equally sophisticated crowd. Reservations are essential, but be warned that regulars reserve the best tables weeks in advance. *Mon-Sat 5:30-9:30pm.* $$$ ⬛ 1 Benvenuto Pl. (Avenue Rd.), 416-961-8011, scaramoucherestaurant.com

7 West Cafe • Bloor/Yorkville • Cafe
Best Late-Night Eats Housed in a semi-detached Victorian house, 7 West charms inside with mirrors and twinkling lights, and the work of local artists on exposed brick walls. With the kitchen open 24/7, this is one of the city's late late-night hot spots, good for a romantic post-night-out meal or for noshing with the crowds who flock

here from the area's many clubs both before and after hours. The menu offers light cafe fare, and the panini come especially recommended, as do the delectable desserts; they're made by Dufflet, one of the city's leading pastry merchants. *Daily 24 hours.* $ = 7 Charles St. W. (Yonge St.), 416-928-9041, 7westcafe.com

Sotto Sotto Trattoria • Bloor/Yorkville • Italian

This romantic subterranean hideaway is a slice of authentic Italy in Yorkville. As well known to the celebrity circuit as to discerning locals, Sotto is located steps below street level, in a warm labyrinthine dining room of ochres accented by wood, stone walls balanced by crisp white linens. Though its reputation makes Sotto Sotto a perennial hot spot for a well-dressed Euro-chic crowd, plenty of quiet nooks and intimate lighting make this the perfect retreat for a romantic tête-à-tête as well. The menu includes no fewer than 15 pasta entrées, including spaghetti al cartoccio with shrimp, king crab, scallops, calamari, and mussels. Other options include risotto, seafood, meats, and a sumptuous dessert menu. The staff is as authentically Italian as the food, and used to catering to famous clientele. *Sun-Thu 5:30-11pm, Fri-Sat 5pm-midnight.* $$$ — 116A Avenue Rd. (Tranby St.), 416-962-0011, sottosotto.ca

Splendido • University of Toronto • Canadian

Sophisticated but fun, Splendido has won the hearts of Toronto's diners and carved a well-deserved niche in the competitive midtown restaurant scene. Servers cater with quiet efficiency to an upscale and sometimes star-studded clientele while chefs craft meals of Canadian-continental fusion behind a glass wall. The dishes they're preparing are breathtakingly good, highlighting local and regional ingredients in elaborately crafted menus—poached Nova Scotia lobster and egg-yolk ravioli with Charlevoix rabbit and Niagara prosciutto, among others. The menu changes monthly, and is complemented by a wine list with over 700 choices, all made most enjoyable in an elegant room brightened by huge paintings of sunflowers. *Tue-Sun 5-10pm.* $$$ = 88 Harbord St. (Sussex Mews), 416-929-7788, splendidoonline.com

Starfish Oyster Bed & Grill • St. Lawrence • Seafood

Best Seafood Restaurants Starfish manages to please patrons consistently, graciously, and with ease. From the chic black awning out front to the sleek interior, it serves up fresh seafood in a room with a New York–style bistro ambience. From lunch through dinner, downtown crowds keep the place humming, and the fragrant smells are a prelude to a delectable menu where mollusks feature prominently: oysters from Malpeque, New Brunswick, and Washington served on ice, or an oyster-stuffed omelette, for example. The lamb and other non-seafood items are also popular. The dining room offers both table and banquette seating in pleasant neutrals as well as a long gleaming bar. The place is busy with a business crowd at lunch, and caters to a more mixed-classic clientele at dinner. *Mon-Fri noon-3pm and 5-11pm, Sat 5-11pm.* $$$ B = 100 Adelaide St. E. (Jarvis St.), 416-366-7827, starfishoysterbed.com

Studio Café • Bloor/Yorkville • Mediterranean

With the Four Seasons' trademark elegance, this polished cafe is stylish but casual. Here, you can enjoy your meal in refined yet relaxed surroundings among the hotel's mainstream, upscale clientele. An artistic look is achieved with white walls, which are separated into sections by glass cases displaying ceramics and glass art, and black lacquer chairs add to the overall sheen. Breakfast classics are superbly prepared, while the lunch and dinner menus offer casual Italian-Mediterranean options. *Mon-Fri 6:30am-11pm, Sat-Sun 7am-11pm.* $$ ≡ Four Seasons Hotel Toronto, 21 Avenue Rd. (Bloor St. W.), 416-928-7330, fourseasons.com

Sunset Grill • The Beaches • Diner

An authentic diner that has existed in the Beaches area of Toronto for generations, the Sunset is the real deal. A sunny interior and congenial service add to the friendly neighborhood vibe. Breakfast is the king of meals here, served in generous portions, with thick slices of toast and copious coffee refills to wash it down. You will find no post-modern irony here, no tongue-in-cheek design elements, just an unfussy menu and a real taste of laid-back Beaches come-one-come-all cool. It's just the fuel you'll need for a walk along Queen or down to the lakeshore. *Daily 7am-6pm.* $ ≡ 2006 Queen St. E. (Bellefair St.), 416-690-9985, sunsetgrill.ca

Tea Room • Bloor/Yorkville • High Tea

Best Ways to Escape a Rainy Day The Tearoom at the Windsor Arms is an ode to the most civilized of Waspy traditions—the high tea. Cushions, velvet drapes, silver, and white linens serve as a backdrop to the Chanel- and Gucci-clad society dames taking a respite from shopping in an atmosphere of quiet yesteryear refinement. Attentive servers bring tiny sandwiches, crumbling scones, and other delicacies, and, of course, a superb cup of tea. In the evenings, the historic room becomes a champagne and caviar bar for a swank crowd. *High tea daily at 1:30pm & 3:30pm.* $$$ ⊔ Windsor Arms Hotel, 18 St. Thomas St. (Bloor St. W.), 416-971-9666, windsorarmshotel.com

Trattoria Giancarlo* • Little Italy • Italian

Best Celebrity Hangouts Sophia Loren came here for the intimate candlelit romance and the authentic Italian cuisine. The Giancarlo was among the vanguard of swank upscale instant-classic eateries that transformed the area from quirky ethnic neighborhood to a stylish destination. The creative nouvelle Italian cuisine features grilled meats and dishes, like swordfish with mint or jumbo quail spiced with sage. If you're here in the summer, you'll want to get a seat on one of Little Italy's busiest patios and settle in to check out the fashionable street scene. *Mon-Sat 6-10pm.* $$$ ≡ 41 Clinton St. (College St. W.), 416-533-9619

Truffles • Bloor/Yorkville • French (G)

Best Romantic Rendezvous This is the epitome of the impossibly posh dining experience, where ceilings soar over wood-inlaid floors, the work of local artists punctuates the rooms, and timeless grandeur trumps up-to-the-minute style. An institution that defies all trends, Truffles is one of Toronto's premier restaurants and has garnered a coveted CAA/AAA five-diamond award for more than a decade running. The pace of a meal here is leisurely, allowing you to savor the chef's continental creations. The service is, of course, impeccable, and local movers and shakers appreciate it as much as visiting glitterati. The menu will seduce you, as will the gracious ambience. So prepare to be impressed—and then relax and simply enjoy every flawless moment of this example of special-occasion dining at its finest. *Tue-Sat 6-10pm.* $$$$ ⊔ Four Seasons Toronto, 21 Avenue Rd. (Bloor St. W.), 416-928-7331, fourseasons.com

Classic Toronto:
The Nightlife

Avenue • Bloor/Yorkville • Hotel Bar

Best Classic Hotel Bars A classic hotel lounge and restaurant with a cosmopolitan edge, this space is dominated by a sleek 20-foot onyx bar that shines against the dark wood railings and set off by white leather furnishings. Stylish Avenue is a terrific spot for a fabulous lunch among the beautiful people. Perfect if you're gearing up for or recovering from a Yorkville shopping spree, Avenue also features a "fashion lunch" special that includes a three-course meal and a small bottle of champagne. The menu features creative casual dishes like quesadillas, crab cakes, gourmet pastas, and pizzas. After the dinner hour, it turns into a swank watering hole for well-heeled locals and visiting VIPs. *Mon-Sat 11:45am-1am, Sun 10:30am-2:30pm and 4:30-11pm.* ≡ Four Seasons Toronto, 21 Avenue Rd. (Cumberland St.), 416-964-0411, fourseasons.com

Azure Restaurant & Bar • Entertainment District • Hotel Bar

Best Classic Hotel Bars Part of the multimillion-dollar renovation of the InterContinental Hotel, Azure is a handsome hotel lounge with a solidly polished and smartly dressed clientele. While drawing its fair share of traveling business accounts, Azure has also won the hearts of locals. Downtown professionals make it a regular stop for happy hour on Thursdays and Fridays. Soaring banks of windows brighten the room with natural light, making it a great cure for bad-weather blues. White linen tablecloths and chandeliers in the dining area add to the bright and open feel. But the scene-stealer without question is the inviting lounge area, dominated by the art installation that anchors the bar. The glassy creation, called Liquid Veil, was commissioned from local artist Stuart Reid, and provides an elegant and artistic foil for the martini-loving crowds. *Daily 5:30am-10:30pm.* ≡ InterContinental Toronto Centre, 225 Front St. W. (Simcoe St.), 416-597-8142, torontocentre.intercontinental.com

BaBaLuu • Bloor/Yorkville • Dance Club

Best Dance Clubs Dress to impress, and you'll have a better chance of getting into this hot Latin dance club. Beyond the velvet rope, a crowd that often includes visiting Hollywood royalty orders bottles of expensive champagne. Mirrored walls, dim lighting, and throbbing Latin rhythms make for a very sexy dance floor. BaBaLuu really heats up after 11pm, so come early or be prepared to wait in line to mingle with that sexy crowd. *Tue-Sun 9pm-2am.* C≡ 136 Yorkville Ave. (Hazelton Ave.), 416-515-0587, babaluu.com

Centro Restaurant and Lounge* • Uptown • Wine Bar

Buzzing before Toronto landed on the global map, this grill manages to draw a well-heeled crowd with its notable wine bar. *See Classic Restaurants (p.123), for details. Restaurant Mon-Sat 5-11pm; lounge Wed-Sat 5pm-1am.* ≡ 2472 Yonge St., upper level (Eglinton Ave.), 416-483-2211, centro.ca

Club 22 • Bloor/Yorkville • Lounge

Tucked away in the Windsor Arms Hotel, this gem provides a sophisticated respite from the hustle and bustle of Yorkville. Supermodel types perch on the white

CLASSIC

leather stools at the polished bar, and well-heeled loungers groove to live piano through the cocktail hour. Then it's on to live bands or DJs in the evening. This is chic clubbing at its best—not for those looking for a raucous party. Posh patrons enjoy private humidor lockers (though the citywide smoking ban means smokers must head for the patio), along with a fine selection of cognacs, ports, and scotches. *Sun-Tue 11am-11pm, Wed-Sat 11am-2am.* ⊟ Windsor Arms Hotel, 18 St. Thomas St. (Bloor St. W.), 416-971-9666, windsorarmshotel.com

Crocodile Rock • Entertainment District • Bar
Best Meet Markets This big, loud crocodile-themed bar is packed with a mixed, urban, 30s-and-up crowd looking to party. Blasting classic-rock standards, Crocodile Rock is something of an anti-hip antidote to Clubland's ultra-stylish and ultra-cool vibe. There's plenty of fun to be had at this multi-level gathering spot where white-collar types let down their hair, and the large main room rocks from after work to late in the evening every night of the week. Known as a thriving meet market, it's also a good place to bump into pro-sports figures and celebs. When you're ordering, keep in mind that brews are the specialty. *Tue-Fri 4pm-2am, Sat 7pm-2am.* Ⓒ⊟ 240 Adelaide St. W. (Duncan St.), 416-599-9751, crocrock.ca

Hair of the Dog • Gay Village • Gay Bar
This is an upscale pub in the heart of Boys' Town, with imaginative pub fare and expertly mixed drinks. There's a steady stream of upscale gays and a few straights coming in the front door of this hugely popular gay-community mainstay. In the summer, the small patio is packed from opening until closing. The owners double as publishers of *Fab*, a high-end gay-lifestyle mag that has featured Toronto's chief of police as cover boy. A casual menu features vegetarian specials, an extensive wine list, and a delectable martini menu that confirms the impression that this is no average pub. *Mon-Fri 11:30am-1am, Sat-Sun 10am-2am.* ⊟ 425 Church St. (Wood St.), 416-964-2708

Hemingway's • Bloor/Yorkville • Bar
Best Celebrity Hangouts Hemingway's is a classic watering hole with a flowery streetside patio in the summer, but the party doesn't end when the nights get colder. A diverse crowd packs it in at Toronto's only year-round heated rooftop terrace. Visiting Hollywood celebs and the usual uptown suspects come to unwind at this perennially popular spot in fashionable Yorkville. A menu of roadhouse classics is spiced with Kiwi and other South Pacific influences, but you're not here for the food so much as the friendly pub-style vibe and great drinks. *Daily 11am-2am.* ⊟ 142 Cumberland Ave. (Avenue Rd.), 416-968-2828, hemingways.to

Jeff Healey's Roadhouse • Entertainment District • Live Music
Best Live Music Created by local blues guitar hero Jeff Healey, the Roadhouse showcases edgier music with rock, blues, and alternative bands from across Canada and touring acts on stage every night. Regular blues and rock faves include Healey's House Band, Danny Marks, and Jack de Keyzer. Walls are adorned with music memorabilia and the décor is simple for a music crowd that favors loud music and cold beer. Tuesday nights feature comedy before the local rock radio station Q107's house band, Michael White's Animal House, takes the stage and Saturdays you can dance to classic rock faves from the '60s and '70s rock era courtesy of Q107 DJ John Garbutt. *Daily 5pm-closing.* Ⓒ⊟ 56 Blue Jays Way (King St. W.), 416-593-2626, jeffhealeysroadhouse.com

Le Saint Tropez • Entertainment District • Cabaret

With walls in ochre washes accented with blue trim and a stylish courtyard that's heated year-round, Le Saint Tropez will make you feel as though you've arrived on the French Riviera. The bistro menu only enhances the illusion. The buzzing pre-theater crowds lap up Provençal-style dishes like steak frites and bouillabaisse, and are then replaced by those who've come to sip wine and watch the live French cabaret–style singers that play nightly. Well-dressed locals looking for a special evening on the town, and a smattering of visitors, love the warm mood, personable service, and French-flavored tunes. Dinner crowds may depend on theater offerings nearby, but you can count on a solid crowd of music lovers on Thursdays and weekends. *Daily 11:30am-midnight; cabaret daily from 8pm.* C= 315 King St. W. (John St.), 416-591-3600, lesainttropez.com

Library Bar • Downtown/Yonge • Hotel Bar

Best Classic Hotel Bars The Library Bar is all sober, old-world elegance. Mahogany paneling, a carved-wood bar, and elegant striped drapes create the feel of your own private library. A favorite of expense accounters and other upscale travelers, it's just the place for a discreet business meeting or contemplative Scotch in the late afternoon as you consider the evening's possibilities. The martinis here change monthly and are considered among the city's best. So order a drink, sink into one of the weighty couches, and watch the business deals going down around you. *Mon-Fri noon-1am, Sat 5pm-1am.* = Fairmont Royal York, 100 Front St. W. (York St.), 416-368-2511, fairmont.com/royalyork

Live @ Courthouse • St. Lawrence • Jazz Club

Best Jazz Clubs With 25-foot-high ceilings, four fireplaces, and hardwood floors, this spacious multi-story venue is a unique combination of dining room, jazz venue, and dance club. At mealtimes, it draws the Bay Street power crowd, who enjoy dishes such as prime rib, ahi tuna, and veal ravioli. At night, the former Courthouse Chamber Lounge transforms into a jazz venue for traditional and contemporary jazz stylings by local and international singers and groups (though avid jazz fans should note that steady conversation competes somewhat with the performers). The 30-plus business crowd carries on the evening sipping single-malt scotches until late in the lower-level bar, which has plasma screens showing the stage. Saturday nights, the spacious club changes to a dance hot spot for the label-conscious crowd that wants a mix of current rap and hip-hop top 10 and 1980s Brit-pop gems. *Mon 11am-3pm, Tue-Sat 11am-3pm and 7pm-2am, Sun 7pm-2am.* C≡ 57 Adelaide St. E. (Yonge St.), 416-214-9379, liveatcourthouse.com

Lolita's Lust & the Chinchilla Lounge* • Greektown • Lounge

This is one of the most popular restaurant-lounges in Greektown, and the crowds love to congregate at the shiny tiled bar. Lolita's Lust has an over-the-top sexy Mediterranean appeal that keeps the sometimes-fickle crowds of Greektown partiers coming in droves. Featuring red accents and exotically draped ceilings, the lounge's décor is a perfect backdrop for its stylish clientele. The restaurant is richly colored with green walls against exposed brick and funky green chandeliers. *Daily 6pm-2am.* = 513 Danforth Ave. (Fenwick St.), 416-465-1751, lolitaslust.ca

Lusso • Harbourfront • Lounge

Best Summer Patios One of the finer ways to take advantage of good weather is to head for an outdoor patio, and you can't do better than Lusso. Join the crowds at this 120-seat patio at the edge of the sparkling dark blue waters of Lake Ontario. Lusso's a hit with locals and travelers alike, with an appeal that goes beyond its fabulous location. Sip a Bloody Mary or martini outside, or perch inside at the wraparound leather bar. *May-late Sep Mon-Fri 8:30am-2am, Sat-Sun 1pm-2am.* ▤ 207 Queen's Quay W. (York St.), 416-848-0005, lussorestaurant.com

Myth* • Greektown • Restaurant/Lounge

Myth beckons with big glass doors that usher you into a funky room—the décor mixes Greek temple grandeur with quirky flair. Offering a Greek- and Mediterranean-inspired menu, the place goes clubby after dark with a well-dressed crowd of young, mainstream partiers. Come early for dinner on Friday or Saturday in the baroque dining area that overlooks the bar-lounge–dance floor, and watch the place fill up as you dine. Later, join the crowds on the dance floor. Seats on the coveted summertime patio go quickly, so come by late afternoon to be sure of securing a spot here. *Daily 4pm-late.* ▤ 417 Danforth Ave. (Chester St.), 416-461-8383, myth.to

N'awlins • Entertainment District • Live Music

N'awlins is an ornate, baroque boîte. Heavy dark carved wood furnishings, arches, and exposed brick conjure up the steamy South. Mixed crowds of music lovers come here for tunes with the same Mississippi Delta flavor. Oversize photographs of the jazz greats remind patrons why this veteran of King West exists as a seven-day-a-week venue for live jazz and blues. The music starts at 8pm Thursday through Saturday and at 7pm the rest of the week. Music lovers and pre-theater crowds come early to dine on Cajun cuisine like Mississippi mussels. Saturday nights are busy after the dinner hour, and you can linger over the music until 1am. *Daily 4pm-late.* ▤ 299 King St. W. (John St.), 416-595-1958, nawlins.ca

One Up Resto/Lounge* • Chinatown • Bar

A popular spot for young professionals looking for after-work drinks. *See Classic Restaurants (p.128) for details. Mon-Thu 11am-3:30pm and 4:30-10pm, Fri 11am-3:30pm and 4:30pm-1:30am, Sat 4:30pm-1:30am.* ▤ 130 Dundas St. W., 2nd Fl. (Bay St.), 416-340-6349, oneup.ca

Reservoir Lounge • St. Lawrence • Jazz Club

This legendary swing-jazz bar where live music plays seven nights a week is well known to an international audience of jazz lovers. Rub shoulders with musicians and visiting glitterati—Nick Nolte drops by when he's in town, as does Chazz Palminteri. Tom Jones has been known to take the stage. Bare brick walls contrasted with white linens and simple furnishings give the music center stage. For hungry listeners, a menu of light fusion cuisine features inventive tapas and reliably excellent thin-crust pizza. *Mon 9pm-2am, Tue-Sat 8pm-2am; live music from 9:30pm.* ⊂▤ 52 Wellington St. E. (Victoria St.), 416-955-0887, reservoirlounge.com

Rex Hotel Jazz & Blues Bar • Entertainment District • Jazz Club

Best Jazz Clubs Serving up live jazz and blues seven days a week has been the Rex Hotel's raison d'être for many years. This institution opened as a local watering hole in 1951 and is now known as a laid-back place to enjoy the music. The old men have largely given way to urban jazz lovers and art-school types who pack the place, but the crowd invariably spans decades and styles. The vibe is casual, but the entire crowd takes the music seriously. *Daily 11am-late. Show times vary; call for details.* C☰ 194 Queen St. W. (St. Patrick St.), 416-598-2475, therex.ca

Roof Lounge • Bloor/Yorkville • Hotel Bar

Best Summer Patios Bartender Joe Gomes has been manning this Toronto institution for 45 years and expert mixology is guaranteed, whether your taste runs to fine Scotch or the signature Park Cosmo. The Roof Lounge is as busy after work and in the early evening as it is late at night. The summertime patio offers a sparkly view of the city lights. The walls of this small lounge are covered in blue suede, and the fireplace and leather couches you can sink into allow you to enjoy the view and the luxurious, timeless ambience. *Daily noon-1am.* ☰ Park Hyatt Toronto, 4 Avenue Rd., 18th Fl. (Bloor St. W.), 416-924-5471, parktoronto.hyatt.com

Rosewater Supper Club* • St. Lawrence • Bar-Lounge

An opulent room popular for after-work drinks, with complimentary hors d'oeuvres on Thursdays. *See Classic Restaurants (p.130) for details. Mon-Fri 11:30am-1:30pm and 5:30-10pm, Sat 5:30-10pm.* ☰ 19 Toronto St. (King St. E.), 416-214-5888, libertygroup.com

Classic Toronto:
The Attractions

Allan Gardens Conservatory • St. Lawrence • Gardens

Best Ways to Escape a Rainy Day A jewel in an urban setting, the Allan offers spacious indoor and outdoor gardens for your enjoyment, making it both the perfect cure for nasty weather and a way to make the most of a sunny day. Grand indoor conservatories feature domed cathedral ceilings and plantings of flowers both domestic and exotic in various environments—tropical house, arid house, and palm house, among others. Outdoor gardens lend themselves to leisurely exploration, with fountains and architectural features that add to Mother Nature's beauty. The facilities are wheelchair accessible and, best of all, free. *Daily 10am-5pm.* 19 Horticultural Ave. (Jarvis St.), 416-392-7288

The Beaches • The Beaches • Neighborhood

Best Ways to Enjoy a Sunny Day While the waterfront extends both east and west of the city, it's the end furthest east that is officially known as the Beaches. Along the lakeshore from about Coxwell Avenue heading east, the Beaches consists of a few miles of pebbly Lake Ontario beach suitable for sunning, strolling, and swimming (but wait until at least July for the lake to warm up). Farther east along the shoreline are the Scarborough Bluffs, cliffs that make the Beaches a more private area. Along with the natural beauty, the area offers diversion in the form of the mega-entertainment complex the Docks, as well as numerous casual burger joints. The Beaches is also the name given to the funky neighborhood centered around Queen Street East, which is lined with eclectic shops, cafes, and restaurants and has a left-of-center vibe that feels light-years away from downtown's bustle. Queen Street from Coxwell east and south to the lakeshore

Casa Loma • Uptown • Historic Site

Best Historic Buildings To glimpse a sumptuous bygone era, come visit the castle built for love. Begun in 1911, architect E.J. Lennox's re-creation of a medieval castle took 300 men nearly three years to complete, and was occupied by its original owners—knighted Canadian financier and entrepreneur Sir Henry M. Pellatt and Lady Mary Pellatt—for less than a decade before financial ruin forced them to abandon it. Today it stands overlooking modern-day Toronto as a monument to the sweeping majesty of that era of unbridled riches. The design incorporates elements of Norman, Gothic, and Romanesque style, and the six-acre estate includes several formal and informal gardens, many with fountains and sculptures, ideal for a leisurely stroll. Inside, grandeur and opulence overwhelm every room—from the impressive Great Hall with its oak-beamed ceiling, to the stained-glass dome in the Conservatory. Be sure to check out the view of the city from the turrets. *Daily 9:30am-5pm (last entry at 4pm); gardens (May-Oct) daily 9:30am-4pm.* $ 1 Austin Terr. (Davenport Rd.), 416-923-1171, casaloma.org

Chinatown • Chinatown • Neighborhood

There are actually no fewer than five Chinatowns in Toronto—a testament to the truth of Toronto's reputation as a welcoming home to the world—but the downtown area is its bustling core. Here, even the signs are bilingual, and on

Saturdays the neighborhood's so busy that the traffic slows to a crawl on Spadina. Come to take in the fresh food markets and the shops of imported clothing and art, gifts, and other curiosities, as well as a wide array of restaurants. You won't doubt the authenticity of this colorful neighborhood. Between Spadina, Queen, College, and Bay Streets, Chinatown

CN Tower • Harbourfront • Viewpoint/Building
Best Views It may be on every kitschy postcard and souvenir of Toronto, but the fact remains that it is a marvel of the modern world, and at 1,815 feet and 5 inches is still its tallest freestanding structure. Initially developed as a telecommunications tower, it has a uniquely flexible concrete construction that allows it to sway with the strong winds. But there's more to it than just the breathtaking view out over Lake Ontario—or for the brave, the view from 1,112 feet straight down through the glass floor on the Observation Deck—as getting up there is half the fun in a glass-fronted elevator that travels 15 mph. The ubiquitous and friendly staff can answer any questions, and the Tower has several casual cafes both at base level and at the Observation Deck, as well as fine dining at 360, the revolving restaurant listed in the *Guinness Book of World Records* as home to the "World's Highest Wine Cellar." *Daily 9am-10pm.* $$ 301 Front St. W. (John St.), 416-868-6937, cntower.ca

Elgin/Winter Garden Theatre • Downtown/Yonge • Historic Site
The imposing arches and marble columns at the entrance stand in stark contrast to the modern glass-and-steel edifices on either side, and provide a taste of the last-century charm that waits to be explored inside. The world's only remaining double-decker theater (two separate performance spaces, one on top of the other) was hopping in the vaudeville era, and may just be the most beautiful theater in existence today. Lovingly restored, it still operates as two separate theater halls with separate performance schedules. Ninety-minute tours are offered year-round Saturday mornings at 11am and Thursday at 5pm, and include a visit backstage, as well as a viewing of the fascinating collection of original vaudeville costumes and props found during restoration. *Tours Thu at 5pm, Sat at 11am. Call for performance schedule.* $ 189 Yonge St. (Queen St.), 416-314-2871, heritagefdn.on.ca

Glen Abbey Golf Club • Oakville • Golf Course
"The Abbey," the first course designed by golf legend Jack Nicklaus, has played host to the PGA's Canadian Open for 20 of the last 25 years. Made famous by Tiger Woods' stunning shot of the year 2000 that won the Bell Canada Open victory and completed his triple crown, this highly ranked course is very popular. It's a rewarding and challenging course of 7,112 feet, slope 140 from the black tees, and known for fiendishly deceptive greens. See how you measure up against the greats, and then relax at the luxurious clubhouse facilities, which include the Gallery Grill & Bistro. $$$$ 1333 Dorval Dr., 905-844-1811, glenabbey.com

Harbourfront Mariposa Tours • Harbourfront • Tour
Along a sparkling waterfront where boat lovers can ogle seaworthy crafts both small and large, Toronto's Harbourfront makes for a gorgeous walk on a nice day. The best views of the harbour, though, are to be had from the water. To truly appreciate the picturesque Great Lakes landscape, take a tour or dinner cruise. Cruises are available from various carriers, including Mariposa Tours, a first-class operator with a

seven-vessel fleet. Mariposa offers harbour tours five times daily, as well as private charters and specialty cruises like Friday night dancing on the water and Sunday brunch. Torontonians love their waterfront just as much as the visitors do, and flock here to spend the warm summer months by the water. $$ 207 Queen's Quay W. (York St.), 416-203-0178, mariposacruises.com

Hockey Hall of Fame • St. Lawrence • Museum

In a country where hockey has iconic status, and a city that was one of the "original six," the Hockey Hall of Fame is a suitably palatial ode to the icy sport. A playful sculpture of hockey players greets you at the entrance. Whether casual or fanatical in your interest, you'll find both the Hall and the exhibits designed to provide maximum entertainment. Several exhibit spaces offer inside details of the sport, as well as interactive games that allow you to test your skills against those of the pros. The centerpiece of the building is a spectacular domed stained-glass ceiling. *Mon-Fri 10am-5pm, Sat 9:30am-6pm, Sun 10:30am-5pm; check for special schedules during the Christmas holidays and spring break.* $ 30 Yonge St. (Front St.), 416-360-7765, hhof.com

Kensington Market • Chinatown • Shopping

Toronto is a city of many ethnicities, and its multicultural heart beats loud and clear in Kensington Market, for 100 years the gateway to Toronto. Today, it's a neighborhood of shops that spill out into the street in the area roughly surrounding the intersection of Baldwin and Augusta. But don't bring your wheels, as this area is best explored on foot. Here, you can buy everything from Ethiopian spices to European linens, funky secondhand clothes and original works of art, and an abundance of fresh food. This is an essential visit for the eclectic shopper, lovers of authentic vintage clothing, or anyone wanting to catch a glimpse of Toronto's multicultural heritage. It's busiest Saturday mornings, with a steady bustle leading up to the weekends. Spadina Ave. (College and Dundas Sts.), kensington-market.ca

Lionhead Golf & Country Club • Brampton • Golf Course

If you like your golf game to be challenging, you'll find two 18-hole courses, Legends and Masters, to test your mettle at Lionhead. Legends, considered one of the most difficult courses in Canada, has a slope rating of 153 and water on 13 holes. Masters offers more lush surroundings, with forests and ravines, and the fifth hole is 411 yards and a par four. A snazzy clubhouse awaits after you're done. $$$$ 8525 Mississauga Rd. (Steels Ave.), 905-455-8400, golflionhead.com

Royal Ontario Museum • Bloor/Yorkville • Museum

Best Ways to Escape a Rainy Day On a fashionable corner near Yorkville, Canada's largest museum occupies palatial digs, complete with grand arches and high ceilings. The ROM houses an internationally recognized collection of over 5 million pieces. As the country's biggest museum, the ROM also aims to be the best, offering fascinating exhibits from its permanent collection as well as blockbuster traveling shows about the natural and human-made world that aim to both educate and entertain. From biodiversity to decorative arts to textiles and dinosaurs, the ROM is a world-class museum and definitely worth making time for. *Hours vary; call or check website for information.* $ 100 Queen's Park (Avenue Rd.), 416-586-5549, rom.on.ca

Spadina Museum • Uptown • Historic Building
Best Historic Buildings Built by wealthy Torontonian James Austin in 1866, this lovely restored Victorian house began as a country estate and saw the city grow up around it. Featuring design elements from the Victorian to Edwardian periods, the regal estate reflects four generations of the Austin family's exquisite tastes. In addition to the meticulously landscaped gardens and furnishings of historic interest, however, the original decorations chronicle the Toronto arts scene of the 19th and 20th centuries. *Sep 4-Dec 31 Tue-Fri noon-4pm, Sat Sun and holidays noon-5pm; May 1-Labor Day Tue-Sun noon-5pm.* $ 285 Spadina Rd. (Davenport St.), 416-392-6910

St. Anne's Anglican Church • Parkdale • Historic Site
The only authentic Byzantine church in Canada, and a scale model of St. Sofia in Istanbul, this designated historic site was built in 1908 by Ford Howland and is decorated with 21 paintings on the domed ceiling and walls done by members of the Group of Seven. The Group of Seven painters took modern art and made it Canadian, and their work is considered important in that context, but you won't need to study beforehand to appreciate the talent and colors under the cathedral's dome. *The church welcomes visitors for self-guided tours every Sun after the 10am service, or by pre-arranged visit.* 270 Gladstone Ave. (Queen St. W.), 416-536-3160, stannes.on.ca

Stillwater Spa • Bloor/Yorkville • Spa
Best Spas This posh spa in the Park Hyatt has been pampering wealthy Torontonians for generations. Stillwater aims to be a relaxed and refined sanctuary from the stresses of the world, and it succeeds beautifully. The entrance alone soothes, bathed in warm neutrals and filled with the sounds of waterfalls and streams. Several rooms offer a range of treatments, including the Stillwater Aqua therapy, during which a therapist uses shiatsu techniques in warm water for the ultimate in relaxation. Choose from massage, manicure and pedicure treatments, or Vichy treatments that incorporate warm cascading water. *Mon-Fri 9am-10pm, Sat 8am-10pm, Sun 10am-6pm.* $$$$ Park Hyatt Toronto, 4 Avenue Rd. (Bloor St. W.), 416-926-2389, stillwaterspa.com

Toronto Antiques on King • Entertainment District • Antique Market
The famed former Harbourfront Antique Market has taken its show indoors to a large and suitably historic building in the Entertainment District. Here you'll find 30 dealers carrying specialty antiques ranging from art and furniture to housewares, wood cabinetry, maps and prints, and militaria, along with more-exotic items like Tibetan jewelry and authentic vintage clothing and accessories. Whether you're buying or not, the bright and pleasant surroundings make it great for browsing, and you may just net that truly unique find. *Tue-Sun 10am-6pm.* 276 King St. W. (Duncan St.), 416-345-9941, torontoantiquesonking.com

Toronto Islands • Harbourfront Park • Island
Best Ways to Enjoy a Sunny Day Don't limit your exploration of Toronto's waterfront to the mainland. Take one of the ferries to the Toronto Islands for a real Toronto summer experience. Once the summer playground of the city, the Islands today are home to a fiercely independent community of locals who pride themselves on the natural beauty of their home just minutes from downtown. Ferries leave from the foot of Bay and Queen's Quay (just west of the Westin Harbour Castle),

every 30 to 45 minutes for three island destinations. At Hanlan's Point, you can rent bicycles, picnic, or explore the 150-year-old Gibraltar Point Lighthouse. Centre Island has its own amusement park. On Ward's Island, you can rent both bicycles and boats, and the charming Rectory Cafe is only a few minutes' walk from the pier. You can enjoy beaches, gardens, art galleries, and bike paths on all the Islands. This relaxed retreat to the great outdoors also offers a splendid view of the Toronto skyline. *Ferry rides approx. 30 min., check schedules online for details.* $ Bay Street (Queen's Quay), 416-392-8193, torontoisland.org

PRIME TIME TORONTO

Everything in life is timing (with a dash of serendipity thrown in). Would you want to arrive in Pamplona, Spain, the day *after* the Running of the Bulls? Not if you have a choice and enjoy the world's most exciting experiences. With our month-by-month calendar of events, there's no excuse for missing out on any of Toronto's greatest moments—when its energy is at its peak. From the classic to the whimsical, the sophisticated to the outrageous, all the events that are worth your time are right here, along with the details you need to plan the perfect trip.

Prime Time Basics

Eating and Drinking

Weekdays, downtown Toronto is working Toronto, and you'll find breakfast served up for the office crowd from 7am, then busy again for coffee breaks at about 10am. There's a coffee shop on almost every corner eagerly catering to the typical Canadian's love of caffeine as bright and early as you want it. Lunch for those same office workers is often a quick bite on the run, but you'll find the downtown is also full of power lunching spots where the midday meal stretches from 11am until 1pm or later. On weekends, though, look for a far more leisurely pace, and brunch to start at 11am and extend till 2pm or 3pm. The after-work crowd fills the bars by 5-ish, with dinner reservations more likely for 7pm or later. The Entertainment District, especially Clubland, is full of dining spots that cater to the late-late-night crowds, and there are a few hot spots in Chinatown ready to dish up noodle favorites till the early morning hours. Bars and clubs get going around 9pm, with the crowds at their peak between 10:30pm or 11pm and last call at 2:30am. Closing time is 3am, with after-hours spots typically open till 5am or 7am.

Weather and Tourism

With the Great Lakes climate of hot summers and cold, blustery winters, the weather certainly plays a role in the flow of visitors to Canada's largest city, but you'll also find many exceptions to the seasonal rule, most of them event driven.

Mar-May: Spring can be a time of extremes in terms of weather, from leftover snow in March to sultry summer-like days in May, and can run the gamut of virtually anything in between. You'll find patios beginning to open, along with a few outdoor events getting underway in May.

Seasonal Changes

Month	Fahrenheit High	Low	Celsius High	Low	Hotel Rates
Jan	30	17	1	-8	L
Feb	30	16	1	-9	L
Mar	37	25	3	-4	L
Apr	52	36	11	2	L
May	63	45	17	7	H
June	73	55	23	13	H
July	79	61	26	16	H
Aug	77	59	25	15	H
Sep	70	52	21	11	H
Oct	57	41	14	5	L
Nov	45	32	7	0	L
Dec	34	22	1	-6	H

H-High Tourist Season; L-Low Tourist Season

June-Aug: Summer is warm to hot, with a mix of absolutely perfect days and blistering heat—and often humidity. Be sure to bring sunscreen and sunglasses. Evenings in late August can be quite cool, making a decent jacket a must-have too.

Sep-Nov: Fall is often an especially lovely time of year in the Toronto area, with the air cleansed of summer's humidity and the trees in a spectacular show of color by mid-October. The flip side of fine weather is occasional rain, although it's not typically heavy till November, with long stretches of perfect sunny weather. November is the most variable month; it's often rainy and may include snow.

Dec-Feb: There's no sugarcoating a Canadian winter. December can be rainy or snowy, cool to downright cold, with a white Christmas in the cards about half the time. Old Man Winter saves his cruelest bite for January and February, when snowstorms are always a possibility.

National Holidays

New Year's Day	January 1
Valentine's Day	February 14
Good Friday	March or April
Easter Monday	March or April
Victoria Day	Monday preceding May 25
Canada Day	July 1
Civic Holiday	First Monday in August
Labor Day	First Monday in September
Thanksgiving	Second Monday in October
Halloween	October 31
Remembrance Day	November 11
Christmas Day	December 25
Boxing Day	December 26

Listings in blue are major celebrations but not official holidays.

The Best Events Calendar

January

- Toronto International Boat Show

February

- Lunar New Year
- Toronto WinterCity Festival

March

- Canada Blooms
- Toronto Wine & Cheese Show

April

- Hot Docs Canadian International Documentary Festival

May

- Sante—the Bloor-Yorkville Wine Fest.
- Inside Out Annual Lesbian and Gay Film & Video Festival
- Toronto Jewish Film Festival

June

- NXNE (North by North East) Music Festival
- Pride Week
- Toronto Downtown Jazz Festival

July

- Canada Day at Ontario Place (Fest. of Fire)
- The Drinks Show
- Grand Prix of Toronto
- Beaches Intl. Jazz Fest.
- Caribana Festival
- Toronto Outdoor Art Ex.

August

- Canadian National Exhibition (CNE)
- Krinos Taste of the Danforth
- Rogers Cup WTA Tennis

September

- Toronto Intl. Film Festival
- Word on the Street
- Nuit Blanche

October

- Harbourfront International Festival of Authors

November

- Royal Agricultural Winter Fair

December

- Cavalcade of Lights

Night+Day's Top Five Events are in blue.

The Best Events

January

Toronto International Boat Show
Direct Energy Centre, Exhibition Place, 905-951-0009, torontoboatshow.com

The Lowdown: There are two ways to cope with winter in the Great White North—cultivate an interest in winter sports, or attend the International Boat Show in January and dream away the weather. Over 100,000 people typically attend this event, which covers 400,000 square feet of exhibition space and features over 1,000 crafts from paddleboats to the latest sport boats and luxury yachts with all the amenities. An indoor lake—the largest in the world—covers 28,000 square feet complete with floating docks and "harborside" dining, and the show features boating and engine repair demonstrations, as well as other educational and entertaining seminars and workshops. This is delightful escapism in the dead of winter. Catch a preview of the show on the Friday evening before it opens in a gala with a different theme each year. Check the website for seminars and presentations by some of the world's preeminent sailors, like Britain's heroine, Dee Caffari, the first woman to sail solo non-stop around the world against prevailing winds.

When and How Much: *Nine days beginning on the second Saturday in January.* The preview gala is $75 per ticket and general admission is $15 for adults, with a two-day pass at $25.

February

Lunar New Year
Direct Energy Building, Exhibition Place, 416-483-8218, torontocelebrates.com

The Lowdown: Join in with the largest Lunar New Year Festival in Canada, the most important holiday of the year for the city's large Chinese population, with the festivities expanded to include traditions from Korea, Vietnam, and other areas that celebrate this holiday. You'll find an abundance of foods, an arts and crafts bazaar, and a full roster of entertainment including everything from Cantonese Opera to kung fu demonstrations to film, dance, and acrobatics. The Saturday afternoon typically features the best selection of entertainment, and look for the Flower Market to be full of plum blossoms, associated with the New Year.

When and How Much: *A long weekend in late January to mid February (the first day of the first lunar month in the Chinese calendar).* Adult admission is $10.

PRIME TIME

Toronto WinterCity Festival

Various downtown venues, 416-394-0490,
city.toronto.on.ca/special_events/wintercity/index.htm

The Lowdown: For two weeks in the dead of winter, the city comes out to play, eat, and be entertained in a citywide festival. The Festival includes free outdoor concerts and performances (yes, outdoor!), as well as events that showcase the rich diversity of Toronto's culinary and performing arts scenes. Indoor events include culinary demonstrations and classes. Watch for the hugely popular special prix fixe Winterlicious menus and special packages at downtown restaurants and hotels, and discount admissions to city attractions and venues. Citywide arts organizations and venues offer behind-the-scenes tours and special shows. Previous highlights have included a spectacular acrobatic performance in downtown's Eaton Centre. Many of the Winterlicious arts events are free of charge, and each weekend during the Festival, you'll find outdoor entertainment and festivities at Nathan Phillips Square (at City Hall), including concerts and performances that typically include acrobatics and dance (to stay warm, of course!) and art exhibits like Vancouver artist Gordon Halloran's ice paintings—a uniquely Canadian art form. Other city venues and establishments like Casa Loma, the Ontario Science Centre, and even the Toronto Zoo offer up special performances, so check the website to get all the details.

When and How Much: *Two weeks from the last Friday in January.* Free.

March

Canada Blooms

Metro Toronto Convention Centre, 222 Bremner Blvd., 416-447-8655,
canadablooms.com

The Lowdown: Gardening enthusiasts won't want to miss Canada's largest horticultural exhibition, bringing the beauties of colorful blooms to the city in early spring. Along with thousands of fragrant flowers and lovely plants, you'll find displays, a cooking school, and a host of nifty gardening gadgets for sale, along with a wine lounge where you can duck in and sample the fruits of the vine. For a preview of the whole show—and how better to view flowers than while sipping vino, with live entertainment?—snag yourself a ticket to the opening-night party at $175.

When and How Much: *A long weekend in early March (timing often depends on local school break).* General admission is $18.

Toronto Wine & Cheese Show

International Centre, 6900 Airport Rd., Mississauga, 416-229-2060,
towineandcheese.com

The Lowdown: This premier vintners' event is billed as "A world of award-winning wines, beers, single-malt whiskeys, specialty foods, and cheeses"—in short, a gourmet's dream of samplings and exhibitions. Leading food and wine experts, including the city's hottest chefs, offer more than 20 free seminars and cooking demonstrations in a gourmet kitchen theater. Preview the latest wines courtesy of the Liquor Control Board of Ontario (LCBO—the province's only liquor retailer and consequently the world's largest buyer of wines and spirits). Look for the wine and beer competitions, and tutorials on how to pair wine with foods. Keep a special lookout for the Vintage Classics Tastings booth for the opportunity to quaff vintage selections like Château Lafite, Château Haut Brion, 1998 Vega Sicilia, and 1999 Duckhorn Howell Mountain Merlot—a treat for oenophiles and wine novices alike.

When and How Much: *Friday to Sunday, between mid-March and early April, typically the the third weekend in March, but it can vary.* Tickets to each day's events run about $18, and are available through the website.

April

Hot Docs Canadian International Documentary Festival

Various venues in the Bloor-Yorkville and Annex area, 416-203-2155, hotdocs.ca

The Lowdown: North America's largest documentary festival screens over 100 works from top-flight Canadian filmmakers and their compatriots from around the world, most of the films receiving their world premiere. Programming includes special retrospective screenings honoring a featured artist, awards, an in-depth look at films from a spotlight country, retrospectives, and much more. If you happen to miss the actual dates, but you're in the city between October and April, the Doc Soup program offers monthly screenings at the venerable Bloor Street Cinema (bloorcinema.com). Join the e-mail list to stay on top of developments. Check out the gala screenings (Retrospective, Canada First), with the artist in attendance for interviews and Q&A sessions after the show. For film professionals, there are networking events, seminars, and workshops, including the Toronto Documentary Forum, where filmmakers pitch their ideas to over 100 broadcasters from around the world—the ideal event to keep on top of the industry. With a mix of public and private events, you'll have to look at the schedule for available parties, but good bets are the opening screening gala and the annual awards presentation.

When and How Much: *Ten days beginning on a Thursday, typically the third Thursday of the month.* Individual tickets typically $10-$15, with premium passes available at $150, and the Hot Docs at Night series, with screenings that start after 11pm, are free.

PRIME TIME

May

Sante—the Bloor-Yorkville Wine Festival

Various locations in Bloor-Yorkville, 416-928-3553 ext. 27,
santewinefestival.net

The Lowdown: Take ultra-posh Yorkville, add vino, and you'll have this fabulous festival of wine, wine education, tastings, and more wine. Creative programming includes many events that combine vintage wines, gourmet dining, and jazz for a delicious experience among a high-end crowd, like a jazz brunch at the ROM, so be sure to check out everything that's available on the website. Gourmets won't want to miss the Ultimate Wine Makers' Dinner each year with celebrity chefs in attendance, and a sumptuous menu prepared by five chefs and featuring ten wines.

When and How Much: *Five days (Tuesday to Saturday) in late April or early May* Tickets range from free lectures to $50 for a tasting to $125 for complete dinner with wines.

Inside Out Annual Lesbian and Gay Film and Video Festival

Various venues, 416-977-6847, insideout.on.ca

The Lowdown: Canada's largest gay and lesbian film fest, Inside Out presents almost 300 films. Inside Out has grown from its humble beginnings to an international showcase that attracts tens of thousands of attendees from all over the globe. In addition to attending the screenings, you can mingle with the film set at panel discussions, director's talks, meet-and-greets, and loads of parties. No one puts on a party like Toronto's gay community, and you can expect a roster of ten parties or more, all of them open to the public and most of them free of charge, (with a $10 or so fee for some). The opening and closing and awards galas are good bets, and expect to find filmmakers, artists, and local celebs in attendance.

When and How Much: *11 days in mid to late May, typically beginning the Tuesday after the Victoria Day long weekend.* Tickets available in early May, with single tickets for $10.50 and galas about $30.

Toronto Jewish Film Festival

Bloor Cinema (bloorcinema.com) and the Al Green Theatre at the Miles Nadel Jewish Centre (milesnadeljewishcentre.com), 416-324-9121, tjff.com

The Lowdown: The largest Jewish film festival in North America, the TJFF showcases films of all kinds that address themes of Jewish culture and identity. Program offerings have typically included films from up to 20 countries, reflecting the diversity of the Jewish experience and the talent it has produced. You'll see animated shorts and feature-length dramas. It's also a chance to connect with Toronto's 180,000-strong Jewish community. Canadian and international filmmakers attend, participating in lectures, discussions, Q&A sessions, and meet-and-greets—in 2006, Academy Award–winning director and actress Lee Grant was a TJFF guest. Box office is open from mid-April.

When and How Much: *Nine days beginning on the first or second Saturday in May.* Tickets to individual screenings $6-$20. The "All You Can Sit" pass is about $200.

June

NXNE (North by North East) Music Festival
Various venues in the downtown, 416-863-6963, nxne.com

The Lowdown: Fans of indie, rock, and alternative can gorge themselves on music, music, and more music as more than 450 bands play at 30 venues in this extravaganza, featuring panels and discussions along with all the performances. Although live music is obviously the draw, you can round out your experience with a selection of features, shorts, and documentary films where music is the star, many screenings with the directors and performers in attendance. NXNE is a music industry conference as well as a showcase for fans, so check out the conference center (location varies) to see the movers and shakers of the music biz. Former panelists and NXNE guests have included Patti Smith, Johnny Rotten, Rolling Stones manager Andrew Loog Oldham, and Stewart Copeland (the Police).

When and How Much: *Thursday to Sunday of the second weekend in June.* Prices for individual shows vary from free to $10-$20, with full passes for $250.

Pride Week
Various venues, 416-927-7433, pridetoronto.com

The Lowdown: For ten days, Toronto comes out to celebrate its gay community, which is second in size only to San Francisco's. Centered around the Gay Village, the festivities include a three-day multistage arts fest and a weeklong street celebration. Look for specials, events, and entertainment throughout the area, culminating in the last weekend that sees several hundred artists performing over three days, spontaneous partying all over the Village, and raucous parades to cap off the experience. There's an official Launch Party, but Pride Week's glamour event is the Pride Awards & Gala dinner on the last evening, held in 2006 at the tony Distillery District and featuring a host of VIP guests, including prominent politicians, and a price tag to go with the crowd, at $250 or so a pop. Many of the arts and entertainment events are free, as are, of course, the Dyke March on the final Saturday, and the no-holds-barred, not-for-the-faint-of-heart Pride Parade extravaganza that occurs on the last Sunday.

When and How Much: *Beginning on a Friday in the last (full) week of June.* Free.

PRIME TIME

Toronto Downtown Jazz Festival

30-plus venues throughout Downtown, 416-928-2033, tojazz.com

The Lowdown: For ten sultry days in the summer, jazz fever takes over downtown. More than 2,000 world-class Canadian and international musicians are showcased at venues ranging from big outdoor concerts to intimate jazz lounges. The lineup of talent has included greats like Oscar Peterson and Wynton Marsalis, and featured Etta James and Dave Brubeck in 2006. The main stage is at Nathan Phillips Square, with most concerts, naturally, spread out over various indoor venues like the venerable Rex Hotel, or Dominion on Queen, all over the downtown. To get the real flavor of jazz, though, check the schedule for late-night jam sessions, it'll include a couple at least, starting at 1am. What could be cooler? And keep your eyes peeled for the luminaries of the jazz world to make impromptu appearances to jam with the locals in the true spirit of improvisation.

When and How Much: *Ten days beginning the last Friday in June.* Admission is purchased to each event, with some free (mostly outdoor concerts), and others ranging from $10 to $25 per ticket.

July

Canada Day at Ontario Place (Festival of Fire)

Ontario Place (various), 416-314-9900,
ontarioplace.com/en/events/festival.htm

The Lowdown: There will be a host of events citywide to help you get into the spirit of celebrating Canada Day, with the spirit of the True North in evidence at concerts and music festivals at the Molson Amphitheatre. Later on, watch a dazzling display of fireworks in the Festival of Fire, a spectacular international pyrotechnics showdown choreographed to music, with the fireworks launched from a lake freighter 700 feet out on Lake Ontario. It's estimated that roughly 2 million spectators take in the show. Of course, it's free to watch anywhere along the lakeshore, but additional great seating—and a cocktail or two—can be had at the Atlantis Pavilions Entertainment Complex on Ontario Place grounds. While the park and lakeshore will be packed with viewers, two of the best vantage points for the fireworks are the CN Tower (maybe a dinner reservation?) and the harbor cruise boats.

When and How Much: *July 1 (Festival of Fire is spread over eight nights, Saturday to Saturday in the week that includes July 1).* Reserved seating on Ontario Place grounds for the fireworks shows runs in the $40 range, with the grand finale and Canada Day itself often sold out well in advance.

The Drinks Show

The Brickworks, drinksshow.com

The Lowdown: This annual celebration of the latest trends in cocktails educates and inspires with its gathering of local and international mixologists over two days. It offers some 100 different libations and even recipe cards to inspire creativity at home. Housed at the historic Evergreen Brickworks, a converted factory area, the open-air cocktail party attracts scenesters who want to know the next "it" cocktail and learn about the latest offerings in whiskey, vodka, gin, tequila, and the ever-increasing number of liqueurs. Don't leave it until late to go; this event hits capacity by dinner time.

When and How Much: *Second weekend in July (Saturday and Sunday).* Tickets ($25) are available online in advance and at the door.

Grand Prix of Toronto

Lakeshore Boulevard and Exhibition Grounds, 416-588-7223, grandprixtoronto.com

The Lowdown: Whether you attend the races or not, you'll know when the Grand Prix is in town by the cars roaring up Lakeshore Boulevard and down a route of curving streets throughout the Exhibition Grounds. Stands and bleachers are set up all along the course, with coveted corporate hospitality tents going for up to $100,000. Thunder Alley is a fan favorite, an area along the fastest part of the track where you can get up close and personal with drivers, quaff a brew in the Beer Garden, catch live entertainment or play interactive games, and more. Practice and qualifying runs are held on Friday and Saturday, with the final race, televised live, held on Sunday.

When and How Much: *Friday to Sunday, the weekend following Canada Day.* Gold seating, directly above pit row, including three days of reserved seating, close access to Thunder Alley and a Champ Car Paddock Pass, runs approximately $200. Non-reserved seating in the Thunder Alley Grandstand, with a lakefront view of the fastest section, runs $60 for the three days.

Beaches International Jazz Festival

Various Beaches venues and Distillery District, main stage at Kew Gardens, 416-698-2152, beachesjazz.com and partigras.com

The Lowdown: Nearly a million people converge on the usually laid-back Beaches neighborhood for this jazz celebration. The music from over 750 bands and solo performers includes not only traditional and experimental forms of the music, but blues, Afro-Canadian influences, world beat, and Latin sounds. And the people come not only for the music, but for the parties, street festivals, dance performances, and workshops where you can learn cool stuff like Cuban drumming or improvisation. The main stage is outdoors at Kew Gardens, and other area venues participate. The Beaches Jazz Fest is really spread over two weekends, launching with PartiGras in the Distillery district the first weekend, and non-stop free outdoor concerts and dancing till you drop. Hang around till late night for impromptu jam sessions at indoor venues like the Boiler House Complex. The following weekend, the festival proper is launched at a party at the Balmy Beach Club on the lakeshore (balmybeachclub.com—check website for ticket details). The music hits fever pitch on this last weekend, with a street fest along blocks of Queen East.

When and How Much: *Eleven days, beginning on a Thursday in mid-July.* Ticket prices vary.

PRIME TIME

Caribana Festival
Various venues, 416-466-0321, caribanafestival.com

The Lowdown: This colorful celebration of Caribbean visual and performing arts is North America's largest street festival. From the opening to the parade that highlights the festivities, it's a feast for the eyes, with lots of steel bands, calypso, and soca to soothe the soul. The parade along 2.2 miles (3.6km) of Lakeshore Boulevard features thousands of costumed masqueraders and floats. Between the opening and closing parades, there's loads to take in, from free outdoor entertainment to a marketplace and cultural village on Olympic Island on the last weekend. Catch the King & Queen Xtravaganza, where the regals of the Festival are chosen and the eye-popping costumes make their public debut at Lamport Stadium (1155 King West near Dufferin), with tickets at $30 each. A highlight for music lovers will be the Steel Band Competition at historic Fort York (toronto.ca/culture/fort_york.htm), tickets for which are $15. Preferred bleacher seating for the parade runs $15, but of course it's free to see along Lakeshore Blvd., with a street party in full swing to get you in that Caribbean mood. Admission to the Arts & Cultural Festival on Olympic Island runs $15.

When and How Much: *18 days beginning on a Friday in mid-July.* Prices are free to $30.

Toronto Outdoor Art Exhibition
Nathan Phillips Square, 416-408-2754, torontooutdoorart.org

The Lowdown: Over three days, over 100,000 converge on Nathan Phillips Square, rain or shine, for this long-running event. It's the largest outdoor art exhibition in Canada, and typically features the work of established artists, undiscovered gems, and talented students. As well as presenting an excellent shopping opportunity for art enthusiasts, it's a way of meeting and networking with artists and art dealers, who routinely cruise the show for new and interesting talent.

When and How Much: *Friday to Sunday, the second or third weekend in July.* Free.

August

Canadian National Exhibition (CNE)
Exhibition Grounds, 416-393-6300, mmi.theex.com

The Lowdown: Founded in 1879, the "Ex," as it's affectionately known to locals, is one of the continent's biggest fairs, with over 500 attractions, 700 exhibitors, and a fab midway with 65 rides. With well over a million visitors, the festivities include something even for those whose tastes don't run to fairs. There's live music on small and midsize stages, a horse show, and the hugely popular Food Building, where you can eat your way through the cultures that make up the city. An on-site casino offers gaming tables and an air-conditioned poker room, along with a pub that features live entertainment. See the human cannonball or the Superdog show, and be sure to catch the Canadian International Air Show on the last weekend.

When and How Much: *18 days from mid-August ending on Labor Day.* About $12 for general admission, and $39 for a "Magic Pass" that includes rides.

Krinos Taste of the Danforth
Greektown, 416-469-5634, tasteofthedanforth.com

The Lowdown: Over a long weekend in August, blocks of Danforth Avenue are shut down, and Greektown takes to the streets. All the local Greek restaurants are represented at booths with savory Greek culinary delights on offer—from souvlaki to calamari—along with the flavors of other Greektown restaurants, from dim sum to chipotle. There are lots of outdoor concerts and other events, all with a multicultural theme that emphasizes Hellenic heritage. Expect to make a day of it, and stay into the evening too, in the company of hordes of other food and entertainment enthusiasts.

When: *Friday to Sunday, first or second weekend in August.* Outdoor events and entertainment is free. Food $1-$5.

Rogers Cup WTA Tennis
Rexall Centre (York University), 416-665-9777, rogerscup.com

The Lowdown: Catch an exciting international tennis tournament with top-seeded players like Martina Navratilova and Nadia Petrova. Tennis Canada cosponsors the annual Tennis Championships held in the new state-of-the-art Rexall Centre on the York University campus. First begun in 1892, this tournament has been around longer than any except Wimbledon and the U.S. Open. Live music and a drink on the patio, along with a little star-gazing (the event is popular among visiting VIPs,) round out your experience.

When and How Much: *Nine days beginning on a Friday in mid-August.* Qualifying rounds tickets range from free to $60 for preferred access that includes parking and access to the VIP lounge. Gold seating ranges from $50 up to $230 per ticket for the finals, and preferred access runs from $60 to $375 for the finals.

September

Toronto International Film Festival
Various venues, 416-968-3456, tiffg.ca

The Lowdown: For two weeks, the streets of Toronto are home to the world's glitterati at the Toronto Film Festival, which is second only to Cannes on the international film calendar. The movie movers and shakers are treated to Toronto's own brand of laid-back hospitality, and increasing numbers of stars in attendance have made celeb-spotting the second-most popular pastime. TIFF is a huge fan favorite because the stars come down to earth—staying, eating, and playing on the streets—and they are often accessible to the public. TIFF is getting a reputation for premiering some of the film industry's hottest new productions thanks to the ongoing efforts of its artistic director, Piers Handling. Between the Hollywood blockbusters, small independents, and illuminating documentaries, you'll never be able to catch everything of interest, but you'll have fun trying. Get the whole TIFF experience by attending a gala screening, especially the opening night gala. Held at Roy Thompson Hall, it's one of the Festival's most glittery and coveted events (tickets $325). Tickets to the closing-night film and all-inclusive after-party also run $300 and the galas are a sure-fire way to fuel your celeb-sighting cred. Your best bet is to plan ahead by a couple of weeks and get a ten-film pass. Otherwise, if you're up for the challenge, most screenings have rush lines, so you can line up to get a single seat at the last minute (be prepared to line up early for popular films). Another option is the Best Bets list at the website tiffg.ca, which has a daily list of available tickets. While the galas are held at Roy Thompson Hall or the Elgin Winter Garden Theatre, screenings take place at theaters throughout the downtown core. If you can find room, camp out in the lobby of the Four Seasons, Windsor Arms, or Hazelton Hotel in Yorkville, for prime celeb-spotting, although other good bets are Yorkville faves such as Avenue Bar, Sotto Sotto, Joso's, and Lobby. Young Hollywood and edgier artists may congregate late night at the über-hip Drake Hotel or C Lounge. Thanks to the city's support of TIFF, many restaurants and lounges stay open until 4am, two hours later than normal closing time.

When and How Much: *Two weeks beginning on the first Thursday in September after Labor Day.* Tickets $10-$20 each. A 10-film pass runs $154.50, other packages $65-$100.

Nuit Blanche

scotiabanknuitblanche.com

The lowdown: In a city that traditionally closes down around 2:30am, the upstart arts festival Nuit Blanche allows art enthusiasts to revel in an all-night celebration of contemporary visual arts. First started in Paris, this arts ritual starts at sunset on the last Saturday in September and goes until 7am Sunday morning. Gallery-rich areas such as Yorkville, the University of Toronto, and the western edge of the Entertainment District along Queen Street host openings and one-night-only exhibitions and performances. Look out for wandering people dressed as monsters and avant-garde arts programming at the Drake and Gladstone Hotels, which benefit from extended bar hours until 4am.

When and how much: *Last Saturday in September.* All events are free.

Word on the Street

Queen's Park, 416-504-7241, thewordonthestreet.ca

The Lowdown: This one-day event takes over Queen's Park for a celebration of the written word. Torontonians are big readers, and they've proven it by making this showcase for independent publishers and booksellers a hugely successful event. The proceedings include over 500 exhibits, readings, book signings, meet-and-greets, and media events. A large selection of books and magazines are for sale, including hard-to-find and out-of-print items.

When and How Much: *The fourth Saturday in September.* Free.

October

Harbourfront International Festival of Authors
Harbourfront Centre for the Arts, 416-973-4000, readings.org

The Lowdown: The Harbourfront Centre becomes a hive of literary activity in October. The International Festival of Authors is a well-attended series of author readings, book signings, and social events, attracting a cross-section of book lovers from around the world. Since 1974, over 4,000 authors have participated, including several Nobel Laureates. Authors in 2006 included Gary Talese and Margaret Atwood, and the organizers produce a stellar line-up of Canadian and internationally recognized artists in a setting with a warm and intimate feel. If you can't make the Festival, a regular reading series runs weekly for most of the year. The opening celebration features an evening of music and entertainment around a chosen theme, but in previous years, the hot ticket has been the PEN Canada benefit gala, with tickets at $20 or $35 depending on seating, and a cool $175 will also get you into the VIP reception afterwards.

When and How Much: *11 days staring on the third Wednesday in October.* Readings are $8.

November

Royal Agricultural Winter Fair
Direct Energy Centre, Exhibition Grounds, 416-263-3400, royalfair.org

The Lowdown: For ten days every November, country comes to the city in a traditional agricultural fair even Martha Stewart loves. This isn't only about pigs and cows and best-in-show, this is the largest indoor combined agricultural, horticultural, canine, and equestrian event in the world. The Royal Horse Show features international-caliber competition in jumping and dressage, as well as carriage-derby racing. The popular Cavalcade of Horses spotlights riding techniques and training. The Celebration of the Dog has also quickly become a crowd favorite, especially the "Raging Jack Russells." There's lots to do and see, including information, shows, and entertaining displays, and of course, no agricultural fair would be complete without the Royal Vineyard wine-tasting bar. The biggest events, like the Royal Horse Show, happen on the last three or four days.

When and How Much: *Ten days beginning the first Friday in November.* General admission about $12.

PRIME TIME

December

Cavalcade of Lights
Various venues throughout downtown, 416-395-0490,
city.toronto.on.ca/special_events/cavalcade_lights/index.htm

The Lowdown: The Cavalcade of Lights Festival officially begins with the lighting of a massive Christmas tree, followed by the lighting of the rest of Nathan Phillips Square with over 100,000 lights, and continues throughout the month of December. Begun in 1967, Canada's centennial year, it includes other events such as a popular outdoor skating rink and several fireworks displays, and, of course, many holiday-themed concerts. Throughout the city, various events include light displays, neighborhood and historic house tours, and a stunning three-day international ice-sculpting competition. All of it culminates in a huge outdoor New Year's Eve celebration that has traditionally featured hot up-and-coming bands, including the now famous Bare Naked Ladies.

When and How Much: *Last weekend in November until New Year's Eve.* Free.

HIT the GROUND RUNNING

In this section, you'll find all the indispensable details to enhance your trip—from tips on what to wear and how to get around, to planning resources that will help your vacation come off without a hitch. You'll also find suggestions for making business trips a pleasure, as well as some fun, surprising facts that will help you impress the locals.

City Essentials

Getting to Toronto: By Air

Lester B. Pearson International Airport (YYZ)
866-207-1690, gtaa.com

The first plane landed at Toronto's airport—then called Malton Airport —back in 1938. Malton Airport later became Toronto International Airport, then got its current moniker in 1984. Lester B. Pearson International Airport was named in honor of Canada's 14th Prime Minister, a Nobel Peace Prize laureate and, incidentally, the designer of the ubiquitous red-and-white maple-leaf Canadian flag. Along the way, the airport's traffic has grown to current levels of 1,200 arrivals and departures per day, on average, and is projected to service 50 million passengers per year by 2020. Often called YYZ (its call letters) the airport is located 21 miles (34km) west of downtown Toronto, and is easily accessible from highways 401, 409, and 427. It takes between a half hour and and an hour to reach from the city, depending on traffic, with the usual workday rush-hour times being most difficult.

The airport's peak times are 7-9:30am and 3-8pm. Travelers leaving for the U.S. will go through U.S. Border pre-clearance right in Pearson (operated by the U.S. Customs & Border Protection Service), so make sure you leave extra time for that process (about two hours is recommended). Once you've cleared customs, you'll enter a "transborder zone" in the airport, considered the legal equivalent of being on U.S. soil. The best thing about it is, of course, that you save all that time and hassle once you've landed since your flight is treated as a domestic arrival.

Sadly, improved facilities haven't included a lot of shopping, with an array of the usual traveler-oriented and touristy Canadiana goods all that is on offer. More shopping and dining is in the works, now that the renos are done, but for the time being, exceptions are few, and include Occhiali da Sole,

Flying Times to Toronto

Nonstop From	Airport Code	Time (hr.)
Boston	BOS	1½
Chicago	ORD	1½
London	LHR	7
Los Angeles	LAX	5½
Miami	MIZ	3½
Montreal	YUL	1
New York	JFK	1½
San Francisco	SFO	5
Vancouver	YVR	5
Washington, D.C.	IAD	1½

Airlines Serving Pearson International Airport

Airline	Website	800 Number	Terminal
Aeroflot Russia	aeroflot.com	416-642-1653	3
Aeromexico	aeromexico.com	800-237-6639	3
Air Canada	aircanada.ca	888-247-2262	
(International and domestic and transborder flights to U.S.)			1
Air Canada Jazz	flyjazz.ca	800-315-1390	
(Domestic and transborder flights to U.S.)			1
Air France	airfrance.us	800-667-2747	3
Air Jamaica	airjamaica.com	800-523-5585	1
Alitalia	alitalia.ca	800-361-8336	1
Air India	airindia.com	800-223-7776	3
All Nippon Airways	fly-ana.com	800-235-9262	1
America West Airlines	americawest.com	800-235-9292	3
American Airlines	aa.com	800-433-7300	3
Austrian Airlines	austrianair.com	888-817-4444	1
British Airways	britishairways.com	888-334-3448	3
BWIA West Indies Airways	bwee.com	800-538-2942	3
Cathay Pacific	cathaypacific.com	888-338-1668	3
Continental Airlines	continental.com	800-784-4444,	3
Cubana Airlines	cubana.cu	416-967-2822	3
Czech Airlines	canada.csa.cz/en/northamerica/us_home.htm	416-363-3174	3
Delta	delta.com	800-221-1212	3
EL AL	elal.co.il	800-361-6174	3
Finnair	finnair.com	800-950-5000	3
Iberia Airlines	iberia.com	800-772-4642	3
Japan Airlines	japanair.com	800-525-3663	3
KLM	klm.com	905-612-0556	3
Korean Air	koreanair.com	800-438-5000	3
LOT Polish Airlines	lot.com	800-668-5928	3
Lufthansa	lufthansa.com	800-563-5954	1
Mexicana	mexicana.com	905-612-8250	1
Northwest Airlines	nwa.com	800-441-1818	3
Olympic Airlines SA	olympicairlines.com	905-676-4841	3
Pakistan International	piac.com.pk	905-677-9479	3
Qantas	qantas.com	800-227-4500	3
SAS Scandinavian Airlines	sas.se	800-221-2350	1
Singapore Airlines	singaporeair.com	800-387-0038	1
Swiss Air Lines	swiss.com	877-359-7947	3
Thai Airways	thaiairways.com	800-426-5204	1
United Airlines	united.com	800-241-6522	1
US Airways	usairways.com	800-943-5436	3
Zoom Airlines	flyzoom.com	866-359-9666	3

HIT THE GROUND

Rental Cars: If you're picking up a car at Pearson Airport, you can do so on the first and/or the basement level of the Terminal 1 parking garage, and/or on the ground level of the parking garages in Terminal 3.

Agency	Website	800 Number	Local Number
Alamo	alamo.com	800-462-5266	905-676-2647
Avis	avis.com	800-879-2847	905-676-1032
Budget	budgettoronto.com	800-561-5212	905-676-1500
Discount/ ACE	discountcar.com	800-259-1638	416-249-5800
Dollar	dollar.com	800-667-2925	905-673-8811
Enterprise	enterprise.com	800-736-8222	416-798-1465
Hertz Canada	hertz.com	800-263-0600	416-674-2020
National	nationalcar.com	800-227-7368	905-676-2647
Thrifty	thrifty.com	800-367-2277	905-673-8811

Luxury

- The Car Rental Place   carrentalplace.com   416-787-0209
  3219 Dufferin St.
  For Jaguar, Porsche, Corvette, and BMW.
- GTA Exotics   gtaexotics.ca   416-253-2180
  1049 The Queensway
  For Porsche, Ferrari, Lamborghini, motorcycles, and more.

a designer sunglass boutique, in Terminal 3; Lush Handmade Cosmetics in Terminal 1; and Roots Canada, hip supplier of casual and especially cool outerwear, in both Terminals 1 and 3. There are duty-free shops in Terminal 1, and in T3 at all departure levels, both pre- and post security.

Perhaps the best new idea to come along in a while is the Made to Fly program, where you can purchase a meal from participating restaurants, packed for travel, to replace airline food. In Terminal 1 you'll find Made to Fly meals post security, around the bridge to level 2. The Arts & Letters Bistro has superior salads and soups, and sushi for something different in flight, and if you want a decent full-menu, sit-down meal before you go, this is the place. The Zyng Noodlery, part of the Kensington Market multicultural food emporium, has noodle bowls, dumplings, and even pad Thai on offer. In Terminal 3, pre-security at the Departures level, you'll find gourmet pizza at Wolfgang Puck Marketplace, or superior made-to-order sandwiches and burgers (including chicken and veggie) at the Yorkville Grille. After you pass through U.S. border pre-clearance, Friday's American Bar has decent take-out, and the cocktails are well mixed if you want to indulge while you wait. If you'd rather escape the airport environment entirely for a sit-down meal, and you're in Terminal 3, scuttle down the climate-controlled walkway to the Sheraton Gateway Hotel, connected to the terminal, where the lounge serves up a nice bistro-style menu in more stylish and relaxed surroundings.

If the weather's good and you have some time on your hands, make the trip to see Art Stage (artstage.ca), an outdoor exhibit of sculptures overlooking the highway from the airport grounds.

Into Town by Taxi: Flat-rate limo or cab fares to downtown are about C$40. and you'll find plenty of drivers waiting for your business in clearly marked areas just outside the arrivals area. You can also try Aerofleet Limousine Services, 905-678-7077 / 800-268-0905.

Into Town by Airport Shuttle Service: Pacific Western Airport Express (905-564-6333 / 800-387-6787, torontoairportexpress.com) operates a regular shuttle service to and from downtown. The bus picks up on the Arrivals Level of Terminal 3, and at Terminal 1 on the Arrivals Level—post B3. All buses are wheelchair accessible and also have front kneeling doors for easier access, and you can get to and from several of the major downtown hotels. Fare is $16.45 one way, $28.35 return.

Into Town by Public Transit: Toronto Transit Commission (TTC) combined bus and subway fare is C$2.75, and provides a number of routes. The 192 Airport Rocket route offers all-day (5:30am to 2:00am) accessible express bus service (only three stops on the way) between the Kipling Station (Bloor-Danforth Subway line) and Pearson Airport, with stops at Terminal 3 at the Arrivals area, and Terminal 1 at ground level. The one-way trip is about 20 minutes. Check toronto.ca/ttc/service_to_airport.htm for additional routes.

Into Town by Car: Theoretically, the drive from Pearson to the downtown core takes about half an hour, but if you're anywhere near the busy, busy workday, expect that time to about double or more. The route takes you south on Highway 427 to the Gardiner Expressway.

Toronto City Centre Airport
416-203-6942, torontoport.com/Airport.asp

Located on the western tip of the Toronto Islands, the island airport handles scheduled, private, and corporate flights. Major airlines include Air Ontario, Trans Capital Airlines, and Grand Aviation.

HIT THE GROUND

Toronto Buttonville Airport

905-477-8100, torontoairways.com

Buttonville Airport is used mainly for flight training, but you can also arrange spectacular aerial sightseeing tours.

Getting to Toronto: By Land

By Car: Highways 2 and 401 and the Queen Elizabeth Way (QEW) enter Toronto from the west. The QEW connects to New York State through Niagara, and Highway 401 connects to Michigan in the west through Windsor and Sarnia, and to the east to New York State at various points. Of the three, Highway 2 is the most scenic route, running along the shores of Lake Ontario. Highway 401 is part of the TransCanada Highway, and runs from the Atlantic to the Pacific coasts. The QEW and Highway 403 (which connects to the QEW

Driving Times to Toronto

From	Distance (mi./km.)	Approx. Time (hr.)
Boston	550/885	9
Chicago	540/870	8
Detroit	230/370	4
Miami	1,530/2,460	24
Montreal	335/540	6
New York	495/800	8
Washington, D.C.	560/900	9

west of Toronto) also connect at various points with Highway 407, a toll road. The 407 runs north of Highway 401, so it's not a good way to get downtown but can be an excellent alternative for getting to the airport. Your license plate will be read electronically as you enter the toll portion of the road, and a bill will then be mailed to your registered address. As an alternative to the often congested 401 or QEW, it can't be beat, but the 407 has the dubious distinction of being the most expensive toll road in the continent. A ride from its western end to Pearson International Airport will run you about C$10.

By Train: Toronto is served by the VIA Rail System (viarail.ca), with connections to the Amtrak system through Niagara Falls to New York City. Union Station is located on Front Street, between Bay and University. The station is connected to Toronto's subway line and GO Transit services.

By Water: Toronto offers docking facilities and complete services for boaters. For information on harbor facilities, call the Toronto Port Authority at 416-863-2000.

Toronto: Lay of the Land

The city of Toronto sits on sedimentary rock, at the eastern edge of the Carolinian Forest zone on the northwestern shore of Lake Ontario. Its sprawling 398 square miles (641 square km) cover a broad, sloping plateau cut by numerous rivers and creeks. The shoreline of Lake Ontario runs along 26 miles (43km) as the crow flies, and is the lowest part of the city. The land rises as you head north, to its highest point in the northwest part of the city, at the intersection of Steeles Avenue and Keele Street.

That basic geography—and the world's tallest structure, sitting right there on the lakeshore—makes Toronto one of the easiest places to find your way around, even if you're a first-time visitor. Just remember that lake equals south, and uphill equals north, and you've got the basics covered. Nothing in the downtown area is far from that CN Tower, with the west end traditionally a hip, artsy hot spot, the north end home to the rich and famous (uphill is upmarket in Toronto,) and the east end home to the Distillery District, and farther still, the more laid-back Beaches.

Yonge Street cuts through the heart of downtown, and is the basic mark for east-west divisions. Most major streets follow a grid pattern, with long, major roads traveling north-south, and often smaller, often one-way streets traveling east-west.

Getting Around Toronto

By Car: Over a million people come into downtown Toronto each weekday to work, leaving by the dinner hour. You can check out the city of Toronto's traffic cams at any time at city.toronto.on.ca/rescu. If you're still mad enough to want to drive around the city, here's a quick lowdown. The speed limit on city streets is 30 miles per hour (50km per hour) unless otherwise noted. Be forewarned that many of the streets that run east-west are one-way. In principle, right turns are allowed on red lights, but you'd be wise to check the signage indicating which turns are restricted. It is common for most corners to be restricted downtown, with no left turns allowed. You can follow the streetcars, but be careful to observe the no-passing rule while the doors are open. A provincial law requires motorists to yield the right of way to a public transit vehicle that is changing lanes.

Parking: There's no getting around the fact that parking in downtown Toronto is a hassle. First, you have to find it, and second, it doesn't come cheap.

HIT THE GROUND

The least expensive option will be street parking, with meter machines located on each block that allows parking where you purchase a ticket to place on your windshield—and gamblers beware, those who issue tickets for the city of Toronto are among the most vigilant timekeepers you'll ever find! The ticket-issuing meters will accept coins or credit cards. Two-hour limits are common up till 6pm, when it may stretch to three hours, with $1.50 an hour a common rate. Parking in the busiest areas of downtown and along thoroughfares is generally restricted between 4pm and 6pm. Hot tip: check for areas where you don't pay at all after 6pm, including Spadina south of King, and if you're out for the evening, try venturing a block or two away from the busy streets to residential areas, where parking is also often unrestricted in the evenings.

Parking Garages

Parking in the city is run by the Greater Toronto Parking Authority, that green P logo you'll find all over town (greenp.com). Here are some of the bigger parking garages in the downtown area:

- Downtown: Carpark 34—Dundas Square Garage (25 Dundas St. E.)

- Lakeshore area: Carpark 32—Bay Street, Lakeshore Blvd. W (45 Bay St.)

- St. Lawrence Market: Carpark 43—St. Lawrence Garage (2 Church St.)

- Entertainment District: Carpark 52—University Avenue Garage (40 York St.)

- Downtown/Financial District: Carpark 36—Nathan Phillips Square Garage (110 Queen St. W.)

- Downtown: Carpark 26—Queen-Victoria Garage (37 Queen St. E.)

By Public Transit: The Toronto Transit Commission (TTC; city.toronto.on.ca/ttc) offers reliable and frequent transport around the city in three different forms—subway, bus, and streetcar. In an integrated network, one fare of C$2.75 can take you from subway to streetcar to bus and back, all the way from the lakeshore to north of Highway 401, east-west from Etobicoke to Scarborough, with transfers beyond to suburbia. Subways run from about 6am, buses and streetcars from about 5am, seven days a week, with service until 1:30am six days a week and reduced services on Sundays. The Blue Night Network, marked at stops with reflective blue bands, runs all night from 1:30am until 5am. A day pass is C$8.50, weekly pass for $30, five tokens for C$10.50.

By Train: The Toronto area is served by an excellent commuter train service—the GO (gotransit.com)—with conjoining bus service that serves
areas well beyond the city limits. Lakeshore service runs from Hamilton
in the west to Pickering in the east, with buses from Union Station to
Newmarket and parts farther north. Most trips originate from downtown
Union Station.

By Taxi:Several cab companies serve the downtown area and well beyond.
You can hail a cab from virtually any downtown street. Taxis typically
congregate around the hotels, and will be lined up on Front Street in
front of Union Station, and at major hotels. Rates are metered and non-
negotiable, but be sure to check out your "Passengers' Bill of Rights,"
which should be clearly posted. These cab companies routinely serve
the downtown area:

• Beck Taxi, 416-449-6911

• Diamond Taxi, 416-366-6868

Other Practical Information

Money Matters (Currency, Taxes, Tipping, and Service Charges): Canadian currency uses dollars and cents (100 cents to the dollar), with $1 and $2
coins and bills for $5 denominations and higher. U.S. dollars are accept-
ed at most businesses, with change, including the exchange premium,
typically returned in Canadian funds. You'll find currency exchange houses all over the downtown area, but you'll get the best rates at any one of
Canada's five chartered banks.

Taxes are levied on goods and services at two levels of government, 8 percent at the provincial level and an additional 5 percent in a federal tax called
the GST. The good news is that for-
eign visitors to Canada can apply for a
rebate on the GST that is paid on
accommodations of up to 30 nights
per visit, and on goods purchased in
Canada and taken out of the country
within 60 days of the purchase. Be
sure to keep your receipts, as you'll
need to have them validated by
Canada Customs at the airport or border crossing when you leave.

Metric Conversion

From	To	Multiply by
Inches	Centimeters	2.54
Yards	Meters	0.91
Miles	Kilometers	1.60
Gallons	Liters	3.79
Ounces	Grams	28.35
Pounds	Kilograms	0.45

For more information about the visitors' tax refund and to obtain an application form, check out the website at cra.gc.ca/visitors or call 800-668-4748 (within Canada) or 902-432-5608 (from outside Canada).

The following companies can facilitate the tax rebate process for a fee, so that you can arrange to receive a cash refund before you leave Canadian soil.

• Global Refund, 905-791-9099, globalrefund.ca

• Premiere Tax-Free Services (Canada), 905-270-2702, taxfree-services.ca

Expect to tip taxi drivers, bar and restaurant servers 15 to 20 percent, and hotel housekeepers $3 or more per day.

Safety: Toronto is one of the safest big cities you'll ever visit anywhere in the world, but a commonsense approach is nonetheless advisable. Use caution in the downtown area, and avoid deserted streets and alleys. With its burgeoning nightlife scene, Toronto has also seen an increase in violent incidents on the weekends, typically centered around closing time at the clubs, so take extra care when you go out for the evening.

Gay and Lesbian Travel: When Canada became the third country in the world to recognize gay and lesbian marriages, it definitely made Toronto a hot spot with GLBT travelers, but with an urban gay, lesbian, bisexual, and transgender population second only to San Francisco's, Toronto has long been a tolerant travel destination. You'll find a wealth of gay-friendly nightclubs and venues well beyond the Gay Village area (centered around Church and Wellesley Streets), particularly in Little Italy. Pick up a copy of *Fab*, the city's gay lifestyle magazine, and pay a visit to the publishers—who also own Hair of the Dog Pub—or check out Fly Nightclub, where they filmed the clubbing scenes for *Queer as Folk*. Toronto's Pride Week is a huge tourist draw for both gays and straights, a veritable city institution along with Caribana. Downtown crowds are very mixed, and you'll find Toronto's much-vaunted tolerance in full force. Check out gaytorontotourism.com for the inside scoop.

Traveling with Disabilities: Disabled travelers will find Toronto a friendly and mainly accommodating city, with even many of the older buildings and attractions made accessible. New facilities at Pearson International Airport are barrier free.

You'll find guides to facilities for disabled people through the Canadian Paraplegic Association, whose national office is in Ottawa. You can contact them directly at 800-720-4933, or through canparaplegic.org.

Radio Stations (a selection)

FM Stations

88.5	CKDX	Unforgettable Hits (Sinatra to Rod Stewart)
88.9	CIRV	Multicultural/Dance Mix
91.1	CJRT	Jazz
91.7	CFUK	Country
92.5	CKIS	Eclectic Hits
93.5	CFXJ	Hip-Hop, R&B
94.1	CBLT	(Radio 2) Classical (Public Broadcaster)
96.3	CFMX	Classical
97.3	CJEZ	Soft Rock
98.1	CHFI	Soft Rock
99.1	CBCS	(Radio One) Public Broadcaster, Various
99.9	CKFM	Contemporary Hits
102.1	CFNY	Alternative Rock
103.5	CIDC	Rock
104.5	CHUM	Adult Contemporary
107.1	CILQ	Classic Rock

AM Stations

590	CJCL	Sports
680	CFTR	All News
740	CHWO	Nostalgia
1010	CFRB	Talk
1050	CHUM	Talk, Oldies
1280	CFYZ	Travel and Airport Information
1540	CHIN	Multinational, Multilingual

Print Media: Torontonians are served by no fewer than four daily newspapers, two city and two national, all of which are published in the city. *The Toronto Star* (torontostar.com) is venerable and slightly left-leaning, with an emphasis on city politics and meaty culture and arts sections even during the week. *The Toronto Sun* (torontosun.com) is its tabloid and right-leaning counterpart, heavy on entertainment, sports, and slightly salacious features. *The Globe & Mail* (globeandmail.com) is a weighty national rag, considered conservative and business oriented, with the *National Post* (nationalpost.com) a more recent challenger to its absolute authority in the financial pages. All four produce thick weekend editions both Saturdays and Sundays.

In addition, there are two tabloid-style weeklies that specialize in entertainment and alternative news reporting, *NOW* magazine (nowtoronto.com) and *eye* magazine (eye.net). Both contain extensive arts and entertainment listings, including current schedules for live music and nightclubs, galleries, and shows, along with restaurant reviews and city news.

HIT THE GROUND

Toronto Life (torontolife.com) is a stylish lifestyle magazine that takes a highbrow look at the city, its people, its dining and entertainment scene, and much more.

Shopping Hours: Most stores are open 10am to 5pm from Monday to Wednesday, and 10am to 9pm Thursday and Friday. Typical Saturday hours run from 10am to 6pm, and Sunday virtually all retail and specialty outlets are also open from noon to 5pm.Most stores are open 10am to 5pm from Monday to Wednesday, and 10 am to 9pm Thursday and Friday. Typical Saturday hours run from 10am to 6pm, and Sunday virtually all retail and specialty outlets are also open from noon till 5pm.

Size Conversion

Dress Sizes

US/Can.	6	8	10	12	14	16
France	36	38	40	42	44	46
Italy	38	40	42	44	46	48
Europe	34	36	38	40	42	44

Women's Shoes

US/Can.	6	6½	7	7½	8	8½
Europe	38	38	39	39	40	41

Men's Suits

US/Can.	36	38	40	42	44	46
UK	36	38	40	42	44	46
Europe	46	48	50	52	54	56

Men's Shirts

US/Can.	14½	15	15½	16	16½	17
UK	14½	15	15½	16	16½	17
Europe.	38	39	40	41	42	43

Men's Shoes

US/Can.	8	8½	9½	10½	11½	12
Europe	41	42	43	44	45	46

Attire: Its lakeside location means Toronto's weather is variable, so layers are advisable no matter what time of year you visit. In summer, the heat may be scorching during the day, but evenings can be cool, so always bring a sweater. In the winter, make sure you have proper footwear, including weatherproof boots, and bundle up in layers along with gloves, hat, and scarf if you plan to be outside for any length of time. Spring and fall are the most variable seasons, and it's essential that you at least have a good rain jacket and umbrella on hand.

Torontonians' dress habits depend largely on the neighborhood. Canadians in general are fairly casual in dress, and often sport jeans and T-shirts. But downtown, you'll find a distinct emphasis on fashion, whether it's in the form of conservative but classy designer suits in the Financial District or chic head-to-toe black on Richmond Street West. High-end restaurants may have a "casual" dress code, but if so, the jeans are $500 designer duds, not department-store specials. On Queen Street West, the black uniform often includes black hair dye and fingernails, and funky, artsy accessories. The Entertainment District is

Numbers to Know (Hotlines)

Emergency, police, fire department, ambulance
and paramedics   911

Poison Control

24-Hour Assaulted Women's Helpline   416-863-0511

24-Hour Mental Health Crisis Lines   416-598-1121 / 416-486-1456

Travelers Aid International   416-366-7788

  Terminal 1   905-676-2868

  Terminal 2   905-626-2869

  Terminal 3   416-776-5890

24-Hour Emergency Rooms

- Mount Sinai Hospital,
  600 University Ave. (between College and Dundas)   416-596-4200

- St. Joseph's Health Centre,
  30 The Queensway (west end of town)   416-530-6000

- St. Michael's Hospital,
  30 Bond St. (right downtown near the Eaton's Centre) 416-360-4000

- Toronto Hospital General Division, 200 Elizabeth St. 416-340-3111
  (near College and University)

24-Hour Shopper's Drug Mart Pharmacy

- Lucliff Place
  700 Bay St.   416-979-2424

HIT THE GROUND

designer hip during the day and competitive Clubland at night, so dress to the nines in your clubby best. Local oddity: you'll find the scantily clad club-goers wandering Clubland in the dead of winter with no coat or jacket—just gets in the way, don't ya know. And definitely dress up a bit in stylish Little Italy. From the Old Town to the groovy Beaches, the city east of Yonge is more casual in tone. But midtown to the Bloor/Yorkville area and into posh North Toronto (where many of the city's wealthiest citizens live), it's all about being chic and fashionable—and flaunting it.

When Drinking Is Legal: The legal drinking age in the Province of Ontario is 19, although you'll find some clubs with a "mature clientele" policy restricting entrance to those 25 and older.

Smoking: As of May 31, 2006, the Smoke Free Ontario Act makes smoking in all restaurants, bars, public places, and work spaces in the entire Province of Ontario illegal, including enclosed patios (those with a roof). You'll find that many bars will have some sort of outdoor area where you can indulge.

Drugs: Yes, relative to many countries in the world, Canada's drug laws seem lax, and yes, particularly and famously in connection with a certain green weed, and yes, you will certainly find it at night clubs and may well catch a whiff of it in the air here and there throughout town, but travelers are well advised to stay away from what is still illegal and will cause foreign nationals to be deported.

Time Zone: Toronto falls within the eastern standard time zone (EST). About daylight saving time: Clocks are set ahead one hour at 2am on the second Sunday in March and set back one hour at 2am on the first Sunday in November. It means the daylight lasts till 9pm or later in mid-summer, and that evening will roll in about 6pm or earlier in mid-winter.

Additional Resources for Visitors

Toronto Convention & Visitors Association/Tourism Toronto
This friendly agency can provide information about member events, attractions, transportation services, shopping, hotels, and entertainment, including package tours and much more. Open Mon-Fri 8:30am-6pm, Sat 10am-4pm. 207 Queen's Quay, 416-203-2600 / 800-499-2514, tourismtoronto.com

Toronto Board of Trade
Founded in 1845, the Board of Trade is Canada's largest local chamber of commerce, serving over 10,000 members and operating the World Trade Centre Toronto. Open Mon-Fri 10am-5pm. Downtown Centre, 1 First Canadian Pl., 416-366-6811, bot.com

Foreign Visitors

Foreign Embassies in Canada: While Ottawa is the nation's capital, Toronto is the capital of Ontario, its most populous province, and the city is home to more than 25 embassies, consulates, and High Commissions. See embassiesabroad.com for a listing. The US Consulate's website is amcits.com/toronto.asp.

Passport requirements: cbsa-asfc.gc.ca/travel/visitors-e.html

Cell phones: North America operates on the 1,900MHz frequency. For cell phone rentals and purchases, try helloanywhere.com, located near the downtown core.

Wireless: wirelesstoronto.ca is a not-for-profit group dedicated to bringing no-fee wireless Internet access (Wi-Fi) to the city. Yonge-Dundas Square, in the heart of downtown, is a Wi-Fi hot spot (1 Dundas St. E, ydsquare.ca, 416-979-9960). Check Wireless Toronto's website for a growing list of Wi-Fi locations throughout town.

Toll-free numbers in Canada: 800, 866, 877, and 888.

Telephone directory assistance in Canada: 411.

Electrical: North American standard is AC, 110 volts/60 cycles, with a plug of two flat pins set parallel to one another.

The Latest-Info Websites

Go to toronto.com, city.toronto.on.ca, thestar.com.
And, of course, check out **pulseguides.com**.

HIT THE GROUND

Party Conversation—A Few Surprising Facts

- Considered "Hollywood North" by the film industry, Toronto ranks fourth in North American TV and film production. Among the more noteworthy films shot here were *Chicago* (in the Distillery District) and the adaptation of *Hairspray*, and television series *Queer as Folk* was filmed here—Fly nightclub stood in for a New York dance club.

- Toronto is the fifth-largest city in North America.

- The Toronto Blue Jays were the first major league baseball team to win the World Championship consecutively in 1992 and 1993.

- Long before the Blue Jays, legendary player Babe Ruth hit his first professional home run in Toronto on September 5, 1914, playing in the minor league AAA team for the Providence Grays. The game was played in the Island Stadium, which used to stand on Hanlan's Point on Toronto Island, and the ball ended up in the bay.

- One-quarter of Canada's population is located within 100 miles (160km) of Toronto, or to look at it another way, about eight per cent of Canada's population lives within the city limits.

- Some of the world's favorite comedians hail from Toronto. Mike Myers based his *Wayne's World* shtick on his teenage years in Scarborough in the city's East End. Superstar Jim Carrey hails from just west of the city limits, and legendary *Saturday Night Live* producer Lorne Michaels is a Toronto native.

- Ernest Hemingway freelanced for the *Toronto Star* just after WWI, and he was on assignment for the *Star* when he returned to Europe in 1921.

- Gooderham & Worts—the "Distillery" in the Distillery District—was the largest distillery in the British Empire in the mid to late 1800s.

- Joe Shuster, creator of Superman, was born in Toronto in 1914, and although he moved to Cleveland ten years later, the *Daily Planet* was originally called the *Daily Star*, after Toronto's venerable *Toronto Star* newspaper, and he said the city of Metropolis was modeled after Toronto.

The Cheat Sheet
(The Very Least You Ought to Know
About Toronto)

Don't look like a tourist! Have more fun and be in the know with this handy countdown of essential Toronto facts and figures.

Neighborhoods

The Beaches This is Toronto's laid-back antidote to the hustle and bustle of downtown and the Financial District. This neighborhood is defined by Queen Street East, a charming and quirky strip of shops and restaurants, as well as the pebbly beaches of Lake Ontario.

Bloor/Yorkville This neighborhood is centered around the intersection of Bloor and Avenue Road, though the chic designer boutiques stretch all the way east along Bloor to Yonge Street, and north to Davenport. In the 1960s, Yorkville was the epicenter of Toronto's hippie counterculture. It's since transformed itself into the place to get designer clothing.

Chinatown and Kensington Market These two areas thrive side by side west of downtown, both constantly bustling with activity. Chinatown offers an intriguing array of Asian restaurants and stores, along with fresh food markets streetside. Just to the north, Kensington Market has been the gateway to Toronto for immigrants for over a century.

Downtown The heart of Toronto is centered along Yonge Street. In the 1970s, it had degenerated into a sleazy run of strip bars and peep shows, with a few hardy retailers. But the sleaze was cleaned out and the big-name retailers moved in, anchored by the huge Eaton's Centre.

Entertainment District/Clubland/Theatre District Back in the 1980s, a few impresarios saw the potential for live theater in the city. In 1993, the Mirvish empire constructed the Princess of Wales Theatre to show what seemed like an endless run of *Phantom of the Opera*. It began the transformation of the area west of Yonge Street into the entertainment hub it is today.

Greektown is centered along Danforth Avenue between Chester and Jones Avenues to the east of downtown. It's is the largest Greek neighborhood in North America.

Harbourfront Toronto's waterfront was at one time home to industrial and utilitarian uses, and the people's reclamation of the city's beautiful natural setting on Lake Ontario is still a work in progress. Theme park Ontario Place really established the Harbourfront as a people-friendly place. You can catch a ferry to the Toronto Islands or hop on a tour boat, and there's always something going on at the Harbourfront Centre for the Arts.

Little Italy This has become a distinct part of the city since the early 1950s, when waves of European immigrants arrived after World War II. With them came a little warmth to counterbalance Toronto's cool Wasp culture—and the city's first sidewalk cafes. The result today is a neighborhood of clubs and restaurants where the hip and beautiful come to play.

St. Lawrence/Old Town/Cabbagetown East of downtown, the venerable St. Lawrence Market has been feeding hungry Torontonians for two centuries. The city grew up around this landmark, and you'll find traces of Victorian and even pre-Victorian architecture, as well as some of the city's best restaurants and clubs.

West Queen West Queen Street West has its own funky appeal starting at the first blocks west of Yonge Street, but it's the area west of Bathurst, dubbed West Queen West, that's really hip. Anchored by the fabulous renovations of the Drake Hotel and the Gladstone, and the Museum of Contemporary Canadian Art (MOCCA), Queen West is home to art galleries and artists' studios, eclectic vintage and designer clothing stores, and clubs and bohemian restaurants.

9   Performing Arts Venues

Buddies in Bad Times Theatre A historic building that has undergone a funky renovation, it's home to one of the world's biggest and best gay and lesbian theater companies. 12 Alexander St., 416-975-8555, buddiesinbadtimestheatre.com

Canon Theatre A plush historic 2,200-seat venue for theater and the performing arts, the Canon began its life in 1920 in the vaudeville circuit, and these days it puts on popular stage shows like the Blue Man Group. 244 Victoria St., 416-364-4100, mirvish.com

Elgin/Winter Garden Theatre A gorgeous and historic double-decker theater that's been packing in the audiences since the days of vaudeville, both the Elgin and Winter Garden venues continue to be home to live theater and musical productions, with a sumptuous interior spectacular enough to visit for its own sake. 189 Yonge St., 416-597-0965, heritagefdn.on.ca

Hummingbird Centre for the Performing Arts An elegant 3,100-seat multipurpose venue that hosts performances from ballet to opera to jazz. 1 Front St. E., 416-393-7469, hummingbirdcentre.com

Massey Hall The grand old lady of Toronto concert halls, Massey Hall is still used today as a venue mainly for musical performances and a favorite of the artists for its intimate atmosphere. There are virtually no bad seats. 178 Victoria St., 416-872-4255, masseyhall.com

Molson Amphitheatre A huge outdoor concert venue that's part of the lakeside festivities at Ontario Place, the Amphitheatre offers both protected and open-air seating, and is a favorite venue for large-scale rock concerts and traveling musical extravaganzas. 909 Lakeshore Blvd. W., 416-260-5600, ontarioplace.com/en/amphitheatre/amphitheatre.html

Princess of Wales Theatre A striking modern venue for theatrical performances, decorated in 10,000 square feet of murals by noted contemporary artist Frank Stella. 300 King St. W., 416-872-1212, mirvish.com

Four Seasons Centre for the Performing Arts Home to the Canadian Opera Company and the highly acclaimed National Ballet, this new world-class opera house features state-of-the-art acoustical engineering and a suspended walkway with a panoramic view. 145 Queen St. W., 416-363-6671, fourseasonscentre.ca

Roy Thompson Hall An impressive concert and performance hall, featuring Canada's Walk of Fame on the sidewalk out front, including impressions from celebrity greats like Jim Carrey and Shania Twain. Roy Thompson is the preferred venue for Film Festival galas and other big events. 60 Simcoe St., 416-872-4255, roythompson.com

City Parks

Ashbridge's Bay Consisting of 300 acres of waterfront, Ashbridge's Bay is located on Lakeshore Boulevard east of Coxwell Avenue, and includes a mile or so of hiking trails, beaches, and fishing. Access from Lakeshore Boulevard.

Cloud Forest Conservatory Located on top of a parking garage, this indoor garden conservatory is bright and airy. Richmond Street at Temperance (just west of Yonge), 416-392-7288, toronto.ca/parks/parks_gardens/bayadelaidegdns.htm.

High Park With 400 acres of tree-filled parkland, (over one-third of it in its natural state), at Bloor Street West and Parkside Drive in the West End, this park is home to the historic Colborne Lodge and hosts outdoor Shakespearean productions (canstage.com), and the Scream Literary Festival (thescream.ca) in the summer, a hugely popular spoken-word event.

Kew Gardens Located right in the heart of the Beaches neighborhood at 2075 Queen Street East, this lovely park hosts the lively Beaches Jazz Festival, along with several other fairs and concerts during the summer months.

Marilyn Bell Park This park follows the shoreline of Lake Ontario in the city's West End and was named after the first person to swim the lake from New York State to Toronto in 1954. You can enter only from Lakeshore Boulevard.

Roundhouse Park A historic patch of green on Bremner Boulevard, in the shadow of the CN Tower and home to the Steamwhistle Brewing Company, this small park gets a visit from virtually every tourist to the city as a vantage point for pics of the ubiquitous Tower, but Steamwhistle's tours may be its hidden gem.

Toronto Island Park There are 569 acres of beaches (including clothing optional at the southern point of Hanlan's Point), and green parklands on the Toronto Islands, with bicycle and boat rentals available.

Trinity Square West of the Eaton's Centre on Yonge Street and south of Dundas, this urban park contains Toronto's only labyrinth, 77 feet in diameter and created as a millennium project.

HIT THE GROUND

Streets

Bathurst Street The official boundary of the city's West End, Bathurst is de facto home to Toronto's Jewish community.

Bay Street This is the heart of the city's bustling Financial District, replete with glass towers and upscale restaurants for the CEO set.

Bloor Street The chic dividing line between downtown and uptown, home to designer boutiques and the gateway to fab Yorkville at Avenue Road. Farther west, Bloor takes you through the Annex, a stylish neighborhood of Victorian townhomes, then farther west still to a scene of trendy lounges and restaurants.

Danforth Avenue Known to locals as simply "the Danforth," it's the home of Greektown and a legendary restaurant and nightclub scene with an unmistakable Mediterranean flavor. It's one of the major arteries in the East End area of town.

Queen Street The coolest street in Toronto, from its laid-back beginnings east at the Beaches, through the Financial District to its West End persona of art galleries and nighttime hot spots.

Richmond Street By day, Richmond is the busy center for fashion and design businesses, and by night it becomes the center of Clubland.

Yonge Street The heart of downtown, Yonge begins at the shores of Lake Ontario and the famous Toronto Star building at number 1. Heading north—or uphill—in Toronto is climbing the social ladder, with some very high-end real estate.

Retail Centers

Atrium on Bay The atrium draws natural light from the height of this skyscraper to the galleria of 50 shops, services, and restaurants. A nice escape in the Financial District. 20 Dundas W., 416-595-1957, atriumonbay.com

BCE Place Includes the airy Allen Lambert Galleria and a second floor devoted to dining establishments and more than 30 shops and services. 161-181 Bay St., 416-777-6480, bceplace.com

Chinatown Centre A shopping mall with an Asian flavor, where you can buy all manner of imported Chinese goods. Located—where else?—in the heart of Chinatown. 222 Spadina Ave., 416-599-8877

Eaton's Centre A huge landmark shopping center, featuring Michael Snow's famous sculptures of Canada geese, along with more than 285 shops and services. Here's a place for shopaholics to indulge till they're bleary eyed. 220 Yonge St., 416-598-8700, torontoeatoncentre.com

Hazelton Lanes Canada's most expensive mall, rife with designer boutiques and high-end goodies, where you may bump into Hollywood royalty. 55 Avenue Rd., 416-968-8680, hazeltonlanes.com

Vaughan Mills Mall Canada's largest outlet mall, located north of the city in Vaughan, with an entertainment complex offering movie theaters, and, as they say, much, much more. 1 Bass Pro Mills Dr. (Vaughan), 905-879-2110, vaughanmills.com

Pro-Sport Teams

Argonauts of the Canadian Football League Its 18-week season of high-flying three-down football runs from exhibition games in June to the championship Grey Cup in late November. This is the league that gave a start to football greats Doug Flutie, Warren Moon and Jeff Garcia, among others, and the ever-hot "Argos" last won the Grey Cup in 2004. 416-341-2700, argonauts.ca

Blue Jays of Major League Baseball It is the only team to have won consecutive World Series in 1992 and 1993, the Jays games are typically a hot ticket. 416-341-1000, bluejays.ca

Maple Leafs of the National Hockey League For hockey afficionados, they are one of the legendary "Original Six." You'll find the local fans devoted, and tickets, as well as ticket prices, at a premium. The city is overcome with playoff fever at playoff time, and you'll find virtually every TV screen in every bar in town following the games if the Leafs make it to the big one. 416-872-5000, torontomapleleafs.com

Raptors of the National Basketball Association This team offers a fast-paced game and high-flying athletics. Hockey is the undisputed king in this town, but the Raptors have made inroads by appealing to younger fans with a great game experience and a talented roster of cheerleaders. 416-366-3865, nba.com/raptors

The Rock of the National Lacrosse League These guys offer an action-packed game that's value priced, routinely packing in crowds of 10,000-plus in a highly competitive North American league. 416-596-3075, torontorock.com

Famous People Who Attended North Toronto Collegiate Institute

David Cronenberg This filmmaker loves to disturb as he entertains with features like 1983's *Videodrome* and *The Dead Zone*, 1986's *The Fly*, 1991's *Naked Lunch*, or most recently, *A History of Violence* (2005).

Roger Paul Neilson The legendary NHL coach was responsible for many innovations in professional hockey, and left his mark on the game after coaching in Buffalo, Vancouver, Los Angeles, New York, Florida, Philadelphia, and Ottawa.

Keanu Reeves *Matrix* made him famous, but long before that, the star of *Bill and Ted's Excellent Adventure* spent his freshman year at North Toronto.

HIT THE GROUND

Amanda Tapping She may not be a household name, but you've likely seen this hard-working British-born actress and North TO grad in *Traffic* (2004), *Proof Positive* (2004), or *Life or Something Like It* (2002), if not on television's *Stargate SG-1* (1997 to present).

Area Codes

416 This is the coolest area code. Once, all of Southern Ontario used 416. When the proliferation of phone numbers necessitated a split, Toronto proper retained 416.

905 This is the area code given to outlying areas after the split. To call someone a "905-er" is to relegate him or her to the uncool world beyond city limits.

647 Now, even two area codes aren't enough, resulting in the creation of 647.

Expressways

Don Valley Expressway Connecting to the Gardiner's east end, it continues north to Highway 401 and eventually turns into Highway 404. It's the quickest route north, unless you happen to get there during rush hour!

Gardiner Expressway It enters the city from the west roughly along the lakeshore, connecting to the QEW (Queen Elizabeth Way) from the west, and is the entry point to downtown.

Singular Sensation

Skypod of the CN Tower Standing here, 1,465 feet above the ground, you can see the mist rise above Niagara Falls some 80 miles (128km) away, or on the glass floor of the Observation Deck, look 1,122 feet (336m) straight down as the world's tallest freestanding structure sways slightly in the wind.

Coffee (quick stops for a java jolt)

Balzac's Café With two locations serving fair trade coffee, freshly roasted from their own roasters, you can choose from artsy chic in the Distillery District or the West End's "Liberty Village" area near King and Dufferin Streets, home to a high concentration of production and design studios. 55 Mill St. (Distillery District) and 43 Hanna Ave., 416-207-1709

Bull Dog Coffee With its coffee-colored décor and handy access to chic shopping in the Yonge/Bloor area, expect an upscale crowd at this location, famous for its signature coffees. 89 Granby St., 416-606-2275

Everyday Gourmet If you're in the St. Lawrence area in need of a caffeine fix, slip into the Market and down to the lower level for this fragrant locale, offering fine coffees roasted on their own roaster, teas, and spices with a funky St. Lawrence flair. The entire St. Lawrence Market is a Wi-Fi hot spot. 79 Front St. E., (lower level), 416-363-7662

Gatto Nero Serving up espresso in Little Italy for four decades has made this West End cafe a neighborhood landmark. You can always catch Euro soccer or Formula One racing on the big screen. 720 College St., 416-536-3132

Jet Fuel Café It's a bit off the beaten track east of downtown, but this is possibly Toronto's coolest coffee emporium, preferred home to the city's caffeine-addicted cycling set. There are no menus or prices on display here, and don't even think about ordering decaf! 519 Parliament St., 416-968-9982

Moonbean Café This place served fair trade coffee here long before it was fashionable, and it still makes up 75 percent of the long list of brews, including signature blends like Morning Buzz, all with the hippie-dippy charm of Kensington Market. 30 St. Andrew St., 416-595-0327

Red Tea Box Sample 32 varieties of tea, including exotic varieties like Crooked Horse Oolong, in posh, elegant surroundings. 696 Queen St. W., 416-203-8882

Roastery Café Have your fair trade brew in an authentic renovated warehouse, with sleek modern furnishings and a curved coffee bar, all of it amidst the artists and arts organizations of 401 Richmond. Wi-Fi access. 401 Richmond St. W. (ground floor), 416-597-8822

Rustic Cosmo Café Soak up the artsy vibe of the "old" Queen West, back in the early '00s when it was a more bohemian artist's hangout, along with a nice selection of baked goods. Wi-Fi access. 1278 Queen St. W., 416-531-4924

Wagamama For those who prefer tea, here's a taste of Japan with homemade sweets, Japan's French-inspired pastries, and tea served in handmade Japanese pottery, in the chic King West 'hood. 766 King St. W., 416-603-0369

HIT THE GROUND

Just for Business and Conventions

Toronto was recently named one of the top three cities in the world in which to hold a business conference by the *World* (a publication of London's prestigious Economist group), and you'll soon see why. The city's largest convention center lies within walking distance of Bay Street, the heart of the Financial District and a good part of Canada's economy, with literally hundreds of restaurants and nightclub options in between, and more attractions, shopping, and things to do than you could possibly shake a stick at. You'll find the city eager to both welcome you and help you get your business done.

Addresses to Know

Convention Centers

• Metro Toronto Convention Centre
255 Front St. W. (York/University),
Downtown, 416-585-8000,
mtcc.com

• Toronto Congress Centre
650 Dixon Rd.,
Etobicoke, ON M9W 1J1,
416-245-5000,
torontocongresscentre.com

• International Centre
6900 Airport Rd.,
Mississauga, ON L4V 1E8,
905-677-6131,
internationalcentre.com

City Information

• Toronto Convention & Visitors Association
P.O. Box 126, 207 Queen's Quay W.,
(York St.), Harbourfront
416-203-2600/800-499-2514,
torontotourism.com

Business and Convention Hotels

You'll find that virtually any hotel in the Toronto Black Book will accommodate your business travel needs, and most are within easy distance of downtown. The airport area, home to two additional convention centers, is also known for business-friendly accommodations and services. Here are some additional choices:

Airport Strip

Sheraton Gateway Hotel Upscale hotel with modern décor, located in Terminal 3 of Pearson Airport. $$$ Toronto International Airport Terminal 3, 905-672-7000, starwoodhotels.com

Toronto Airport Hilton Reliable quality with modern, comfortable, and ergonomic business furnishings. $$$ 5875 Airport Rd., Mississauga, 905-677-9900, hilton.com

Downtown

Cambridge Suites Refined, classy business hotel in the Financial District. $$ 15 Richmond St. E., 416-368-1990, cambridgesuitestoronto.com

Renaissance Hotel at the Rogers Centre Polished hotel with some rooms that look right into the Rogers Centre arena itself. $$ 1 Blue Jays Way, 416-341-7100, marriott.com

Sheraton Centre Large upscale hotel near City Hall and Financial District. $$$ 123 Queen St. W., 416-361-1000 / 866-716-8101, starwood.com

Business Entertaining

Need to impress a client or network over drinks? These places will help seal the deal in great style.

Bistro 990 A French bistro with a touch of Hollywood stardust in the Financial District (p.120). $$$ 990 Bay St., 416-921-9990, bistro990.ca

Bymark An elegant dining room and sexy lounge, where Bay Street comes to play (p.121). $$$$ 66 Wellington St. W., 416-777-1144, bymarkdowntown.com

Oro Superb cuisine and stunning private dining rooms for the ultimate meeting place (p.129). $$$ 45 Elm St., 416-597-0155, ororestaurant.com

Zachary's Highbrow and much-acclaimed continental cuisine in the airport strip. $$$ Wyndham Bristol Place Hotel, 950 Dixon Rd. (Etobicoke), 416-675-9444

Also See: **Best Fine Dining** (p.24)

    Best Power Lunches (p.37)

Ducking Out for a Half-Day

All work and no play can't be good for you, so try one of these liberating pursuits.

Art Gallery of Ontario It has a huge permanent collection and blockbuster traveling shows (p.74). 317 Dundas St. W. (McCaul St.), 416-979-6648

Hockey Hall of Fame A lavish shrine to Canada's national sport (p.140). 30 Yonge St. (BCE Place, Front St.), 416-360-7765

Toronto Islands Escape the city altogether and catch a ferry to one of the islands (p.141). Toronto Harbourfront, 416-392-8193

Also See: **Best Only-in-Toronto Museums** (p.36)

Gifts to Bring Home

Don't leave Toronto without a fabulous souvenir. Check out these places for the best of the lot.

Queen's Quay Terminal A historic lakeside center offering art, crafts, and other Canadiana. 207 Queen's Quay W. (Bay St.), 416-203-0510

Textile Museum Gift Shop Fab gift shop with artisan scarves, purses, and more. 55 Centre St. (Bay St.), 416-599-5321

HIT THE GROUND

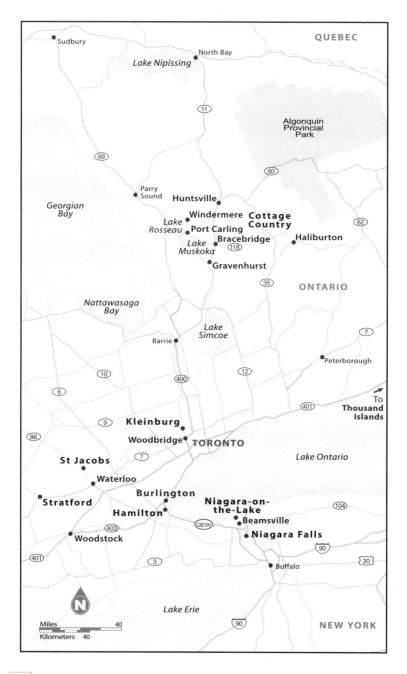

Sudbury

QUEBEC

North Bay

Lake Nipissing

11

Algonquin
Provincial
Park

69

60

Parry
Sound

Huntsville

Georgian
Bay

Windermere Cottage
Lake   Country
Rosseau Port Carling
                              Haliburton
          Bracebridge
Lake   118
Muskoka

62

Gravenhurst

35

ONTARIO

Nattawasaga
Bay

Lake
Simcoe

7

Barrie

Peterborough

10

12

6

400

401

9   Kleinburg

To
Thousand
Islands

86

Woodbridge   TORONTO

St Jacobs

7

Lake Ontario

Waterloo

Burlington

Stratford

Niagara-on-
the-Lake

104

Hamilton

Beamsville

QEW

Woodstock

Niagara Falls

90

401

3

Buffalo

20

Lake Erie

N

Miles   40
Kilometers   40

90

NEW YORK

LEAVING TORONTO

When you've had your fill of urban fun, it's time to head out of town and discover what the area has to offer beyond Toronto. From a trip to Niagara Falls to a tour of Ontario's burgeoning wine country, from a night at exclusive Niagara-on-the-Lake to an evening of gambling in the Thousand Islands region, you have a rich and diverse list of attractions to choose from, many of them within a few hours' drive.

Cottage Country

Hot Tip: For a taste of real wilderness, where you can hear the howling of wolves, go camping, canoeing, or backcountry skiing—drive about 31 miles (50km) from Huntsville further north on Highway 60 to Algonquin Park, a legendary provincial park consisting of 4,800 sq. miles (7,725 square km) of lakes, woods, and rivers.

The Lowdown: "Cottage Country" exists in the Canadian psyche as a near-mythical landscape of woodland and lakes, a pristine wilderness where the silence is broken only by the shrill of the loon or the howl of the wolf. It begins with the area called the "Near North." Upscale Torontonians and a large quotient of wealthy Americans (even Goldie and Kurt) have long been making their summer homes in the Muskoka Lakes area of the province, an area loosely based around Lakes Muskoka, Rosseau, and Joseph, and encompassing over 1,000 freshwater lakes. The nearest towns are Bracebridge, Port Carling, and Huntsville, which has a charming tree-lined downtown of shops and boutiques. The nearby town of Haliburton is central to the Haliburton Highlands region of lakes, woodlands, and rolling hills.

The best accommodations and other facilities here typically are to be found in resort complexes, which offer a wide range of outdoor activities, from boating and fishing to cross-country skiing, along with several dining options, spas, and other luxe touches.

Best Attractions

Aveda Spa at Deerhurst Resort Enjoy the luxuries of a spa in a jewel of a setting. Book ahead for a full range of spa services, including the signature Muskoka Maple Body Scrub or Algae Thalasso Wrap. $$$$ 1235 Deerhurst Dr., Huntsville, 705-789-6411 / 800-461-4393, deerhurstresort.com/spa.html

Echo Valley Observatory Delta Grandview Resort Gaze up at stars, nebula, and far-away galaxies at this ideally situated observatory, outfitted with cutting-edge equipment, including an equatorial mounted 16-foot LX 200 Schmidt-Cassegrain telescope. $$ 939 Hwy. 60, Huntsville, 705-789-1871 / 877-472-6388

Hidden Valley Highlands Ski Area Hit the slopes for a day with 14 runs to choose from, from easy to freestyle levels. Over 100 professionals offer lessons. Snowboarding too! $$$ 1655 Hidden Valley Rd., Huntsville, 705-789-1773 / 800-398-9555, skihiddenvalley.on.ca

Lady Muskoka Cruises Take a tour on this 104-foot-long fully furnished vessel, complete with licensed bar. $$ 300 Ecclestone Dr., Bracebridge, 705-646-2628 / 800-263-5239, ladymuskoka.com

Taboo Golf Course Test your game on 2003 Masters Champion Mike Weir's home course, a challenging and exciting 18-hole golf course of 7,123 yards. $$$$ Muskoka Beach Road, R.R. 1, Gravenhurst, 705-646-5800, tabooresort.com/golf_intro.php

Best Restaurants and Nightlife

Eclipse Restaurant Deerhurst Resort A wine list of over 300 selections (earning it a *Wine Spectator* award every year since 2000), and eight executive chefs create fusion with international influences. The dining room overlooks Peninsula Lake through a ring of evergreens. $$-$$$ 1234 Deerhurst Dr., Huntsville, 705-789-6411 deerhurstresort.com

Sherwood Inn Dining Room Enjoy lunch or dinner in a charming country house, with a view from the dining room to lush well-tended gardens. 1090 Sherwood Rd., Port Carling, 705-765-3131, deltahotels.com

Tall Trees Restaurant Country-style décor and continental-inspired fine dining in an intimate country dining room. $$ 87 Main St. W., Huntsville, 705-789-9769 spencerstalltrees.com

Best Hotels

Cedarwood Resort Fully furnished, Wi-Fi accessible luxury suites and stunning cottages right on picturesque Lake Muskoka. $$$$ Box 262, Bracebridge/Port Carling, 705-645-8558 / 866-252-0223, cedarwoodresort.ca

Deerhurst Resort A landmark resort since 1896 on Peninsula Lake, Deerhurst offers the epitome of the all-inclusive luxury experience, including fab accommodations, two challenging golf courses, live entertainment, an Aveda spa, and more. $$$ 1235 Deerhurst Dr., Huntsville, 705-789-6411, deerhurstresort.com

Delta Grandview Resort Set on the shores of pretty Fairy Lake, this premium luxury resort was built onto an existing historic inn and has two golf courses, an indoor and outdoor pool, an ecotourism program, and an observatory. $$$ 939 Hwy. 60, Huntsville, 705-789-1871 / 877-472-6388, deltahotels.com

Domain of Killien This 5,000-acre exclusive and private resort in the Haliburton Highlands offers hiking, biking, and swimming (among other activities), with a French chef on hand. $$ P.O. Box 810, Haliburton, 705-457-1100 / 800-390-0769, domainofkillien.com

Taboo Golf & Conference Centre An ultra-posh and high-end modern design complex that features deluxe accommodations, fine dining, upscale spa, and golf course. $$$ Muskoka Beach Rd., R.R. 1, Gravenhurst, 705-687-2233 / 800-461-0236, tabooresort.com

Windermere House Resort Right on the scenic shores of Lake Rosseau, this resort has a real Old Muskoka ambience. $$ 2508 Windermere Rd., Box 68, Windermere, 705-769-3611 / 888-946-3376, windermerehouse.com

Contacts

Muskoka Tourism Highway 11 Visitor Centre, Kilworthy, Hwy. 11 Northbound (1.2 miles or 2km north of Severn Bridge), 800-267-9700, muskoka-tourism.on.ca

LEAVING

Getting There: Huntsville—take the Gardiner Expy. westbound, exiting at Hwy. 427 north. From the 427, exit to Hwy. 401 eastbound to Hwy. 400 north. From Hwy. 400 north, take Hwy. 11 exit and watch for the signs for Huntsville on Hwy. 11.

80 mi.
129 km
SW

Niagara Falls

Hot Tip: The Friendship Festival straddles one international border (Canada-U.S.) and two national holidays (Canada Day and July 4) to create one giant festival of music and fun that takes place just a little farther south down the QEW into Fort Erie and Buffalo, New York.

The Lowdown: Gushing over the brink with an awe-inspiring might that transcends all the honeymoon retro kitsch, the Falls are always spectacular. From the 1940s and '50s, the moniker of "Honeymoon City" stuck, and to this day you'll see heart-shaped jacuzzis advertised in even the lowliest of motels. A strip of old-school amusements evolved to cater to honeymooners and nature gawkers—Tussaud's Wax Museum, fun houses, and the like. That was then, and this is now, when casino dollars have transformed the entire area, resulting in a score of upscale accommodations and restaurants. One relatively new development has been the proliferation of world-class golfing clubs—over 40 public and private—earning it the nickname "Myrtle Beach of the North." And shopping opportunities—from outlet malls to high-end designer boutiques—abound. In the end, of course, these attractions can't compete with Mother Nature, who remains the star of this show. The Falls are especially pretty in the winter, when the outer fringes of water begin to ice. The city hosts light shows and fireworks, concerts, and other outdoor events year round.

Best Attractions

Butterfly Conservatory One of North America's largest exhibits of free-flying butterflies, it's housed year-round in climate-controlled greenhouses that are landscaped to resemble a rain forest. $ 2405 Niagara River Pkwy., 905-356-8119, niagaraparks.com/nature/butterfly.php

Great American Balloon Company Slip stateside for a ride in the Flight of Angels, an exciting 15-minute ride over Niagara Falls in a helium-filled balloon. May-Oct. $$ 310 Rainbow Blvd. S., Niagara Falls (U.S.) 716-278-0824 or 716-278-0825, flightofangels.net

Konica Minolta Tower See the Falls from an observation deck 25 floors up. $-6732 Fallsview Blvd., 905-356-1501, niagaratower.com

Legends on the Niagara Golf Course Legends is a stunning 700-acre, 5-star, 45-hole course and resort, featuring two 18-hole courses, a 9-hole executive course, and a unique 360-degree practice course. $$$$ 9561 Niagara Pkwy., 905-295-9595 / 866-465-3642, niagaraparksgolf.com/legends

Maid of the Mist Steamboat Company It may be touristy, but this 30-minute ride is a fantastic way to experience the Falls up close. Allow an hour and a quarter, including waiting in line and getting off. 905-358-7581, maidofthemist.com

Niagara Fallsview Casino Vegas-level glitz and glamour, including a $100,000 fountain and art installation, an 180,000-square-foot facility with 3,000 slot machines, and 150 gaming tables. It also has a great spa. 6380 Fallsview Blvd., 905-358-7654 / 888-325-5788, fallsviewcasinoresort.com

Niagara Helicopters This sweeping 12-minute tour of the Falls is the ultimate photo opportunity. 3731 Victoria Ave., 905-357-5672, niagarahelicopters.com

Whirlpool Jet Tours Get up close and personal with the might of the Falls in a jet boat—you'll go as close as safety allows in the whirlpool just where the water comes rushing down. $$$$ 61 Melville St., P.O. Box 1215, Niagara-on-the-Lake, 905-468-4800 / 888-438-4444, whirlpooljet.com

Best Restaurants and Nightlife

Millery Dining Room Old Stone Inn Enjoy a meal in historic splendor, complete with stone walls, fireplace, and chandeliers. $$$ 5425 Robinson St., 905-357-1234 / 800-263-6208, oldstoneinn.on.ca

Penthouse Fallsview Dining Room Sheraton on the Falls Hotel The home of Niagara's best chef combines gourmet fare and the best view of the Falls. $$$ 5875 Falls Ave., Niagara Falls, 905-374-4444 / 800-263-7135, niagarafallshotels.com

Pinnacle Restaurant Konica Minolta Tower With a dining room that rises 525 feet above the Niagara River, the Pinnacle commands one of the most dramatic views in a town that's built on them. $$-$$$ 6732 Fallsview Blvd., Niagara Falls, 905-356-1501, pinnacleniagara.com

Queenston Heights Fine dining and a great local VQA wine list in period architecture with a view of the Niagara River as it flows into Lake Ontario. Ask about the popular Niagara Grand Dinner Theatre. $$ 14184 Niagara Pkwy., 905-262-4274, niagaraparks.com/planavisit/queenstonres.php

17 Noir This sleek, contemporary space with a knockout view is the perfect place to indulge in an upscale dinner. $$$$ 6380 Fallsview Blvd., 905-358-7654 / 888-325-5788, fallsviewcasinoresort.com

Skylon Tower With a revolving dining room that rises a stunning 775 feet above the Falls, it will be hard to take your eyes off the view to enjoy your flawlessly executed meal. $$$$ 6732 Fallsview Blvd., Niagara Falls, 905-356-1501, pinnacleniagara.com

Best Hotels

Sheraton Fallsview Hotel Benefitting from outstanding views and a great location one block from the Fallsview Casino, this is an excellent home base for your visit. $$ 6755 Fallsview Blvd., 905-374-1077 / 800-618-9059, fallsview.com

Hilton Niagara Falls This 34-story luxury hotel has over 500 oversize rooms and suites above the Falls. Check out the nine-story atrium lobby with 40-foot trees and a waterfall. $$ 6361 Fallsview Blvd., 905-354-7887 / 888-370-0700, niagarafallshilton.com

Niagara Fallsview Casino Resort The Fallsview offers upscale accommodations, with a view of the Falls from every room. Ask for a view of Horseshoe Falls. $$ 6380 Fallsview Blvd., 905-358-7654 / 888-325-5788, fallsviewcasinoresort.com

Contacts

Tourism Niagara 424 S. Servia Rd., Grimsby, 800-263-2988, tourismniagara.com

Getting There: Take the Gardiner Expy. westbound to the QEW Hamilton. Stay on the QEW in the direction of Niagara to the Niagara River.

LEAVING

Niagara-on-the-Lake

Hot Tip: The region is one of the few in the world to produce "ice wines." Watch for festivals and packages.

The Lowdown: In 1896, writer William Kirby wrote, "Niagara is as near Heaven as any town whatever," and succeeding generations have continued to vote it one of the prettiest towns in the country. Strict bylaws mean that the main street and older parts of town have retained their lovely 19th-century character, and Mother Nature has blessed this area with lush, fertile soil—none of which has escaped the notice of film directors, who have often used the small-town streetscape in movies. The surrounding lush agricultural lands are mostly planted with soft-fruit trees and increasingly vineyards. Some of Canada's finest wines are produced here, and the wineries now cater to visitors with luxury accommodations and gourmet dining. This pretty historic town is said to be home to more ghosts per capita than anywhere else in North America, with hauntings that include Fort George (now a museum and tourist attraction) and even some high-end accommodations like the Oban Inn. Together with the Shaw Festival Theatre, the town has also become quite an upscale party town, boasting the most expensive hotel rooms in Canada.

Best Attractions

Hillebrand Estates Visit Canada's leading producer of VQA wines. Tour the vineyards, cellars, and wine-making facilities. Stop at the boutique and acclaimed Hillebrand Vineyard Cafe. $$ Hwy. 55, 800-582-8412, hillebrand.com

Inniskillin Winery This grand estate winery offers tours year round. Ask about the limited edition tour, which includes private tastings of older vintage and rare premium wines. $$ Wine Boutique, 1499 Line 3 off the Niagara Pky., 888 466-4754 ext 311, inniskillin.com

Niagara-on-the-Lake Golf Club The historic nine-hole course—North America's oldest—features lush greens and a newly renovated clubhouse. $$$$ 143 Front St., 905-468-3424, notlgolf.com

Niagara Riding Stables Ride the scenic trails along the Niagara Escarpment on horseback April to December. $$$ 471 Warner Rd., 905-262-5101, niagarariding.com

Niagara Wine Tours International Explore award-winning wineries with tastings and shopping opportunities along the way. $$$$ 92 Picton St., 905-468-1300 / 800-680-7006, niagaraworldwinetours.com

100 Fountain Spa Choose from a full range of European spa treatments in a lavish setting. $$$$ Pillar & Post Inn, 48 John St., 905-468-1362 / 888-669-5566, vintageinns.com/niagara-on-the-lake/spa/pillar-and-post.php

Shaw Festival Theatre A highly acclaimed theater festival that runs April to November. Based on the works of George Bernard Shaw, but the Festival also includes musicals and classic theater. $$$ 10 Queen's Parade, 800-511-7429, shawfest.com

Steve Bauer Bike Tours Let Olympic cycling medalist Steve Bauer's team take you on a cycling tour of the region. $$$$ 224 Glenridge Ave., St. Catherine's, 905-704-1224, stevebauer.com

Best Restaurants and Nightlife

Escabeche Canadian and regional cuisine, featuring produce grown locally and picked daily in season, with an extensive wine list. $$$$ Prince of Wales Hotel, 6 Picton St., 905-468-3246 / 888-669-5566, vintageinns.com

Zees Patio & Grille A chic, lighthearted addition to the area, with French classics and continental-inspired fare in cool contemporary surroundings. $$$ Shaw Club Hotel, 92 Picton St., 905-468-5715 / 800-511-7070, zees.ca

On the Twenty Restaurant On the Twenty is the height of country elegance. $$$ Cave Spring Cellars, 3836 Main St., Jordan, 905-562-7313, innonthetwenty.com

Restaurant at Peninsula Ridge Located on the Peninsula Ridge Estates Winery, it offers fine dining with vineyard views. Also lovely for an evening glass of wine. $$$ 5600 King St. W., Beamsville, 905-563-0900 ext 35, peninsularidge.com

Ristorante Giardino This dining room is a bubble of contemporary luxury in this historic town. $$ Gate House Hotel, 142 Queen St., 905-468-3263, gatehouse-niagara.com

Tiara Queen's Landing An opulent spot overlooking the Niagara River, and a menu of continental inspirations and cocktails. $$$ 155 Byron St., 905-468-2195 / 888-669-5566, vintage-hotels.com

Best Hotels

Harbour House Hotel Bright, airy rooms in a luxury small hotel on the scenic riverfront. $$$ 86 Melville St., 905-468-4683/866-277-6677 harbourhousehotel.ca

Inn on the Twenty This Jordan Village winery, inn, and restaurant offers luxury accommodations, superb tippling and dining. $$ Cave Spring Cellars, 3845 Main St., Jordan, 905-562-5336, 800-701-8074 innonthetwenty.com

Oban Inn The 21 luxury rooms are furnished in period style, many with canopy beds. $$ 160 Front St., 866-359-6226, obaninn.ca

Prince of Wales Hotel This palatial landmark property comes complete with a liveried doorman. $$$ 6 Picton St., 905-468-3246 / 888-669-5566, vintageinns.com/niagara-on-the-lake/hotels/prince-of-wales.php

Queen's Landing A stately Georgian mansion overlooking the Niagara River. Ask about the Lakefront Villa and Waterfront Cottage for an exclusive experience. $$$ 155 Byron St., 905-468-2195 / 888-669-5566, vintageinns.com

Shaw Club Hotel An ultra-modern, ultra-posh boutique hotel. $$$ 92 Picton St., 905-468-5711 / 800-511-7070, shawclub.ca

Contacts

Niagara-on-the-Lake Visitor & Convention Bureau, 26 Queen St., 905-468-1950, niagaraonthelake.com

LEAVING

Getting There: Take the Gardiner Expy. westbound to the QEW Hamilton, following it to the QEW Niagara. Once you're over the Garden Skyway Bridge, take the exit for Hwy. 55 and follow it to the end.

Stratford

Hot Tip: A sweet rural village with inns, restaurants, and a real Ontario country flavor, nearby St. Mary's—a mere 15 minutes west on Hwy. 7— is also worth a visit.

The Lowdown: In 1828, Stratford was little more than a tavern and a few houses along a small river they called "Little Thames" when the area was first surveyed. In 1832, Thomas Mercer Jones gave a picture of William Shakespeare to William Sargint, the owner of the Shakespeare Hotel. Sargint named the blossoming town Stratford and renamed the river Avon, and the rest, as they say, is history. The first formal Stratford Festival began in 1953, featuring Alec Guinness playing Shakespeare under a temporary tent. A permanent theater (based on Shakespeare's original theater-in-the-round in England) was built four years later.

The Stratford of today is a thriving small town in the midst of bucolic agricultural lands, focused on theater. The Festival has become an entire industry, with costume and set makers working year-round. Another offshoot has been the creation of the prestigious Stratford Chef School, where many of Canada's finest chefs have studied, obviously resulting in a wealth of culinary delights far beyond what you'd expect for a town of this size.

Best Attractions

Birtch Farms and Estate Winery Balance the intellectual pursuits of highbrow theater with a taste of farmland Ontario at this estate winery and farm a mere 25 minutes south of Stratford. $-$$ 655514 15th Line, R.R. 7, Woodstock, 519-469-3040, birtchfarms.com

Gallery Stratford Gallery Stratford houses a permanent collection of over 2,000 works. 54 Romeo St., 519-271-5271, gallerystratford.on.ca

Stratford Country Club A beautiful, mature 18-hole golf course (par 71) that follows the Avon River for a challenging round in a pastoral setting. $$$$ 53 Romeo St. N., 519-271-4212, stratfordcountryclub.com

Stratford Festival Theatre The Festival hosts sophisticated shows of the highest caliber. The playbill is based in Shakespearean plays, but also includes musicals and more modern offerings. $$$$ 55 Queen St., 800-567-1600, stratfordfestival.ca

Best Restaurants and Nightlife

Annex Cafe & Lounge A wood bar, a leather couch, a martini or two, and a nice menu selection of pasta, thin-crust pizza, and more make this a relaxing escape. $$ 38 Albert St., Stratford, 519-271-1407 / 800-361-5322, bentleys-annex.com

Bijou Restaurant The contemporary French menu uses fresh, local ingredients, and is matched by a carefully chosen wine list, all served in a Parisian-style bistro. $$ 105 Erie St., Stratford, 519-273-5000, bijourestaurant.com

The Church Restaurant/The Belfry Housed in the vaulted-ceiling splendor of an old church, the Church downstairs is open seasonally with the Festival, while the casual Belfry upstairs is open year-round. $$ 70 Brunswick St., 519-273-3424, churchrestaurant.com

The Old Prune The Old Prune, an Edwardian mansion in a verdant garden setting, offers informed and much-acclaimed service along with superb modern cuisine. $$ 151 Albert St., 519-271-5052, oldprune.on.ca

Rundles Rundles has a longstanding tradition of faultless service and innovative cuisine, thanks to the constant stream of young chefs from the town's fabled Chef School. 9 Cobourg St., 519-271-6442, rundlesrestaurant.com

Best Hotels

Annex Inn Each room features tasteful furnishings in elegant neutrals, a comfortable sitting area with a gas fireplace, and a large whirlpool tub. $$ 38 Albert St., 519-271-1407 / 800-361-5322, bentleys-annex.com

Bentley's Inn Bentley's offers spacious two-level suites or an upscale loft with exposed brick walls, both with period furnishings and stylish, contemporary touches. $$ 99 Ontario St., 519-271-1121 / 800-361-5322, bentleys-annex.com

Rundles Morris House, Chosen as a "Record House" by *Architectural Record* magazine, Rundles Morris House features a fireplace and queen-size beds on three floors. $$$$ 7 Cobourg St., 519-271-6442, rundlesrestaurant.com/housemain.html

Sally's Place Executive Suites, This luxury boutique hotel in a Victorian townhouse offers stylish self-contained apartment suites appropriate to the historic setting. $$$ 28 Waterloo St. and 299 Ontario St., 519-272-0022, sallysplace.com

Contacts

Tourism Stratford, 47 Downie St., 800-561-7962, city.stratford.on.ca

LEAVING

Getting There: Take the Gardiner Expy. westbound to Hwy. 427 North, then onto Hwy. 401 westbound. From the 401, take exit 278 Hwy. 8 west toward Kitchener/Waterloo and watch for the signs as Hwy. 8 W merges with Hwy. 7 W, direction Stratford. After about 30 miles, look for the various exits to town.

Thousand Islands

Hot Tip: Lovers of everything apple will want to stop at the "Big Apple" in Courtice along the way (and once you spot it beside Highway 401, no explanation will be necessary), for mouthwatering pies and other treats.

The Lowdown: Early Native American dwellers called this place, where the St. Lawrence River spills into Lake Ontario and straddles both the Province of Ontario and New York State, "the Garden of the Great Spirit," and you won't question why for a moment. One of the first French explorers to set eyes on this unusually beautiful area enthusiastically declared that there had to be a thousand islands—there's actually over 1,700, but the name remains. In the Gilded Age of the industrial era, this is where the richest families of New York and Toronto came to play in the summer months. Nowadays, visitors can enjoy the splendid Victorian and Edwardian mansions, posh historic accommodations, and equally fine dining.

Tourism in the area is based around two centers, Kingston—a small historic city that's home to the Royal Military College and prestigious Queen's University—and Gananoque. Kingston, located where the Rideau Canal meets Lake Ontario near the St. Lawrence, is the freshwater sailing capital of North America, and you'll soon conclude that virtually everyone in this area owns a boat! Gananoque is an upscale resort town with a small but pretty public beach and a fabulous marina.

Best Attractions

Bellevue House National Historic Site of Canada Visit the Italianate villa where Canada's first Prime Minister—as well known for his flamboyant behavior and copious drinking as for his political acumen—lived and worked. $ 35 Centre St., Kingston, 613-545-8666 / 800-230-0016, pc.gc.ca

Boldt Castle A lavish historic home begun by George Boldt, former owner of New York's Waldorf Astoria Hotel, for his wife. Self-guided tours available mid-May through mid-October. $$ Heart Island International Region of northern New York State, 800-847-5263, boldtcastle.com

Gananoque Boat Line Cruise Relax on triple-decker boats and sip a drink as you marvel at the lavish summer estate islands and the quiet beauty of the scenery and wildlife. Sunset cruises also available. $ 6 Water St., Gananoque, 613-382-2146, ganboatline.com

Spa at the Mill A full range of services is on offer at this luxurious spa housed in a renovated mill. 8 Cataraqui St., Kingston, 613-544-1166 / 877-424-4417

Thousand Islands Charity Casino This multimillion-dollar facility includes 450 slot machines and many gaming tables. 380 Hwy. 2, Gananoque, 866-266-8422 corporate.olgc.ca/olg-casinos/thousand_islands.jsp

Thousand Islands Country Club This prestigious golf and country club has a long history of distinguished members. $$$$ 46433 County 100, Wellesley Island, 800-928-8422, ticountryclub.com

Thousand Islands Playhouse Enjoy a professionally produced program of comedies, dramas, and musicals. $$ Box Office: 690 Charles St. S., Gananoque, 613-382-7020, 1000islandsplayhouse.com

Best Restaurants and Nightlife

Aqua Terra Bistro This classic steak-and-seafood house is right on the waterfront with a gorgeous view. Live jazz Fri-Sat. $$$ Radisson Hotel, 1 Johnson St., Kingston, 613-549-8100, aquaterrarestaubistro.com

Athlone Inn Restaurant Athlone serves French and continental cuisine in the romantic ambience of a historic B&B. $$ 250 King St. W., Gananoque, 613-382-3822 / 888-382-7122

Casa Bella Restaurant and B&B Bella serves up imaginative fusion in style in a warm and elegant dining room. $$-$$$ 110 Clarence St., Gananoque, 613-382-1618 / 866-382-1618, eatatbella.com

The Gananoque Inn Dining Room An elegant dining room with a gorgeous view over the water and a menu of updated continental classics; alfresco dining is available when weather permits. $$$ 550 Stone St. S., Gananoque, 613-382-2165 / 800-465-3101, gananoqueinn.com

General Wolfe Restaurant A free 20-minute ferry ride across the scenic St. Lawrence River takes you to Wolfe Island and a 150-year-old dining room that overlooks the storied waterway. $$$$ 1237 Main St., Wolfe Island, 613-385-2611 / 800-353-1098, generalwolfehotel.com

Trinity House Inn This elegant award-winning restaurant serves an inventive continental menu. $$ 90 Stone St. S., Gananoque, 613-382-8383 / 800-265-4871, trinityinn.com

Best Hotels

The Gananoque Inn & Spa This historic inn with elegant furnishings is set in lush gardens by the water, with a newly refurbished spa with facial and body treatments. $$$ 550 Stone St. S., Gananoque, 613-382-2165 / 800-465-3101, gananoqueinn.com

Hochelaga Inn This historic French Victorian style inn has a tower, and rooms are furnished with antiques. $$ 24 Sydenham St., Kingston, 613-549-5534 / 877-933-9433, hochelagainn.com

Sleepy Hollow Bed & Breakfast Stay in a gorgeous three-story mansion, professionally decorated in grand period style. $ 95 King St. W., Gananoque, 613-382-4377, sleepyhollowbb.ca

Victoria Rose Inn This Victorian mansion with turret, ornate brickwork, and gingerbread trim has romantic suites on two acres of gardens. $$ 279 King St. W., Gananoque, 613-382-3368 / 888-246-2893, victoriaroseinn.com

Contacts

1000 Islands International Tourism Council: 800-847-5263, visit1000islands.com

LEAVING

Getting There: From downtown Toronto, take the Gardiner Expy. eastbound. When the Gardiner ends, stay left to merge onto the Don Valley Expy. Exit the Don Valley at Hwy. 401 east, staying on the 401 approximately 2 1/2 hours to exit at either Gananoque or Kingston.

Hamilton and Burlington

Hot Tip: The highway is quickest, but if you have the time, take a leisurely drive west along Lakeshore Road all the way from Toronto's downtown, and about halfway to Hamilton and Burlington, you'll drive through what is known as "Millionaire's Row" in Oakville, the richest concentration of real estate in Canada.

The Lowdown: Hamilton and Burlington share the Royal Botanical Gardens and a location at the head of Lake Ontario. The spectacular Gardens are the region's most popular tourist attraction and straddle the two municipalities almost equally. But that's where the similarities end. Hamilton is a small industrial steel city with a blue-collar feel, while Burlington is its more upscale cousin with parklands and expensive yacht clubs. Together, however, they make an ideal day visit or refreshing pause along the way to Niagara.

Best Attractions

Art Gallery of Hamilton Canada's third-largest public art gallery, the AGH houses a collection of Canadian art through the centuries. 123 King St. W., Hamilton, 905-527-6610, artgalleryofhamilton.on.ca

Canadian Warplane Heritage Museum The museum's collection includes aircraft dating from World War II to the present. $ 9280 Airport Rd., Hamilton, 905-679-4183, warplane.com

Royal Botanical Gardens Visit Canada's largest botanical garden at over 2,700 acres in several adjacent sites. $ 680 Plains Rd. W., Hamilton, 905-527-1158, rbg.ca

Best Restaurants and Nightlife

Bistro Parisien A classic bistro menu with a nice wine list and warm contemporary décor. $$$ 150 James St. S., Hamilton, 905-546-0003,bistroparisien.com

Main Street Desserts If all you want is a big bowl of latté and a slab of cheesecake, then head to this chic cafe. $ 344 Main St. W., Hamilton, 905-522-2232

Koi Restaurant & Cocktail Boutique A modern and minimalist high-end Japanese eatery and martini lounge. $$$$ 27 Hess St. S., Hamilton, 905-308-7507, koirestaurant.ca

Contacts

Tourism Hamilton myhamilton.ca/myhamilton/TourismAndVisitorInfo
Tourism Burlington 414 Locust St., Burlington, 877-499-9989, tourismburlington.com

Getting There: Take the Gardiner Expy. westbound till it merges with the QEW Hamilton. Take the QEW Niagara, then the Woodward St. exit to reach the east end of Hamilton (H.M.C.S. Haida). For other attractions, take Hwy. 403 west and the York Blvd. or Main St. E. exits.

25 mi.
40 km
N

Kleinburg

Hot Tip: This lovely escape from the city is accessible even by public transit!

The Lowdown: Atop the Humber River Ridge and surrounded by glorious views, this country village just north of Toronto was founded in 1848 by John Kline, a Swiss watchmaker. Early Canadiana lives on here in lovingly restored and tended architecture. Kleinburg is full of city dwellers who came for a visit and decided to stay, as did Robert and Signe McMichael. The wealthy couple were so charmed by the town that they not only stayed, but built an estate that they eventually donated to the Province of Ontario—along with, most importantly, their large collection of art by the famed Group of Seven, which eventually became the renowned McMichael Gallery.

The town that's grown around the McMichael is lined with historic streets that offer eclectic shops, galleries, and exhibits with a definite artsy flair.

Best Attractions

Kleinburg Golf & Country Club There are three different nine-hole courses here, each with its own particular terrain. $$$$ 115 Putting Green Cr., 905-893-1900, kleinburg-golf.com

Kortright Conservation Centre Over 10 miles (16km) of hiking trails through meadows and forests and across a marsh. $- 9550 Pine Valley Dr., Woodbridge, 905-832-2289, kortright.org

McMichael Gallery The premier collection of Group of Seven paintings, and other fine exhibits and shows. $$ 10365 Islington Ave., 905-893-1121 / 888-213-1121, mcmichael.com

Best Restaurants and Nightlife

Chartreuse Two old-fashioned dining rooms and traditional French cuisine. $$$$ 10512 Islington Ave., 905-893-0475, chartreuserestaurant.com

Doctor's House & Lounge Continental classics and an extensive wine list. Drinks and casual fare in the lounge. $$$$ 21 Nashville Rd., 905-893-1615, thedoctorshouse.ca

Contacts

Kleinburg, Ontario kleinburgvillage.com, city.vaughan.on.ca/tourism/tourattraction.cfm

LEAVING

Getting There: Take the Gardiner Expy. eastbound, staying left as it turns into the Don Valley Expy. Exit onto Major Mackenzie Dr., heading west (left) to Islington Ave. Turn north (right) on Islington to reach the village.

St. Jacobs

Hot Tip: You'll find plenty of goodies at the Farmer's Market, but take a drive down a country road or two in the area, and you'll discover perhaps the best pies, sausages, and other traditional Mennonite fare you've ever tasted for sale at roadside stands along the way.

The Lowdown: West of Toronto, the cities become smaller and thin out into pastures and bucolic rolling hills. Tiny and historic St. Jacobs was founded in 1852 as the marketplace for area farmers and developed Ontario's first creamery in 1872. But as far back as the late 1700s, the area was being settled and farmed by Mennonites who traveled there in wagons from Pennsylvania. Today, the area is known as Mennonite country, and you'll see Old Order Mennonites in horse-drawn buggies and traditional dress. The area has retained its rural charm, and along with the Mennonites and their wares, you'll find a picturesque village and shopping opportunities, with over 100 retailers, including galleries, studios, and an antique market.

Best Attractions

The Mennonite Story Visitor Centre Learn about the history and culture of the Mennonites. 1406 King St. N., St. Jacobs, 519-664-3518

St. Jacobs Antique Market Forty-five antique dealers offering an array of antique furniture and collectibles. $$$ 8 Spring St., St. Jacobs, 519-664-1243

St. Jacobs Farmer's and Flea Markets Festive farmer's market with hundreds of vendors and delicious Mennonite fare. Thu and Sat only 7am-3:30pm year-round, and Tue during the summer. $ 878 Weber St. N. (1.2 miles or 2km south of St. Jacobs), Waterloo, 519-747-1830 / 800-265-3353

Best Restaurants

Benjamin's Restaurant Experience contemporary Canadian cuisine in a refurbished 1852 inn. $$ 1430-1 King St. N., 519-664-3731

Stone Crock Get a taste of local history with Waterloo County recipes and home-style cooking. $$ 1396 King St. N., 519-664-2286

Vidalia's Market Dining This casual eatery features open kitchens where your food is prepared as you watch. $$ 1398 King St. N., 519-664-2575

Contacts

St. Jacobs Tourism 1386 King St. N., 800-265-3353 ext. 212, stjacobs.com

Getting There: Take the Gardiner Expy. westbound just out of town, then exit to Hwy. 427 north. From 427, get on Hwy. 401 west (direction London). Take exit 278 to Hwy. 8 west (toward Kitchener-Waterloo). After merging onto Hwy. 8 west, exit to Hwy. 85 toward Waterloo. Follow Hwy. 85 to 15 exit for the farmer's market. Turn left onto King St. (Rd. 15), then left onto Farmers Market Rd. For St. Jacobs, continue on Highway 85. Turn left at the traffic lights onto Sawmill Rd. (Rd. 17) and follow the signs to the Village.

TORONTO BLACK BOOK

You're solo in the city—where's a singles-friendly place to eat? Is there a good lunch spot near the museum? Will the bar be too loud for easy conversation? Get the answers fast in the *Black Book*, a condensed version of every listing in our guide that puts all the essential information at your fingertips.

A quick glance down the page and you'll find the type of food, nightlife, or attractions you are looking for, the phone numbers, and which pages to turn to for more detailed information. How did you ever survive without it?

BLACK BOOK

Toronto Black Book

Hotels

NAME TYPE (ROOMS)	ADDRESS (CROSS STREET) WEBSITE	AREA PRICE	PHONE 800 NUMBER	EXPERIENCE	PAGE
Cosmopolitan Hotel Trendy (97 Rms)	8 Colborne St. (Yonge St.) cosmotoronto.com	DT $$$	416-350-2000 800-958-3488	Hot & Cool	57
The Drake Hotel Trendy (19 Rms)	1150 Queen St. W. (Beaconsfield St.) thedrakehotel.ca	WQ $$$	416-531-5042 866-372-5386	Hip	87
Fairmont Royal York Grand (1,376 Rms)	100 Front St. W. (York St.) fairmont.com/royalyork	DT $$$$	416-368-2511 800-441-1414	Classic	115
The Four Seasons Toronto Timeless (380 Rms)	21 Avenue Rd. (Bloor St.) fourseasons.com/toronto	BY $$$$	416-964-0411 800-332-3442	Hot & Cool	57
The Gladstone Hotel Trendy (37 Rms)	1214 Queen St. W. (Gladstone Ave.) gladstonehotel.ca	WQ $$$	416-531-4635 n/a	Hip	87
Hazelton Hotel Trendy (77 Rms)	118 Yorkville Ave. (Avenue Rd.) thehazeltonhotel.com	BY $$$$	416-963-6300 866-473-6300	Hot & Cool	58
Hilton Toronto Timeless (601 Rms)	145 Richmond St. W. (University Ave.) hilton.com	FD $$$$	416-869-3456 800-445-8667	Classic	115
InterContinental Toronto Centre Timeless (586 Rms)	225 Front St. W. (Simcoe St.) torontocentre.intercontinental.com	ED $$$	416-597-1400 800-422-7969	Classic	115
Hôtel Le Germain Trendy (122 Rms)	30 Mercer St. (Blue Jays Way) germaintoronto.com	ED $$$$	416-345-9500 866-345-9501	Hot & Cool	58
Madison Manor Timeless (25 Rms)	20 Madison Ave. (Bloor St. W.) madisonavenuepub.com	BY $$$	416-922-5579 877-561-7048	Hip	87
Le Meridien King Edward Hotel Grand (298 Rms)	37 King St. E. (Victoria St.) lemeridien.com	SL $$$$	416-863-9700 800-543-4300	Classic	116
Metropolitan Hotel Timeless (422 Rms)	108 Chestnut St. (Dundas Ave.) metropolitan.com/toronto	CT $$$	416-977-5000 800-668-6600	Classic	116
Pantages Hotel Suites Trendy (111 Rms)	200 Victoria St. (Shuter St.) pantageshotel.com	DT $$$$	416-362-1777 866-852-1777	Hot & Cool	58
Park Hyatt Toronto Timeless (346 Rms)	4 Avenue Rd. (Bloor St. W.) parktoronto.hyatt.com	BY $$$$	416-925-1234 800-633-7313	Classic	117
The SoHo Metropolitan Trendy (92 Rms)	318 Wellington St. W. (Blue Jays Way) sohomet.com	ED $$$$	416-599-8800 866-764-6638	Hot & Cool	59
Sutton Place Timeless (375 Rms)	955 Bay St. (Gerrard St. W.) toronto.suttonplace.com	FD $$$$	416-924-9221 866-378-8866	Classic	117

Neighborhood (Area) Key

BE = Beaches	**FD** = Financial District	**QS** = Queen Street
BY = Bloor/Yorkville	**GT** = Greektown	**SL** = St. Lawrence
CT = Chinatown	**GV** = Gay Village	**UP** = Uptown
DD = Distillery District	**HF** = Harbourfront	**VA** = Various
DT = Downtown/Yonge	**LI** = Little Italy	**WQ** = West Queen West
ED = Entertainment Dis.	**PD** = Parkdale	

NAME	ADDRESS (CROSS STREET)	AREA	PHONE	EXPERIENCE	PAGE
TYPE (ROOMS)	WEBSITE	PRICE	800 NUMBER		
Westin Harbour Castle	1 Harbour Sq. (York St.)	HF	416-869-1600	Classic	117
Timeless (97 Rms)	westin.com/harbourcastle	$$$	800-228-3000		
Windsor Arms Hotel	18 St. Thomas St. (Bloor St. W.)	BY	416-971-9666	Classic	118
Grand (28 Rms)	windsorarmshotel.com	$$$$	877-999-2767		

Restaurants

NAME	ADDRESS (CROSS STREET)	AREA	PHONE	EXPERIENCE	PAGE
TYPE	WEBSITE	PRICE	SINGLES/NOISE	99 BEST	PAGE
Annona	4 Avenue Rd. (Bloor St. W.)	BY	416-324-1567	Classic	119
Continental	parktoronto.hyatt.com	$$$	≡		
Auberge du Pommier	4150 Yonge St. (York Mills St.)	UP	416-222-2220	Classic	119
French	oliverbonacini.com	$$$	–	Fine Dining	24
Babur	273 Queen St. W. (McCaul St.)	ED	416-599-7720	Hip	119
Indian	babur.ca	$$	≡	Ethnic Dining	23
Balzac's Café	55 Mill St. (Parliament St.)	DD	416-207-1709	Hot & Cool	*51*, 60
Cafe	balzacscoffee.com	$	≡		
✔ Bar Italia	582 College St. W. (Manning St.)	LI	416-535-3621	Hip	*84*, 89
Italian	bar-italia.ca	$$$	≡		
✔ Bar One*	924 Queen St. W. (Shaw St.)	WQ	416-535-1655	Hip	89
Italian	bar-one.com	$$$	Ⓑ ≡		
The Beaconsfield*	1154 Queen St. W. (Beaconsfield Ave.)	WQ	416-516-2550	Hip	89
International	thebeaconsfield.com	$$	Ⓑ ≡		
Beaver Café	1192 Queen St. W. (Northcote St.)	WQ	416-537-2768	Hip	*83*, 89
Cafe		$	≡		
Beer Bistro	18 King St. E. (Yonge St.)	DT	416-861-9872	Hip	*83*, 90
French	beerbistro.com	$$	Ⓑ ≡		
Biagio Ristorante	155 King St. E. (Jarvis St.)	SL	416-366-4040	Classic	119
Italian		$$$	–		

Restaurant and Nightlife Symbols		
Restaurants	**Nightlife**	**Restaurant + Nightlife**
Singles Friendly (eat and/or meet)	Price Warning	Prime time noise levels
⒤ = Communal table	Ⓒ = Cover or ticket charge	– = Quiet
Ⓑ = Food served at bar		= = A buzz, but still conversational
		≡ = Loud
(G) = Gourmet destination		
Venues followed by an * are those we recommend as both a restaurant and a destination bar.		

Note regarding page numbers: Italic = itinerary listing; Roman = description in theme chapter listing.

BLACK BOOK

Restaurants (cont.)

NAME	ADDRESS (CROSS STREET)	AREA	PHONE	EXPERIENCE	PAGE
TYPE	WEBSITE	PRICE	SINGLES/NOISE	99 BEST	PAGE
Biff's French	4 Front St. E. (Yonge St.) oliverbonacini.com	SL $$$	416-860-0086 B ▤	Classic	120
Bistro & Bakery Thuet French	609 King St. W. (Bathurst St.) thuet.ca	ED $$$	416-603-2777 ▤	Classic Hot Chefs	120 28
Bistro 990 French	990 Bay St. (Wellesley St.) bistro990.ca	FD $$$	416-921-9990 B ▥	Classic	120
Bistro 333 International	333 King St. W. (Widmer St.) clubmenage.ca	ED $$$	416-971-3336 ▥	Classic Late-Night Eats	112, 120 30
Bloor Street Diner & Bistro Express International	145 King St. W. (University Ave.) bloorstreetdiner.com	FD $	416-928-3105 ▤	Classic	109, 121
Blowfish Restaurant + Sake Bar* Fusion	668 King St. W. (Bathurst St.) blowfishrestaurant.com	ED $$	416-860-0606 B ▤	Hot & Cool Nouvelle Asian Restaurants 34	52, 60
Boba International	90 Avenue Rd. (Elgin St.) boba.ca	BY $$$$	416-961-2622 ▭	Classic	111, 121
Brassaii International	461 King St W. (Spadina Ave.) brassaii.com	ED $$$	416-598-4730 B ▤	Hot & Cool Romantic Rendezvous	53, 60 39
Bright Pearl Seafood Asian	346-348 Spadina Ave. (St. Andrew St.) brightpearlseafood.com	CT $$	416-979-3988 ▤	Classic	112, 121
Bymark Continental (G)	66 Wellington St. W. (Bay St.) bymarkdowntown.com	FD $$$$	416-777-1144 B ▤	Classic	110, 121
Byzantium* International	499 Church St. (Wellesley St.)	GV $$$	416-922-3859 B ▥	Hip Gay Scenes	83, 90 25
C'est What? International	67 Front St. E. (Church St.) cestwhat.com	SL $$	416-867-9499 B ▤	Classic	110, 122
Cafe Diplomatico Cafe	594 College St. W. (Clinton St.) diplomatico.ca	LI $	416-534-4637 ▤	Hip	84, 90
Café Supreme Cafe	40 University Ave. (Wellington St.) cafesupreme.ca	FD $	416-585-7896 ▤	Classic	111, 122
Caju Brazilian	922 Queen St. W. (Crawford St.) caju.ca	WQ $$	416-532-2550 ▤	Hip Ethnic Dining	82, 90 23
Canoe Restaurant & Bar* Canadian (G)-	66 Wellington St. W., 54th Fl. (Bay St.) canoerestaurant.com	FD $$$	416-364-0054 B ▤	Classic Canadian Cuisine	110, 122 18
Caren's Wine and Cheese Bar Continental	158 Cumberland St. (Avenue Rd.) carenswineandcheese.com	BY $$$	416-962-5158 B ▤	Classic	111, 122
Centro Restaurant and Lounge* Italian	2472 Yonge St. (Eglinton Ave.) centro.ca	UP $$	416-483-2211 B ▥	Classic	123
Coco Lezzone Grill and Porto Bar Italian	602 College St. W. (Clinton St.) cocolezzone.com	LI $$$	416-535-1489 B ▥	Classic	123
Colborne Lane International	45 Colborne St. (Leader Ln.) colbornelane.com	SL $$$	416-368-9009 B ▯ ▥	Hot & Cool Hot Chefs	60 28
Coppi Ristorante Italian	3363 Yonge St. (Golfdale Rd.) coppiristorante.com	UP $$	416-484-4464 ▭	Classic	123
Corner House Continental	501 Davenport Rd. (Madison Ave.) cornerhouse.sites.toronto.com	UP $$$	416-923-2604 ▭	Classic	123

NAME TYPE	ADDRESS (CROSS STREET) WEBSITE	AREA PRICE	PHONE SINGLES/NOISE	EXPERIENCE 99 BEST	PAGE PAGE
Courtyard Cafe Continental	18 St. Thomas St. (Bloor St. W.) windsorarmshotel.com	BY $$$	416-971-9666 ⌐	Classic	*112*, 124
Crepes à Go Go French	18 Yorkville Ave. (Yonge St.) crepesagogo.com	BY $	416-922-6765 =	Classic	124
✓ Crush Wine Bar French	455 King St. W. (Spadina Ave.) crushwinebar.com	ED $$$	416-977-1234 Ⓑ =	Hot & Cool	*54*, 61
✓ Czehoski* Canadian	678 Queen St. W. (Euclid Ave.) czehoski.com	QS $$	416-366-6787 Ⓑ =	Hip Canadian Cuisine	*84*, 91 18
Doku 15 Asian	8 Colborne St. (Yonge St.) doku15.com	DT $$	416-368-3658 Ⓑ =	Hot & Cool Nouvelle Asian Restaurants	61 34
Drake Dining Room and Raw Bar* Canadian	1150 Queen St. W. (Beaconsfield St.) thedrakehotel.ca	WQ $$	416-531-5042 ⌐	Hip Canadian Cuisine	*82*, 91 18
Esplanade Bier Markt* Belgian	58 The Esplanade (Church St.) thebiermarkt.com	SL $$	416-862-7575 Ⓑ =	Hip	*83*, 91
The Fifth Grill French	225 Richmond St. W. (Duncan St.) thefifthgrill.com	ED $$$$	416-979-3005 =	Classic	124
Futures Bakery & Cafe Bakery/Cafe	483 Bloor St. W. (Bathurst St.)	BY $	416-922-5875 =	Hip	*82*, 92
Fuzion Resto-Lounge & Garden* Fusion	580 Church St. (Wellesley St.) fuzionexperience.com	GV $$$	416-944-9888 Ⓑ =	Hot & Cool Gay Scenes	61 25
Gallery Grill Continental (G)	7 Hart House Cir., 2nd Fl. (Queen's Park) gallerygrill.com	VA $$	416-978-2445 ⌐	Classic Brunches	124 17
Gamelle French	468 College St. W. (Markham St.) gamelle.com	LI $$$	416-923-6254 =	Classic	125
George International	111 Queen St. E. (Church St.) georgeonqueen.com	SL $$$	416-863-6006 =	Classic	*109*, 125
Globe Bistro Canadian (G)	124 Danforth Ave. (Broadview) globebistro.com	GT $$$	416-466-2000 =	Classic	125
Harbour 60 Steak House	60 Harbour St. (Bay St.) harboursixty.com	HF $$$$	416-777-2111 =	Classic	*110*, 125
Hemispheres Lounge & Bistro International	110 Chestnut St (University Ave.) metropolitan.com/toronto/hemis/	CT $$$	416-599-8000 =	Classic	*112*, 125
Holt's Café International	50 Bloor St. W. (Bay St.) holtrenfrew.com	BY $$	416-922-2333 =	Hot & Cool	*52*, 61
Hot House Cafe Continental	35 Church St. (Front St. E.) hothousecafe.com	SL $$	416-366-7800 =	Classic	126
Il Posto Italian	148 Yorkville Ave. (Hazelton Ave.) ilposto.ca	BY $$$	(416) 968-0469 =	Classic Power Lunches	126 37
Jamie Kennedy at the Gardiner Canadian	111 Queen's Park (Bloor St.) jkkitchens.com	BY $$	416-362-1957 ⌐	Hot & Cool Power Lunches	*52*, 62 37
Jamie Kennedy Wine Bar Canadian	9 Church St. (Front St.) jkkitchens.com	SL $$$$	416-362-1957 =	Hot & Cool Brunches	*53*, 62 17
Joso's Seafood (G)	202 Davenport Rd. (Avenue Rd.) josos.com	BY $$$	416-925-1903 =	Classic Seafood Restaurants	*111*, 126 41

Restaurants (cont.)

NAME TYPE	ADDRESS (CROSS STREET) WEBSITE	AREA PRICE	PHONE SINGLES/NOISE	EXPERIENCE 99 BEST	PAGE PAGE
✓ Kalendar International	546 College St. W. (Euclid St.) kalendar.com	LI $$	416-923-4138	Hip	84, 92
✓ KitKat2/Club Lucky Italian	117 John St. (Adelaide St.) kitkattoronto.com	ED $$$	416-977-8890	Classic	126
✓ KiWe Kitchen Fusion	587 King St. W. (Portland St.) kiwekitchen.com	ED $$$	416-203-0551	Hot & Cool	53, 62
Kultura International	169 King St. E. (Lower Jarvis St.) kulturarestaurant.com	ED $$	416-363-9000	Hot & Cool Of-the-Moment Dining	53, 62 35
La Maquette French	111 King St. E. (Church St.) lamaquette.com	SL $$	416-366-8191	Classic	127
Lai Wah Heen Asian	108 Chestnut St., 2nd Fl. (University Ave.) metropolitan.com/lwh	CT $$$	416-977-9899	Classic	127
Le Petit Déjeuner Cafe	191 King St. E. (Frederick St.) petitdejeuner.ca	SL $	416-703-1560	Hip	82, 92
✓ Lee Fusion	603 King St. W. (Bathurst St.) susur.com	ED $$	416-504-7867	Hot & Cool Always-Trendy Tables	63 16
Liberty Bistro/Bar Cafe	25 Liberty St. (Atlantic St.) theliberty.ca	WQ $$	416-533-8828	Hip	81, 92
Li'ly Resto-Lounge* Italian	656 College St. (Grace St.) lilylounge.com	LI $$	416-532-0419	Hot & Cool Restaurant Lounges	52, 63 38
Lobby* Fusion	192 Bloor St. W. (Avenue Rd.) lobbyrestaurant.com	BY $$	416-929-7169	Hot & Cool	63
Lolita's Lust & the Chinchilla Lounge*　Greek	513 Danforth Ave. (Fenwick St.) lolitaslust.ca	GT $$	416-465-1751	Classic	127
Maro Fusion	135 Liberty St. (Fraser Ave.) maro.ca	ED $$	416-588-2888	Hot & Cool Of-the-Moment Dining	63 35
Michelle's Brasserie French	162 Cumberland Ave. (Yorkville Ave.) michellesbrasserie.ca	BY $$	416-944-1504	Classic	127
Mitzi's Café & Gallery Cafe	100 Sorauren Ave. (Pearson Ave.) mitzissister.com	PD $	416-588-1234	Hip Brunches	92 17
Mitzi's Sister* Pub Grub	1554 Queen St. W. (Dowling Ave.) mitzissister.com	PD $	416-532-2570	Hip	93
Monsoon* Asian (G)	100 Simcoe St. (Peter St.) monsoonrestaurant.ca	ED $$	416-979-7172	Hot & Cool Nouvelle Asian Restaurants	51, 64 34
Moonbean Coffee Company Cafe	30 St. Andrews St. (Kensington St.) moonbeancoffee.com	KM $	416-595-0327	Hip	84, 93
Myth* Mediterranean	417 Danforth Ave. (Chester St.) myth.to	GT $$$	416-461-8383	Classic	127
Niagara Street Cafe French	169 Niagara St. (Wellington St. W.) niagarastreetcafe.com	ED $$	416-703-4222	Classic	128
North 44° Continental	2537 Yonge St. (Briarhill Ave.) north44restaurant.com	UP $$$	416-487-4897	Classic	111, 128
One Up Resto/Lounge* Continental	130 Dundas St. W., 2nd Fl. (Bay St.) oneup.ca	CT $$	416-340-6349	Classic Restaurant Lounges	112, 128 38

NAME / TYPE	ADDRESS (CROSS STREET) / WEBSITE	AREA PRICE	PHONE SINGLES/NOISE	EXPERIENCE 99 BEST	PAGE PAGE
One* / French (G)	118 Yorkville Ave. (Avenue Rd.) / thehazeltonhotel.com	BY $$$	416-963-6300 =	Hot & Cool	52, 53, 64
Opus / French (G)	37 Prince Arthur Ave. (St. George St.) / opusrestaurant.com	BY $$$	416-921-3105 –	Classic / Fine Dining	128 24
Oro / International	45 Elm St. (Bay St.) / ororestaurant.com	FD $$	416-597-0155 =	Classic	129
Ouzeri / Greek	500A Danforth Ave. (Logan St.) / ouzeri.com	GT $$	416-778-0500 =	Classic / Ethnic Dining	129 23
Oyster Boy / Seafood	872 Queen St. W. (Crawford St.) / oysterboy.ca	WQ $$	416-534-3432 =	Hip	82, 93
Pangaea / Continental (G)	1221 Bay St. N. (Bloor St. W.) / pangaearestaurant.com	BY $$$	416-920-2323 =	Classic / Power Lunches	111, 129 37
Perigee / International	55 Mill St. (Parliament St.) / perigeerestaurant.com	DD $$$$	416-364-1397	Hot & Cool	64
Prego Della Piazza / Italian	150 Bloor St. W. (Avenue Rd.) / pregodellapiazza.ca	BY $$$	416-920-9900 B =	Classic	129
Provence Delices / French	12 Amelia St. (Parliament St.) / provencerestaurant.com	SL $$$	416-924-9901 –	Classic	129
Pure Spirits Oyster House & Grill / Seafood	55 Mill St. (Parliament St.) / purespirits.ca	DD $$$	416-361-5859 B ≡	Hot & Cool / Seafood Restaurants	51, 64 41
Queen Mother / Asian	208 Queen St. W. (University Ave.) / queenmothercafe.ca	QS $	416-598-4719 =	Hip	93
Rain* / Asian	19 Mercer St. (Blue Jays Way) / rainrestaurant.ca	ED $$$	416-599-7246 B ☐ =	Hot & Cool	53, 65
Revival* / International	783 College St. W. (Shaw St.) / revivalbar.com	LI $$	416-535-7888 =	Hip	94
Richtree / International	42 Yonge St. (Front St.) / richtree.ca	DT $$$	416-366-8986 =	Classic	130
Rivoli* / International	332 Queen St. W. (Peter St.) / rivoli.ca	QS $$	416-596-1908 =	Hip / Restaurant Lounges	83, 94 38
Rosewater Supper Club* / Fusion	19 Toronto St. (King St. E.) / libertygroup.com	SL $$$	416-214-5888 B =	Classic / Romantic Rendezvous	110, 130 39
Sassafraz* / French	100 Cumberland St. (Bellair St.) / sassafraz.ca	BY $$$	416-964-2222 B =	Hot & Cool / Always-Trendy Tables	52, 65
Scaramouche / Continental	1 Benvenuto Pl. (Avenue Rd.) / scaramoucherestaurant.com	UP $$$	416-961-8011 –	Classic / Views	130 45
Sen5es Restaurant & Lounge / International	318 Wellington St. W. (Blue Jays Way) / senses.ca	ED $$$	416-935-0400 B =	Hot & Cool / Fine Dining	65 24
7 West Cafe / Cafe	7 Charles St. W. (Yonge St.) / 7westcafe.com	BY $	416-928-9041 =	Classic / Late-Night Eats	111, 130 30
Shanghai Cowgirl* / International	538 Queen St. W. (Bathurst St.) / shanghaicowgirl.com	QS $	416-203-6623 =	Hip	94
Sotto Sotto Trattoria / Italian	116A Avenue Rd. (Tranby St.) / sottosotto.ca	BY $$$	416-962-0011 –	Classic	131

Restaurants (cont.)

NAME TYPE	ADDRESS (CROSS STREET) WEBSITE	AREA PRICE	PHONE SINGLES/NOISE	EXPERIENCE 99 BEST	PAGE PAGE
Splendido Canadian	88 Harbord St. (Sussex Mews) splendidoonline.com	VA $$$	416-929-7788 ☰	Classic	*112*, 131
Starfish Oyster Bed & Grill Seafood	100 Adelaide St. E. (Jarvis St.) starfishoysterbed.com	SL $$$	416-366-7827 Ⓑ ☰	Classic Seafood Restaurants	*110*, 131 41
Studio Café Mediterranean	21 Avenue Rd. (Bloor St. W.) fourseasons.com	BY $$	416-928-7330 ☰	Classic	*110*, 131
Sunset Grill Diner	2006 Queen St. E. (Bellefair St.) sunsetgrill.ca	BE $	416-690-9985 ☰	Classic	*112*, 132
Susur Fusion (G)	601 King St. W. (Bathurst St.) susur.com	ED $$$$	416-603-2205 ☰	Hot & Cool Hot Chefs	*53*, 65 28
Swan Diner	892 Queen St. W. (Crawford St.)	WQ $$	416-532-0452 ☰	Hip Always-Trendy Tables	*83*, 94 16
Tea Room High Tea	18 St. Thomas St. (Bloor St. W.) windsorarmshotel.com	BY $$$	416-971-9666 —	Classic Ways to Escape a Rainy Day	131 47
Tequila Bookworm Café and Books Cafe	512 Queen St. W. (Denison Ave.) tequilabookworm.blogspot.com	QS $	416-504-7335 ☰	Hip	*83*, 94
Tomi-Kro Fusion	1214 Queen St. E. (Leslie St.)	VA $$	416-463-6677 Ⓑ ☰	Hot & Cool	*52*, 66
Trattoria Giancarlo Italian	41 Clinton St. (College St. W.)	LI $$$	416-533-9619 ☰	Classic Celebrity Hangouts	132 19
Trevor Kitchen and Bar* Continental	38 Wellington St. E. (Leader Ln.) trevorkitchenandbar.com	SL $$$	416-941-9410 Ⓑ ☰	Hot & Cool Of-the-Moment Dining	66 35
Truffles French (G)	21 Avenue Rd. (Bloor St. W.) fourseasons.com	BY $$$$	416-928-7331 —	Classic Romantic Rendezvous	*111*, 132 39
Ultra Supper Club* International	314 Queen St. W. (Soho St.) ultrasupperclub.com	ED $$$	416-263-0330 ☰	Hot & Cool	66
Zelda's Diner	542 Church St. (Wellesley St.) zeldas.ca	GV $	416-922-2526 Ⓑ ☰	Hip	*82*, 95

Nightlife

NAME TYPE	ADDRESS (CROSS STREET) WEBSITE	AREA COVER	PHONE NOISE	EXPERIENCE 99 BEST	PAGE PAGE
Afterlife Nightclub Dance Club	250 Adelaide St. W. (Duncan St.) afterlifenightclub.com	ED Ⓒ	416-593-6126 ☰	Hot & Cool Dance Clubs	*53*, 67 22
Andy Pool Hall Lounge	489 College St. W. (Bathurst St.) andypoolhall.com	LI Ⓒ	416-923-5300 ☰	Hip	*83*, 96
Avenue Hotel Bar	21 Avenue Rd. (Cumberland St.) fourseasons.com	BY	416-964-0411 ☰	Classic Classic Hotel Bars	*111*, 133 20
Azure Restaurant & Bar Hotel Bar	225 Front St. W. (Simcoe St.) torontocentre.intercontinental.com	ED	416-597-8142 ☰	Classic Classic Hotel Bars	133 20

Nightlife

NAME	ADDRESS (CROSS STREET)	AREA	PHONE	EXPERIENCE	PAGE
TYPE	WEBSITE	COVER	NOISE	99 BEST	PAGE
BaBaLuu	136 Yorkville Ave. (Hazelton Ave.)	BY	416-515-0587	Classic	133
Dance Club	babaluu.com	C	≡	Dance Clubs	22
Bar One*	924 Queen St. W. (Shaw St.)	WQ	416-535-1655	Hip	96
Restaurant/Bar	bar-one.com		≡		
The Beaconsfield*	1154 Queen St. W. (Beaconsfield Ave.)	WQ	416-516-2550	Hip	83, 96
Restaurant/Bar	thebeaconsfield.com		≡		
Blowfish Restaurant + Sake	668 King St. W. (Bathurst St.)	ED	416-860-0606	Hot & Cool	67
Bar* Bar	blowfishrestaurant.com		≡		
Boiler House	55 Mill St. (Parliament St.)	DD	416-203-2121	Hip	96
Jazz Club	boilerhouse.ca	C	≡		
Bovine Sex Club	542 Queen St. W. (Ryerson Ave.)	QS	416-504-4239	Hip	83, 96
Bar	bovinesexclub.com	C	≡		
Budo Liquid Theatre	137 Peter St. (Richmond St. W.)	ED	416-593-1550	Hot & Cool	53, 67
Lounge	budolt.com	C	≡	Sexy Lounges	42
Byzantium*	499 Church St. (Wellesley St.)	GV	416-922-3859	Hip	97
Lounge			≡	Gay Scenes	25
C-Lounge	456 Wellington St. W. (Draper St.)	ED	416-260-9393	Hot & Cool	53, 67
Lounge	libertygroup.com	C	≡	Meet Markets	33
The Cameron Public House	408 Queen St. W. (Vanauley St.)	QS	416-703-0811	Hip	84, 97
Live Music	thecameron.com	C	≡		
Centro Restaurant & Lounge*	2472 Yonge St. (Eglinton Ave.)	UP	416-483-2211	Classic	133
Wine Bar	centro.ca		≡		
Century Room	580 King St. W. (Portland St.)	ED	416-203-2226	Hot & Cool	67
Lounge	centuryroom.com	C	≡		
Cheval	606 King St. W. (Portland St.)	ED	416-363-4933	Hot & Cool	68
Lounge	chevalbar.com	C	≡		
Circa	126 John St. (Richmond St. W.)	ED	416-979-0044	Hot & Cool	68
Nightclub	circatoronto.com	C	≡		
Club 22	18 St. Thomas St. (Bloor St. W.)	BY	416-971-9666	Classic	133
Lounge	windsorarmshotel.com		−		
The Communist's Daughter	1149 Dundas St. W. (Ossington Ave.)	WQ	647-435-0103	Hip	81, 97
Bar			≡		
The Comrade Bar	758 Queen St. E. (Broadview)	VA	416-778-9449	Hip	97
Bar			−		
Crocodile Rock	240 Adelaide St. W. (Duncan St.)	ED	416-599-9751	Classic	110, 134
Bar	crocrock.ca	C	≡	Meet Markets	33
Czehoski*	678 Queen St. W. (Euclid Ave.)	QS	416-366-6787	Hip	97
Lounge	czehoski.com		≡		
The Dakota	249 Ossington Ave. (Dundas St. W.)	WQ	416-850-4579	Hip	97
Bar/Live Music	thedakotatavern.com		≡		
Drake Lounge*	1150 Queen St. W. (Beaconsfield St.)	WQ	416-531-5042	Hip	82, 98
Lounge	thedrakehotel.ca	C	≡		
El Convento Rico	750 College St. W. (Shaw St.)	LI	416-588-7800	Hip	84, 98
Dance Club	elconventorico.com	C	≡		

BLACK BOOK

Nightlife (cont.)

NAME TYPE	ADDRESS (CROSS STREET) WEBSITE	AREA COVER	PHONE NOISE	EXPERIENCE 99 BEST	PAGE PAGE
Esplanade Bier Markt* Pub	58 The Esplanade (Church St.) thebiermarkt.com	SL	416-862-7575 ≡	Hip	98
Flow Restaurant + Lounge* Lounge	133 Yorkville Ave. (Hazelton Ave.) flowrestaurant.com	BY	416-925-2143 ≡	Hot & Cool Martinis	68 32
Fly Nightclub Dance Club	8 Gloucester St. (Yonge St.) flynightclub.com	GV C	416-410-5426 ≡	Hot & Cool Gay Scenes	54, 68 25
Foundation Room Lounge	19 Church St. (Front St.) foundationroom.ca	SL	416-364-8368 ≡	Hot & Cool Scene Bars	53, 69 40
Fuzion Resto-Lounge & Garden* Restaurant-Lounge	580 Church St. (Wellesley St.) fuzionexperience.com	GV	416-944-9888 ≡	Hot & Cool Gay Scenes	53, 69 25
Gallery Dance Club	132 Queen's Quay E. (Lower Jarvis St.) theguvernment.com	HF C	416-869-1462 ≡	Hot & Cool Dance Clubs	69 22
The Gladstone Hotel Bar/Lounge	1214 Queen St. W. (Gladstone Ave.) gladstonehotel.com	WQ	416-531-4635 ≡	Hip	98
Habitat Lounge Lounge	735 Queen St. W. (Manning St.) habitatlounge.com	QS	416-860-1551 ≡	Hip Sexy Lounges	82, 99 42
Hair of the Dog Gay Bar	425 Church St. (Wood St.)	GV	416-964-2708 ≡	Classic	110, 134
Hemingway's Bar	142 Cumberland Ave. (Avenue Rd.) hemingways.to	BY	416-968-2828 ≡	Classic Celebrity Hangouts	111, 134 19
Jeff Healey's Roadhouse Live Music	56 Blue Jays Way (King St. W.) jeffhealeysroadhouse.com	ED C	416-593-2626 ≡	Classic Live Music	110, 134 31
Le Saint Tropez Cabaret	315 King St. W. (John St.) lesainttropez.com	ED C	416-591-3600 ≡	Classic	135
Library Bar Hotel Bar	100 Front St. W. (York St.) fairmont.com/royalyork	DT	416-368-2511 ≡	Classic Classic Hotel Bars	112, 135 20
Light Lounge	134 Peter St. (Richmond St. W.) lightlounge.ca	ED C	416-597-9547 ≡	Hot & Cool	69
Li'ly Resto-Lounge* Lounge	656 College St. W. (Grace St.) lilylounge.com	LI	416-532-0419 ≡	Hot & Cool	52, 70
Live @ Courthouse Jazz Club	57 Adelaide St. E. (Yonge St.) liveatcourthouse.com	SL C	416-214-9379 ≡	Classic Jazz Clubs	112, 135 29
Lobby* Bar	192 Bloor St. W. (Avenue Rd.) lobbyrestaurant.com	BY	416-929-7169 ≡	Hot & Cool Scene Bars	69 40
Lolita's Lust & the Chinchilla Lounge* Lounge	513 Danforth Ave. (Fenwick St.) lolitaslust.ca	GT	416-465-1751 ≡	Classic	112, 135
Lusso Lounge	207 Queen's Quay W. (York St.) lussorestaurant.com	HF	416-848-0005 ≡	Classic Summer Patios	110, 136 44
Martini Lounge Lounge	200 Victoria St. (Shuter St.) pantageshotel.com	DT	416-362-1777 ≡	Hot & Cool Martinis	51, 70 32
Mitzi's Sister* Bar	1554 Queen St. W. (Dowling Ave.) mitzissister.com	PD	416-532-2570 ≡	Hip	82, 99
Mod Club Theatre Live Music/Dance Club	722 College St. W. (Crawford St.) themodclub.com	LI C	416-588-4663 ≡	Hip Live Music	83, 99 31

NAME TYPE	ADDRESS (CROSS STREET) WEBSITE	AREA COVER	PHONE NOISE	EXPERIENCE 99 BEST	PAGE PAGE
Monsoon* Lounge	100 Simcoe St. (Peter St.) monsoonrestaurant.ca	ED	416-979-7172 ≡	Hot & Cool	70
Myth* Restaurant-Lounge	417 Danforth Ave. (Chester St.) myth.to	GT	416-461-8383 ≡	Classic	112, 136
N'awlins Live Music	299 King St. W. (John St.) nawlins.ca	ED	416-595-1958 ≡	Classic	136
One Up Resto/Lounge* Bar	130 Dundas St. W. 2nd Fl. (Bay St.) oneup.ca	CT	416-340-6349 ≡	Classic	112, 136
One* Restaurant Bar	118 Yorkville Ave. (Avenue Rd.) thehazeltonhotel.com	BY	416-963-6300 ≡	Hot & Cool	52, 53, 70
Opal Jazz Lounge Jazz Club	472 Queen St. W. (Augusta Ave.) opaljazzlounge.com	ED C	416-646-6725 ≡	Hot & Cool Jazz Clubs	70 29
Panorama Lounge	55 Bloor St. W., 51st Fl. (Bay St.) panoramalounge.com	BY	416-967-0000 ≡	Hot & Cool Views	70 45
Phoenix Concert Theatre Live Music	410 Sherbourne St. (Carlton St.) libertygroup.com/phoenix/phoenix.html	SL C	416-323-1251 ≡	Hip Live Music	84, 99 31
Pravda Vodka Bar Bar	36 Wellington St. E. (Victoria St.) pravdavodkabar.ca	SL	416-306-2433 ≡	Classic	71
Rain* Bar	19 Mercer St. (Blue Jays Way) rainrestaurant.ca	ED	416-599-7246 ≡	Hot & Cool Martinis	71 32
Reservoir Lounge Jazz Club	52 Wellington St. E. (Victoria St.) reservoirlounge.com	SL C	416-955-0887 ≡	Classic	136
Revival* Bar/Live Music	783 College St. W. (Shaw St.) revivalbar.com	LI C	416-535-7888 ≡	Hip	83, 100
Rex Hotel Jazz & Blues Bar Jazz Club	194 Queen St. W. (St. Patrick St.) therex.ca	ED C	416-598-2475 ≡	Classic Jazz Clubs	110, 137 29
Rivoli* Bar/Live Music	332-334 Queen St. W. (Peter St.) rivoli.ca	QS C	416-596-1908 ≡	Hip Restaurant-Lounges	100 38
Rockwood Lounge/Nightclub	31 Mercer St. (John St.) rockwoodclub.com	ED C	416-979-7373 ≡	Hot & Cool Scene Bars	54, 71 40
Roof Lounge Hotel Bar	4 Avenue Rd., 18th Fl. (Bloor St. W.) parktoronto.hyatt.com	BY	416-924-5471 ≡	Classic Summer Patios	111, 137 44
Rosewater Supper Club* Bar/Lounge	19 Toronto St. (King St. E.) libertygroup.com	SL	416-214-5888 ≡	Classic	137
Sassafraz* Restaurant Bar	100 Cumberland St. (Bellair St.) sassafraz.ca	BY	416-964-2222 ≡	Hot & Cool	71
Seven Lounge Lounge	224 Richmond St. W. (Simcoe St.) sevenlounge.ca	DT C	416-599-9797 ≡	Hot & Cool	54, 71
Shanghai Cowgirl* Lounge	538 Queen St. W. (Bathurst St.) shanghaicowgirl.com	QS	416-203-6623 ≡	Hip	100
Sky Bar Lounge	132 Queen's Quay E. (Lower Jarvis St.) theguvernment.com	HF C	416-869-0045 ≡	Hot & Cool Summer Patios	54, 72 44
Sneaky Dee's Live Music	431 College St. W. (Bathurst St.) sneaky-dees.com	LI	416-603-3090 ≡	Hip Late-Night Eats	100 30

BLACK BOOK

Nightlife (cont.)

NAME TYPE	ADDRESS (CROSS STREET) WEBSITE	AREA COVER	PHONE NOISE	EXPERIENCE 99 BEST	PAGE PAGE
Stones Place Bar/Live Music	1225 Queen St. W. (Duffren St.) stonesplace.ca	PD C	416-536-4242 ≡	Hip	*82*, 101
✓ Sutra Tiki Bar Bar	612 College St. W. (Clinton St.) 	LI C	416-537-8755 =	Hip	*84*, 101
✓ Sweaty Betty's Bar	13 Ossington Ave. (Queen St. W.) sweatybettysbar.com	WQ 	416-535-6861 ≡	Hip	*84*, 101
Therapy Ultra Lounge Lounge	203 Richmond St. W. (Bedford St.) therapylounge.com	ED C	416-977-3089 =	Hot & Cool Sexy Lounges	*54*, 72 42
This Is London Lounge/Dance Club	364 Richmond St. W. (Peter St.) thisislondonclub.com	ED C	416-351-1100 ≡	Hip Celebrity Hangouts	*84*, 101 19
Trevor Kitchen and Bar* Bar	38 Wellington St. E. (Leader Ln.) trevorkitchenandbar.com	SL 	416-941-9410 =	Hot & Cool	*52*, 72
✓ 2 Cats Cocktail Lounge Lounge	569 King St. W. (Portland St.) 2cats.ca	ED 	416-204-6261 =	Hot & Cool	*53*, 72
Ultra Supper Club* Lounge	314 Queen St. W. (Soho St.) ultrasupperclub.com	ED C	416-263-0330 ≡	Hot & Cool	*54*, 72
Velvet Underground Lounge	510 Queen St. W. (Portland St.) libertygroup.com	QS C	416-504-6688 ≡	Hip	*83*, 102
West Lounge Lounge	510 King St. W. (Bathurst St.) westlounge.com	ED C	416-361-9004 =	Hot & Cool Meet Markets	*52*, 73 33

Attractions

NAME TYPE	ADDRESS (CROSS STREET) WEBSITE	AREA PRICE	PHONE	EXPERIENCE 99 BEST	PAGE PAGE
Allan Gardens Conservatory Gardens	19 Horticultural Ave. (Jarvis St.)	SL	416-392-7288	Classic Ways to Escape a Rainy Day	138 47
Art Gallery of Ontario Art Gallery	317 Dundas St. W. (McCaul St.) ago.net	CT $	416-979-6648	Hot & Cool	74
Artinsite Tour	artinsite.com	VA $$	416-979-5704	Hot & Cool Guided Tours	*52*, 74 26
Bata Shoe Museum Museum	327 Bloor St. W. (St. George St.) batashoemuseum.ca	BY $	416-979-7799	Hot & Cool Only-in-Toronto Museums	*52*, 74 36
The Beaches Neighborhood	Queen Street East from Coxwell east and south to the lakeshore	BE		Classic Ways to Enjoy a Sunny Day	*112*, 138 46
Body Blitz Spa: Health by Water Spa	471 Adelaide St. W. (Portland St.) bodyblitzspa.com	ED $$$$	416-364-0400	Hot & Cool Spas	*82*, 74 43
Camera Bar and Media Gallery Art Cinema/Gallery	1028 Queen St. W. (Ossington Ave.) camerabar.ca	WQ $	416-530-0011	Hip	*84*, 103
Casa Loma Historic Site	1 Austin Terrace (Davenport Rd.) casaloma.org	UP $	416-923-1171	Classic Historic Buildings	*111*, 138 27

NAME TYPE	ADDRESS (CROSS STREET) WEBSITE	AREA PRICE	PHONE	EXPERIENCE 99 BEST	PAGE PAGE
CHUM/Citytv Building Tour	299 Queen St. W. (John St.)	ED $	416-591-5757	Hot & Cool Guided Tours	75 26
Cinematheque Ontario Art Cinema	317 Dundas St. W. (McCaul St.) cinemathequeontario.ca	CT $	416-968-3456	Hip	103
CN Tower Viewpoint/Building	301 Front St. W. (John St.) cntower.ca	HF $$	416-868-6937	Classic Views	109, 139 45
Corkin Gallery Art Gallery	55 Mill St. (Parliament St.) corkingallery.com	DD	416-979-1980	Hot & Cool Only-in-Toronto Museums 36	75
Design Exchange Museum	234 Bay St. (Wellington St.) dx.org	FD $	416-363-6121	Hip Contemporary Art & Design 21	83, 103
The Distillery District Site	55 Mill St. (Parliament St.) thedistillerydistrict.com	DD		Hot & Cool	75
Eagles Nest Golf Club Golf Course	10000 Dufferin St. (Major McKenzie Dr.) eaglesnestgolf.com	VA $$$$	905-417-2300	Hot & Cool	53, 75
Elgin/Winter Garden Theatre Historic Site	189 Yonge St. (Queen St.) heritagefdn.on.ca	DT $	416-314-2871	Classic	139
401 Richmond Art Space	401 Richmond St. W. (Spadina Ave.) 401richmond.net	ED	416-595-5900	Hip Contemporary Art & Design 21	82, 104
Gardiner Museum of Ceramic Art Museum	111 Queen's Park (Bloor St.) gardinermuseum.on.ca	BY $	416-586-8080	Hot & Cool Only-in-Toronto Museums 36	52, 76
Glen Abbey Golf Club Golf Course	1333 Dorval Dr. (Oakville) glenabbey.com	VA $$$$	905-844-1811	Classic	110, 139
Got Style Shop	489 King St. W. (Spadina Ave.) gsmen.com	ED	416-260-9696	Hot & Cool	76
Harbourfront Centre Art Space/Park	235 Queen's Quay W. (York St.) harbourfrontcentre.com	HF $	416-973-4000	Hip	83, 104
Harbourfront/Mariposa Tours Tour	207 Queen's Quay W. (York St.) mariposacruises.com	HF $$	416-203-0178	Classic	139
High Park Park	1873 Bloor St. W. (High Park Ave.) city.toronto.on.ca/parks	PD		Hip Ways to Enjoy a Sunny Day 46	82, 104
Hockey Hall of Fame Museum	30 Yonge St. (Front St.) hhof.com	SL $	416-360-7765	Classic	109, 140
Joe Rockhead's Sports	29 Fraser Ave. (Liberty St.) joerockheads.com	WQ $$$	416-538-7670	Hip	82, 104
Kensington Market Shopping	Spadina Ave. (College/Dundas Sts.) kensington-market.ca	CT		Classic	112, 140
Lionhead Golf & Country Club Golf Course	8525 Mississauga Rd. (Steels Ave.) golflionhead.com	VA $$$$	905-455-8400	Classic	140
Made Design Shop	867 Dundas St. W. (Manning Ave.) madedesign.ca	WQ	416-607-6384	Hot & Cool WQW Art Spaces 48	76
Mercer Union Centre for Contemporary Art Art Space	37 Lisgar St. (Queen St. W.) mercerunion.org	WQ	416-536-1519	Hip WQW Art Spaces 48	81, 104
Ministry of the Interior Shop	80 Ossington Ave. (Queen St. W.) ministryoftheinterior.net	QS	416-533-6684	Hot & Cool	77

Attractions (cont.)

NAME TYPE	ADDRESS (CROSS STREET) WEBSITE	AREA PRICE	PHONE	EXPERIENCE 99 BEST	PAGE PAGE
Moksha Yoga Downtown Sports	860 Richmond St. W., 3rd Fl. (Strachan St.)　mokshayogadowntown.com	WQ $$	416-361-3033	Hip	*82*, 105
Museum of Contemporary Canadian Art (MOCCA)　Museum	952 Queen St. W. (Shaw St.) mocca.toronto.on.ca	WQ	416-395-0067	Hip WQW Art Spaces	105 48
Museum of Television Museum	550 Queen St. E. (River St.) mztv.com	QS $	416-599-7339	Hot & Cool	77
National Film Board/ Mediatheque　Film Museum	150 John St. (Richmond St.) nfb.ca/mediatheque	ED $	416-973-3012	Hip	*82*, 105
The Oasis Wellness Centre and Spa　Spa	55 Mill St. (Parliament St.) experienceoasis.ca	DD $$$$	416-364-2626	Hot & Cool	77
Ontario College of Art & Design Art Gallery	100 McCaul St. (Dundas St. W.) ocad.on.ca	CT	416-977-6000	Hip	105
Pantages Spa and Wellness Center　Spa	200 Victoria St. (Shuter St.) pantagesspa.com	DT $$$$	416-367-1888	Hot & Cool Spas	*53*, 77 43
Power Plant Gallery Art Gallery	231 Queen's Quay W. (York St.) thepowerplant.org	HF $	416-973-4949	Hip Contemporary Art & Design 21	*84*, 105
Rogers Centre Tour Tour	1 Blue Jays Way (Front St. W.) rogerscentre.com	ED $	416-341-2770	Hot & Cool	78
Royal Ontario Museum Museum	100 Queen's Park (Avenue Rd.) rom.on.ca	BY $	416-586-5549	Classic Ways to Escape a Rainy Day 47	*112*, 140
Rudsak Shop	315 Queen St. W. (John St.) rudsak.com	QS	416-595-9661	Hot & Cool	78
Satori Urban Wellness Spa	33 Hazelton Ave. (Scollard St.) satoriwellness.com	BY $$$	416-972-9355	Hot & Cool	78
Spadina Museum Historic Site	285 Spadina Rd. (Davenport Rd.) 	UP $	416-392-6910	Classic Historic Buildings	*111*, 141 27
St. Anne's Anglican Church Historic Site	270 Gladstone Ave. (Queen St. W.) stannes.on.ca	PD	416-536-3160	Classic	141
St. Lawrence Market Market	92 Front St. E. (Jarvis St.) stlawrencemarket.com	SL	416-392-7219	Hip Historic Buildings	*83*, 106 27
Steam Whistle Brewing Co. Tour	The Roundhouse, 255 Bremner Blvd. (Blue Jays Way)　steamwhistle.ca	HF $	416-362-2337	Hip Guided Tours	*82*, 106 26
Stillwater Spa Spa	4 Avenue Rd. (Bloor St. W.) stillwaterspa.com	BY $$$$	416-926-2389	Classic Spas	*111*, 141 43
Textile Museum of Canada Museum	55 Centre Ave. (Dundas St. W) textilemuseum.ca	CT $	416-599-5321	Hot & Cool	78
Toronto Antiques on King Antique Market	276 King St. W. (Duncan St.) torontoantiquesonking.com	ED	416-345-9941	Classic	*110*, 141
Toronto Islands Island	Bay Street (Queen's Quay) torontoisland.org	HF $	416-392-8193	Classic Ways to Enjoy a Sunny Day 46	*110*, 141
Toronto Music Garden Garden	475 Queen's Quay W. (Lower Portland St.) toronto.ca/parks/musicgarden	HF	416-973-4000	Hip	*84*, 106

NAME TYPE	ADDRESS (CROSS STREET) WEBSITE	AREA PRICE	PHONE	EXPERIENCE 99 BEST	PAGE PAGE
Toronto School of Art Gallery Art Gallery	410 Adelaide St. W., 3rd Fl. (Spadina Ave.) tsa-art.ca	CT	416-504-7910	Hip	107
Ukula Shop	492 College St. (Bathurst St.) ukula.com	LI	416-619-9282	Hip	*84*, 106
The Yorkville Club Health Club	87 Avenue Rd. (Elgin Ave.) theyorkvilleclub.com	BY $$	416-961-8400	Hot & Cool	79
Yorkville Shopping District Shopping	Around Bloor & Avenue Rds.	BY		Hot & Cool	*54*, 79

Notes

BLACK BOOK

Toronto Black Book By Neighborhood

Beaches

R	Sunset Grill		132
A	The Beaches	46	138

Bloor/Yorkville

H	The Four Seasons Toronto		57
	Hazelton Hotel		58
	The Madison Manor		87
	Park Hyatt Toronto		117
	Windsor Arms Hotel		118
R	Annona		119
	Boba		121
	Caren's Wine and Cheese Bar		122
	Courtyard Cafe		124
	Crepes à Go Go		124
	Futures Bakery & Café		92
	Holt's Café		61
	Il Posto	37	126
	Jamie Kennedy at the Gardiner	37	62
	Joso's	41	126
	Lobby*		63
	Michelle's Brasserie		127
	One*		64
	Opus	24	128
	Pangaea	37	129
	Prego Della Piazza		129
	Sassafraz*	16	65
	7 West Café	30	130
	Sotto Sotto Trattoria		131
	Studio Café		131
	Tea Room	47	131
	Truffles	39	132
N	Avenue	20	133
	BaBaLuu	22	133
	Club 22		133
	Flow Restaurant + Lounge*	32	68
	Hemingway's	19	134
	Lobby*	40	70
	One*		70
	Panorama	45	70
	Roof Lounge	44	137
	Sassafraz*	16	71
A	Bata Shoe Museum	36	74
	Gardiner Museum of Ceramic Art	36	76
	Royal Ontario Museum	47	140
	Satori Urban Wellness		78
	Stillwater Spa	43	141
	The Yorkville Club		79
	Yorkville Shopping District		79

Chinatown

H	Metropolitan Hotel		116
R	Bright Pearl Seafood		121
	Hemispheres Lounge & Bistro		125
	Lai Wah Heen		127
	Moonbean Coffee Company		93
	One Up Resto/Lounge*	38	128
N	One Up Resto/Lounge*		136
A	Art Gallery of Ontario		74
	Cinematheque Ontario		103

Code: H-Hotels; R-Restaurants; N-Nightlife; A-Attractions. Blue page numbers denote listings in 99 Best. Black page numbers denote listings in theme chapters. The Toronto Neighborhoods Map is on p. 219.

	Kensington Market		140
	Ontario College of Art & Design		105
	Textile Museum of Canada		78
	Toronto School of Art Gallery		107

Distillery District

R	Balzac's Café		60
	Perigee		64
	Pure Spirits Oyster House		
	& Grill	41	64
N	Boiler House		96
	Gallery	22	69
A	Corkin Gallery	36	75
	The Distillery District		75
	The Oasis Wellness Centre		
	and Spa		77

Downtown/Yonge

H	Cosmopolitan Hotel		57
	Fairmont Royal York		115
	Pantages Hotel Suites		58
R	Beer Bistro		90
	Doku 15	34	61
	Richtree		130
N	Library Bar	20	135
	Martini Lounge	32	70
	Seven Lounge		71
A	Elgin/Winter Garden Theatre		139
	Pantages Spa and		
	Wellness Center	43	77

Entertainment Dis.

H	InterContinental Toronto		
	Centre		115
	Hôtel Le Germain		58
	The SoHo Metropolitan		59

R	Babur	23	119
	Bistro & Bakery Thuet	28	120
	Bistro 333	30	120
	Blowfish Restaurant		
	+ Sake Bar*	34	60
	Brassaii	39	60
	Crush Wine Bar		61
	The Fifth Grill		124
	KitKat2/Club Lucky		126
	KiWe Kitchen		62
	Kultura	35	62
	Lee	16	63
	Maro	35	63
	Monsoon*		64
	Niagara Street Cafe		128
	Rain*		65
	Sen5es Restaurant		
	& Lounge	24	65
	Susur	28	65
	Ultra Supper Club*		66
N	Afterlife Nightclub	22	67
	Azure Restaurant & Bar	20	133
	Blowfish Restaurant		
	+ Sake Bar*		67
	Budo Liquid Theatre	42	67
	C-Lounge	33	67
	Century Room		67
	Cheval		68
	Circa		68
	Crocodile Rock	33	134
	Jeff Healey's Roadhouse	31	134
	Le Saint Tropez		135
	Light		69
	Monsoon*	34	70
	N'awlins		136
	Opal Jazz Lounge	29	70

Entertainment Dis. (cont.)

	Rain*	32	71
	Rex Hotel Jazz		
	& Blues Bar	29	137
	Rockwood	40	71
	Therapy Ultra Lounge	42	72
	This Is London	19	101
	2 Cats Cocktail Lounge		72
	Ultra Supper Club*		72
	West Lounge	33	73
A	Body Blitz Spa: Health		
	By Water	43	74
	CHUM/Citytv Building	26	75
	401 Richmond	21	104
	Got Style		76
	National Film Board/		
	Mediatheque		105
	Rogers Centre Tour		78
	Toronto Antiques on King		141

Financial District

H	Hilton Toronto		115
	Sutton Place		117
R	Bistro 990		120
	Bloor Street Diner &		
	Bistro Express		121
	Bymark		121
	Café Supreme		122
	Canoe Restaurant & Bar	18	122
	Oro		129
A	Design Exchange	21	103

Gay Village

R	Byzantium*	25	90
	Fuzion Resto-Lounge		
	& Garden*	25	61
	Zelda's		95

Greektown

N	Byzantium*		97
	Fly Nightclub	25	68
	Fuzion Resto-Lounge		
	& Garden*		69
	Hair of the Dog		134

R	Globe Bistro		125
	Lolita's Lust & the		
	Chinchilla Lounge*		127
	Myth*		127
	Ouzeri	23	129
N	Lolita's Lust & the		
	Chinchilla Lounge*		135
	Myth*		136

Harbourfront

H	Westin Harbour Castle		117
R	Harbour 60		125
N	Lusso	44	136
	Sky Bar	44	72
A	CN Tower	45	139
	Harbourfront Centre		104
	Harbourfront/Mariposa Tours		139
	Power Plant Gallery	21	105
	Steam Whistle Brewing		
	Company	26	106
	Toronto Islands	46	141
	Toronto Music Garden		106

Little Italy

R	Bar Italia		89
	Cafe Diplomatico		90
	Coco Lezzone Grill & Porto Bar		123
	Gamelle		125
	Kalendar		92
	Li'ly Resto-Lounge*	38	63

Revival*   94
Trattoria Giancarlo   19 132
N   Andy Pool Hall   96
El Convento Rico   98
Li'ly Resto-Lounge*   70
Mod Club Theatre   31   99
Revival*   100
Sneaky Dee's   30 100
Sutra Tiki Bar   101
A   Ukula   107

Parkdale

R   Mitzi's Café & Gallery   17   92
Mitzi's Sister*   93
N   Mitzi's Sister*   99
Stones Place   101
A   High Park   46 104
St. Anne's Anglican Church 141

Queen Street

R   Czehoski*   18   91
Queen Mother   93
Rivoli*   94
Shanghai Cowgirl*   94
Tequila Bookworm Café & Books 94
N   Bovine Sex Club   96
The Cameron Public House   97
Czehoski*   97
Habitat Lounge   42   99
Rivoli*   38 100
Shanghai Cowgirl*   100
Velvet Underground   102
A   Ministry of the Interior   77
Museum of Television   77
Rudsak   78

St. Lawrence

H   Le Meridien King Edward Hotel 116
R   Biagio Ristorante   119
Biff's   120
C'est What?   122
Colborne Lane   28   60
Esplanade Bier Markt*   91
George   125
Hot House Cafe   126
Jamie Kennedy Wine Bar 17   62
La Maquette   127
Le Petit Déjeuner   92
Provence Delices   129
Rosewater Supper Club* 39 130
Starfish Oyster Bed & Grill 41 131
Trevor Kitchen and Bar* 35   66
N   Esplanade Bier Markt*   98
Foundation Room   40   69
Live @ Courthouse   29 135
Phoenix Concert Theatre 31   99
Pravda Vodka Bar   71
Reservoir Lounge   136
Rosewater Supper Club*   137
Trevor Kitchen and Bar*   72
A   Allan Gardens
Conservatory   47 138
Hockey Hall of Fame   140
St. Lawrence Market   27 106

Uptown

R   Auberge du Pommier   24 119
Centro Restaurant & Lounge* 123
Coppi Ristorante   123
Corner House   123
North 44°   128

Uptown (cont.)

    Scaramouche   45 130

N Centro Restaurant & Lounge* 133

A Casa Loma   27 138

    Spadina Museum   27 141

West Queen West

H Drake Hotel   87

    Gladstone Hotel   87

R Bar One*   89

    The Beaconsfield*   89

    Beaver Café   89

    Caju   23 90

    Drake Dining Room

      and Raw Bar*   18 91

    Liberty Bistro/Bar   92

    Oyster Boy   93

    Swan   16 94

N Bar One*   96

    The Beaconsfield*   96

    The Communist's Daughter 97

    The Dakota   97

    Drake Lounge*   98

    Gladstone Hotel   98

    Sweaty Betty's   101

A Camera Bar & Media Gallery 103

    Joe Rockhead's   104

    Made Design   48 76

    Mercer Union Centre for

      Contemporary Art 48 104

    Moksha Yoga Downtown 105

    Museum of Contemporary

      Canadian Art (MOCCA) 48 105

Notes

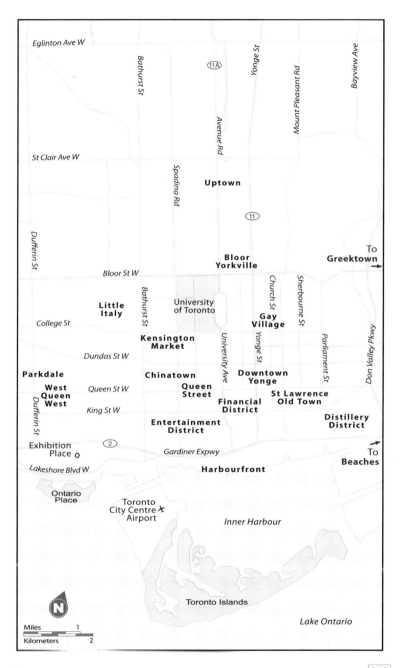

Eglinton Ave W

Bathurst St

11A

Yonge St

Mount Pleasant Rd

Bayview Ave

Avenue Rd

St Clair Ave W

Spadina Rd

Uptown

11

Dufferin St

Bloor Yorkville

To **Greektown**

Bloor St W

Church St

Sherbourne St

Little Italy

Bathurst St

University of Toronto

Gay Village

College St

University Ave

Yonge St

Parliament St

Don Valley Pkwy

Kensington Market

Dundas St W

Chinatown

Parkdale

Downtown Yonge

West Queen West

Queen St W

Queen Street

Dufferin St

King St W

Financial District

St Lawrence Old Town

Entertainment District

Distillery District

Exhibition Place o

2

Gardiner Expwy

To **Beaches**

Lakeshore Blvd W

Harbourfront

Ontario Place

Toronto City Centre Airport

Inner Harbour

Toronto Islands

Lake Ontario

N

Miles 1
Kilometers 2

Toronto Unique Shopping Index

NAME	PHONE	AREA	PRODUCTS	PAGE
Anti-Hero	416-924-6121	BY	Men's apparel	56
The Bay	416-861-9111	DT	Luxury department store	114
The Cashmere Shop	416-925-0831	BY	Sweaters and accessories	114
Coast Mountain Sports	416-598-3785	DT	High-performance clothing	114
Doll Factory by Damzels	416-598-0509	QS	Funky women's apparel	86
Fleurtje	416-504-5552	QS	Handbags and accessories	86
Fluevog Shoes	416-581-1420	QS	Canadian-designed footwear	114
Fresh Collective	416-594-1313	QS	Locally designed apparel	86
The Guild Shop	416-921-1721	BY	Jewelry, ceramics, textiles	56
Harry Rosen	416-972-0556	BY	Men's apparel	56
Heffel Gallery	416-961-6505	BY	Art gallery	114
Holt Renfrew	416-922-2333	BY	Luxury department store	56
Indigo Books and Music	416-591-3622	DT	Bookstore	114
Lileo	416-413-1410	DD	Trendy gifts, books, and other	56
Lilliput Hats	416-536-5933	LI	Hats and other headwear	86
Lululemon Athletica	416-964-9544	BY	Upscale athletic apparel	56
Lush Cosmetics	416-599-5874	QS	Handmade cosmetics	114
Magic Pony	416-861-1684	QS	Hip clothing, books, gifts, art	86
Nathalie Roze & Co.	416-792-1699	QS	Funky women's apparel	86
Noir	416-962-6647	BY	Men's and women's apparel	56
Peach Beserk	416-504-1711	QS	Locally designed women's apparel	86
Roots	416-323-3289	BY	Athletic clothing, leather goods	114
Sandra Ainsley Gallery	416-214-9490	DD	Art gallery	56
Silver Snail	416-593-0889	QS	Comics and graphic novels	114
Soma Chocolate Maker	416-815-7662	DD	Decadent chocolates	56
Soundscapes	416-537-1620	LI	Hipster music	86
Stollery's	416-922-6173	BY	British goods	114
Thompson Landry Gallery	416-364-4955	DD	Art gallery	56
Thrill of the Find	416-461-9313	QS	Vintage couture	86
Ukula	416-619-9282	LI	Trendy women's apparel	86
Uncle Otis	416-920-2281	BY	Trendy women's apparel	56

For Neighborhood (Area) Key, see p.200.

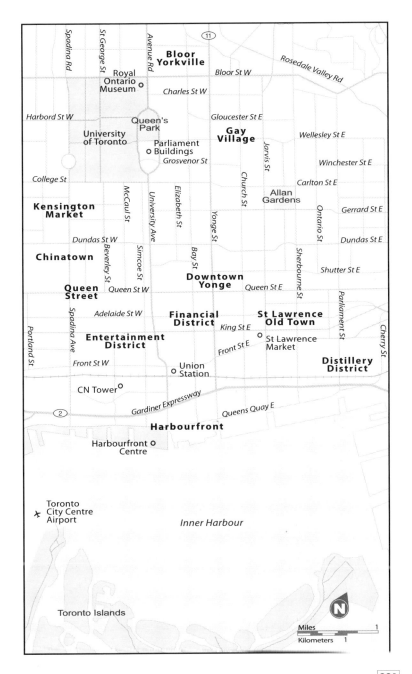

Notes

About the Author

Neil Carlson is a Toronto-born journalist who lives in the Netherlands and in Canada. As the Travel and Design Editor of *Highrise Magazine* and a freelance journalist, Neil has traveled to over 65 countries. From interviewing Renzo Piano to covering the 2006 Winter Olympics in Torino, he has written for numerous print and online publications, including Fodor's, Sherman's Travel, and Slate. Neil's interests include sustainable tourism, architecture, food, culture, southern Africa, the Balkans, and sport. Neil is also the author of *Night + Day Amsterdam.*

Acknowledgments

I'd like to thank Joyce for her patience, understanding, and unwavering support through my many deadlines. I want to extend a special thank you to my editors Anita and Christina for their guidance and vision for the project, and to Alan for giving me the chance to write about my hometown. I thank my family for instilling in me a love of travel and books, and I wish to thank Vivian Vassos, whose enthusiasm for the city is rivaled only by her knowledge of its hotspots. My most heartfelt gratitude is reserved for Cynthia Cully, whose generosity and insights made this book possible. Finally, I wish to thank the people of Toronto—especially the fabulous concierges and restaurateurs—who were quick to share their love of the city.—Neil Carlson

About the Contributors

Waheeda Harris is a Toronto-based freelance writer who always has a suitcase ready and passport in hand. After spending her twenties learning the intricacies of book publishing, she now focuses on writing about travel, architecture, design and fashion. She has contributed to the *National Post*, *CanWest News Services, Canadian House & Home, Access Magazine, Tremblant Resort Magazine, Style, LouLou, Wish, Life & Fashion, VIA Rail Destinations,* and *2 Magazine.*

Anya Wassenberg has been a freelance writer of short stories and non-fiction articles for several years. Her eclectic interests have led her to cover a wide range of topics, from Canadian football to lifestyle, the arts, and travel features, and her work has appeared in a variety of media, from print to web to radio. Her short fiction has appeared in magazines and anthologies throughout North America, as well as in the U.K.

It's New. It's You.
Night+Day online
@ pulseguides.com

a travel web site designed to
complement your lifestyle

Today's urbane, sophisticated traveler knows
how fast things change in the world. What's hot,
and what's not? Now you have access to the
insider information you need, whenever you
need it—**Night+Day**—at pulseguides.com.

We're committed to providing the latest, most
accurate information on the hottest, hippest,
coolest, and classiest venues around the world,
which means keeping our listings current—
even after you've purchased one of our
Night+Day guides.

Visit pulseguides.com and browse your way to any
destination to view or download the most recent
updates to the **Night+Day** guide of your choice.

Online and in print, **Night+Day** offers independent travel advice tailored to suit your lifestyle,
capturing the unique personality of each city.
From uptown chic to downtown cool, our guides
are packed with opinionated tips, and selective,
richly detailed descriptions geared toward the
discerning traveler.

Enhance your travel experience online:
- Zero in on hot restaurants, classic
  attractions, and hip nightlife
- Print out your favorite itinerary to keep
  in your purse or pocket as you travel
- Update your **Night+Day** guide with
  what's new
- Read news and tips from around the world
- Keep the world's most up-to-date guides
  even more current by downloading the
  latest reviews

Night+Day—online now at pulseguides.com.

All You Need To Know

Best of the Best   15

The Black Book
All our recommended
hotels, restaurants,
nightlife, attractions,
and shopping   199

If you're looking for ...

Airports   160

Clothes Size
  Conversion   170

Coffee Shops   181

Day Trips   196

Drinking and
  Smoking Laws   171

Events   146

Gay and Lesbian
  Travel Resources   168

Getting Around Town   165

History   9

Holidays   145

Important Numbers   172

Money Matters   167

Overnight Trips   186

Parks   177

Performing Arts   176

Print Media   169

Radio Stations   169

Safety   168

Shopping Hours   170

Sports Teams   179

Weather   144